POWERING

FORWARD

What Everyone Should Know about
AMERICA'S ENERGY REVOLUTION

FULCRUM

Bill Ritter, Jr.

Cover image: Thank you to the National Renewable Energy Laboratory (NREL), a Department of Energy laboratory in Colorado, for the use of this image of a hydrogen flame. Hydrogen, when burned with oxygen or used in a contained cell, is a zero-emission fuel that can power internal engines, vehicles, and electronic devices. (Warren Gretz / NREL)

Library of Congress Cataloging-in-Publication Data

Names: Ritter, Bill, 1956-
Title: Powering forward : what everyone should know about America's energy
  revolution.
Description: Golden, CO : Fulcrum Publishing, [2016] | Includes
  bibliographical references.
Identifiers: LCCN 2015046356 (print) | LCCN 2015047653 (ebook) | ISBN
  9781936218219 | ISBN 9781933108889 ()
Subjects: LCSH: Clean energy--United States | Clean energy--Colorado. |
  Renewable energy sources--United States | Renewable energy
  sources--Colorado. | Climatic changes--United States. | Climatic
  changes--Colorado. | Energy policy--United States. | Energy
  policy--Colorado.
Classification: LCC TJ807.9.U6 R58 2016 (print) | LCC TJ807.9.U6 (ebook) |
  DDC 333.790973--dc23
LC record available at http://lccn.loc.gov/2015046356
978-1-936218-21-9

Printed in the United States.

Fulcrum Publishing
4690 Table Mountain Drive, Suite 100
Golden, Colorado 80403
(800) 992-2908 • (303) 277-1623
www.fulcrumbooks.com

Praise for *Powering Forward*

"Governor Bill Ritter has long been in the vanguard of leaders on energy and climate policy. *Powering Forward* is the best, most thorough, and sensible analysis of the energy-climate policy issues I've seen in recent years. It should launch a long overdue national discussion about the most urgent challenges and opportunities Americans face. It is a practical and farsighted guide to a decent, prosperous, and durable future."

– David Orr, Counselor to the President, Oberlin College

"Governor Ritter has written an important book for anyone interested in energy and the challenge of climate change. Drawing on his experiences as governor and now as Founder and Director of the Center for the New Energy Economy at Colorado State University, he details the progress made in Colorado and other western states to transition to a clean energy economy. Here's hoping more governors and more states will use this as a blueprint for action."

– Jeff Bingaman, Former US Senator (NM) and Former Chair, Senate Committee on Energy and Natural Resources

"America faces a moment of enormous danger but also opportunity. The threat of climate change has opened the way for a boom in renewable energy sources that could benefit both our economy and our planet. In this essential book, Governor Ritter analyzes the choice we face between designing our future or being its victims. He shows how success will require rethinking not only our energy policies but also our politics."

– Walter Isaacson, CEO of the Aspen Institute

"As a longtime student and policy maker regarding America's energy future in the 21st century, I am aware of no book that addresses our energy challenges more comprehensively than Governor Bill Ritter's new book, *Powering Forward*. This book should become a standard text in high school and college political sciences classes across our nation. It includes economics, technology, history, public policy, environment and climate science, and Bill Ritter's own rich experiences in all these fields. As the founder of the Center for the New Energy Economy at Colorado State University, Governor Ritter is now recognized as one of our country's leading experts on achieving the sustainable, climate-friendly energy economy America's twenty-first century requires."

– Gary Hart, US Senator, Colorado (Ret.)

"Few energy experts bring the well-rounded, pragmatically grounded and ethical viewpoint that Bill Ritter articulates in this book. Bill knows this subject cold, and writes in a personal and compelling voice. In doing so, he provides one of the best chances of any book around to inform fence-sitters and draw them into the critically important conversation about our nation's clean energy transformation. Please read this inspiring book and share it widely."

– Susan Tierney, 2009 candidate to become
Deputy Secretary of Energy for the US Department of Energy

"*Powering Forward* is a must read for both advocates of a low energy carbon future and those who despair that there appears to be no leadership. With his passionate commitment to revolutionary energy changes, Governor Ritter shows us the way forward with the winning evolutionary approach outlined in this book."

– Mark Udall, US Senator, Colorado (Ret.)

"In *Powering Forward*, Bill Ritter lays out in concrete terms how we must begin the just transition to a new clean energy economy. He takes what seems to be a daunting task and breaks it down into key steps, making it clear why and how states are leading the way. This book takes us to the ground level and gives us a much-needed guide to a real and exciting clean energy future."

– Maggie Fox, former CEO of the Climate Reality Project and former
Deputy Executive Director of the Sierra Club

"There are many books about the energy revolution, but this one is different. Bill Ritter, who invented the concept of 'unleashing the new energy economy,' tells us how to root the emerging renewable energy economy in ethics, vision, truth-telling, and compassion."

– Hunter Lovins, the founder and president of
Natural Capitalism Solutions

"Every elected official in the United States should read this book. It is the owner's manual to a new American century and clean energy economy. A pragmatic road map to a vibrant, sustainable economy that leaders across the political spectrum can proudly support."

– Robert C. Sisson, Executive Director, ConservAmerica

"An informative why-and-how book about preventing climate change by making the transition to clean energy. The former governor of Colorado and founder and director of the Center for the New Energy Economy at Colorado State University, Ritter expands on the center's "Powering Forward" plan sent to President Barack Obama outlining actions the executive branch could take to help the United States meet climate and energy goals. First, the author describes the actions he took as governor to make Colorado a leader in clean energy – actions that other states might learn from. In straightforward prose interspersed with bulleted lists and numerous charts, diagrams, maps, and tables, Ritter tells it like it is, showing what the challenges are, where we have failed, and why. When Congress created the Department of Energy in 1977, it required the development of a coherent national energy plan. Today, however, 'our de facto national energy policy consists of a hodgepodge of government market interventions, many of them created for the benefit of influential special interests.' Ritter faults Congress for failing to lead, arguing about the science, and collaborating with a denial campaign. Still, the author notes, an energy revolution is already under way, with states setting clean energy standards, communities and individuals turning to wind and solar energy, corporations adopting greening tactics, and entrepreneurs developing new technologies. Ritter writes persuasively that while Congress seems paralyzed, the United States can and should lead the world, and he calls for a redistribution of political power back to the voters to ensure that this happens. Interestingly, for readers of Gary Sernovitz's *The Green and the Black* (2016), Ritter sees natural gas as an important part of the energy mix for decades to come.

– *Kirkus Reviews*

Contents

Foreword

Never before has the world been as interdependent as it is today. We see this new reality in financial markets, in transportation and trade, and in patterns of health and migration. Most profound of all is the degree to which we are linked by threats to the Earth's life support systems – our atmospheric, oceanic, freshwater, and other key natural resources.

The reality of this kind of interdependence is entirely new in human history. Never before have the fates and responsibilities of the world's people been as intertwined. Never before have we borne such heavy moral responsibilities to our children and grandchildren.

Unhappily, we are not living up to those responsibilities. In fact, we are failing badly as stewards of the natural systems that make human life and planetary productivity possible.

And our use of the atmosphere as a vast garbage dump is the most far-reaching failure of all. The global climate is changing even faster than many scientists anticipated only a few years ago.

The facts are indisputable. The primary global warming pollutant in our atmosphere has increased from 300 to more than 400 parts per million in a century. Over that same period, sea levels have increased by seven inches, and the acidity in the oceans has grown by more than 30 percent. The world's great ice sheets are shrinking, led by rapid losses in Arctic sea ice at a rate of 3.5–4 percent per decade in the last 30 years. Glaciers are retreating the world over. The range and activities of species are changing on land, at sea, and in freshwater ecosystems. Weather patterns are changing, and extreme weather events – droughts, wildfires, floods, and heat waves – are increasing.

These realities have been rigorously documented by the world's best scientists – peer reviewed and widely popularized. Scientific consensus tells us that unless we significantly change course and reduce emissions, catastrophic climate change is likely in this century.

For too long, the political response to this mountain of scientific evidence has been utterly insufficient. We have squandered years, even decades in the fight against global climate change because too many elected leaders have refused to acknowledge how much our long-term economic and national security is linked to the health of the planet's life support systems. Virtually all economic activity is dependent in some way on the environment and its underlying resource base – everything from food and fuel to water and fiber. These are the foundations of the vast majority of all economic activity and most jobs. Over the long term, living off our ecological capital is a bankrupt economic strategy. Moreover, it is a recipe for global instability as climate changes inflict devastating and destabilizing consequences on the world's poorest islands and coastal regions, on agriculture and food security, and on disease and global health.

To prevent this kind of a future, the science tells us that we need to stabilize carbon dioxide emissions immediately and begin rolling them back to achieve an 80 percent reduction from 1990 levels by 2050. Central to this agenda is the challenge of transforming the world's energy systems to low and no-carbon fuels and electricity. The requirements are clear:

- Using energy more efficiently is the low-hanging fruit of the world's low carbon future. Massive opportunities exist for increased productivity in the transportation, building, and industrial sectors.

- We need to facilitate rapid fuel-switching, so that we can move from the most carbon-intensive fuels, such as coal and oil, toward cleaner burning fuels, such as natural gas and renewables.

- For the long term, we need to continue accelerating deployment of the clean energy technologies and jobs that are expanding rapidly in the solar, wind, and biomass industries.

- And we have to set the right incentives for soil, wetland, and forest preservation, so that farmers can make money through sustainable practices and carbon sequestration.

With the world's largest economy, and as the greatest long-term contributor to the global warming problem, the United States bears special responsibility in taking on the greatest economic, social, political, and moral challenge of the twenty-first century.

Bill Ritter has emerged as a highly unlikely guiding light for the kind of American political leadership that is required. As a former missionary, Ritter has long possessed a resolute moral compass and compassion for the poor. But he is a relatively new evangelist for climate action and energy innovation. This passion evolved from his decision to jump into politics. Many were perplexed when the tough-on-crime, pro-life Denver District

Attorney announced his intention to run for governor in 2006. Few could envision what his platform might be. Even fewer gave him a chance of winning.

Throughout 2005 and 2006, Bill Ritter traveled the state of Colorado, hunting for votes. It was an expedition that changed him and the state completely. Ritter did what good politicians do – he listened and learned. With a prosecutor's attention to detail, he came to understand the changing energy landscape unfolding across Colorado and the nation. As a gifted political leader, he took what he learned, looked over the horizon, and defined an agenda for a new energy economy around which he could base his campaign and his administration as governor.

As governor, Bill Ritter implemented his plan for a new energy future by simultaneously harnessing responsible natural gas development and rapidly deploying energy efficiency and renewable energy. He reformed the state's Oil and Gas Commission, dramatically expanded Colorado's renewable energy standard to 30 percent by 2020, attracted numerous clean energy businesses and jobs, and launched a major effort to replace 900 megawatts of coal-fired electricity with cleaner alternatives.

This book, in part, chronicles the governor's remarkable journey and ultimate embrace of global climate change and the clean energy challenge. It is a testament to the kind of change one individual can experience, and one individual can create. Moreover, it provides a roadmap for the future – for how governors, states, and countries everywhere can become a part of the new energy future that Bill Ritter has helped usher in.

Today, there are nearly 400 solar energy companies in Colorado, providing more than 4,000 jobs. Colorado is among the top 10 states for per capita solar capacity. In the wind industry, Colorado hosts 23 manufacturing facilities and ranks fifth in the nation for wind energy jobs. All totaled, the state ranks in the top 10 nationally for installed wind and solar capacity.

The climate and energy challenge is the essential, existential priority for the future of humanity. All who want to join in forging solutions for the future will find in Bill Ritter and this book an example of the kind of political and moral courage that is required to change course and preserve the planet's life support systems. And they will see that this is both a worthy challenge and a compelling opportunity for the work of this and future generations.

– Timothy E. Wirth

Introduction

Why We Need an Energy Revolution

*An archer aimed at an eagle and let loose an arrow.
The eagle was struck. As he turned and looked at the
shaft, he saw that it was tipped with his own feathers,
and he said, "Many are betrayed by the very things
that they themselves have wrought."*

– An Aesop Fable[1]

When educator Katharine Lee Bates arrived in Colorado Springs in 1893
after traveling across the country, the sight of Pikes Peak inspired her to
write the poem that became the lyrics of "America the Beautiful." For those
of us who have been here for generations, it has been too easy to take the
natural beauty of this place for granted and to assume it always will be
what it always has been. I grew up working the fields in Colorado, hiking
its mountains, fishing in its streams, and hunting on its prairies. Nothing
would give me greater joy than to know my grandchildren will share those
experiences in years to come.

But when we drive west into the mountains today, the purple
mountain majesties have been replaced by dead trees. There are enormous
expanses of pine forests where trees have fallen as far as the eye can see,
like millions of flammable pick-up sticks. The elk, deer, longhorn sheep,
and black bear habitat is gone in those places. The erosion that was once
held in check by healthy forests threatens to choke Colorado's storied
trout streams with silt. A profound ecological chain reaction is under way,
started by the Japanese bark beetle – an insect the size of a grain of rice
that has proliferated in part because the weather has warmed enough to
allow it to have two life cycles each year, rather than one. The infestation
will only end when the insects die because there are no trees left.

At the same time, as a westerner and a Coloradan, I know the
value we in the United States have derived from fossil fuels, nuclear

power, and the generations of people who produced them. Fossil energy production is part of Colorado's history and remains an important part of its economy. The problems caused by conventional energy resources here and elsewhere around the world can no longer go unaddressed, however. There can be no question that the quality of life we enjoy today, the incredible innovations in technology we have witnessed, the competitiveness of our economy, and indeed life as we know it have been built on the foundation created by men and women working in coal mines, oil and gas fields, power plants, and laboratories. They have been the sinew and bone of prosperity and national security for the past 200 years. We should hope that 200 years from now our descendants will conclude that we achieved the same degree of hard work, genius, and entrepreneurial spirit as those early energy industries.

These are the two Colorados that, like the rest of America, are on the cusp between the fossil energy economy of the twentieth century and the low-carbon economy of the twenty-first. The transition from the old energy economy to the new is both necessary and disruptive, with real impacts on real people. Regardless of differences of opinion on how we actually make this transition, there is one indisputable fact: We saw trouble coming long ago but we did virtually nothing to stop it.

Some historians consider 1970 the beginning of both our energy insecurity and the roller-coaster ride our economy has taken with its reliance on fossil fuels. That is the year we began consuming more oil than we produced, the year when the era of oil imports began. It took only three years to find out the hard way how vulnerable we are to political and economic forces we do not control.

Late in 1973, President Richard Nixon began providing material support to Israel during the Yom Kippur War. The Organization of Petroleum Exporting Countries (OPEC) responded by suspending oil shipments to the United States. Oil prices shot from $3 to $12 a barrel. The embargo resulted in gasoline shortages, shocks to the US automobile industry, and even an appeal that Americans forgo Christmas lights that year. Eventually, it resulted in an international energy crisis.

The First Presidential Alert

We have known about the dangers of global climate change for generations. Scientists began understanding the link between carbon dioxide and the greenhouse effect in the late 1800s. As far as we know, the first US president alerted to climate change was Lyndon Johnson in 1965. That November, his science advisors gave him a report warning that carbon emissions "will modify the heat balance of the atmosphere to such an extent that marked changes in climate... could occur." The White House release of the report summarized its findings:

> *Carbon dioxide is being added to the earth's atmosphere by the burning of coal, oil, and natural gas at the rate of six billion tons a year. By the year 2000, there will be about 25 percent more carbon dioxide in our atmosphere than at present...*

> *Pollution is an inevitable consequence of an advanced society, but we need not suffer from the intensity and extent of pollution we now see around us... Society must take the position that no citizen, no industry, no municipality has the right to pollute.*

President Johnson told the US Congress in a special address that year that, "This generation has altered the composition of the atmosphere on a global scale through... a steady increase in carbon dioxide from the burning of fossil fuels." His advisors recommended that special taxes be levied against polluters. It is an idea our political leaders are still debating a half century later.[2]

Had we confronted climate change and oil addiction when they first came to our attention, addressing these problems would have been far cheaper and less disruptive than it will be today. With market-based actions and regulations when necessary, including a price on carbon pollution, the United States could have engaged in a more gradual evolution to a clean and stable energy economy. We might have avoided the oil shocks that helped trigger "stagflation" and the stock market crash of 1973, as well as the succession of painful economic recessions that hit the American people in the early 1980s, 1990s, and 2000s. It can be argued that the extreme weather events causing great suffering today would be significantly less extreme, and their impact on federal spending much lower.

Acting today can still reduce the impacts of climate change in the future, but it will require from us nothing short of an energy revolution.

Bloodless and Green

The word *revolution* carries heavy connotative baggage, because it usually refers to the violent overthrow of an established order. The revolution we need today would definitely disrupt the established order – our fossil energy economy – but it is neither subversive nor violent. It is bloodless, but far from gutless. It would fundamentally change the way we produce and consume energy to provide maximum benefit to our citizens while strengthening and expanding our economy. It would be profoundly patriotic. In fact, revolution is an American tradition "as necessary in the political world as storms in the physical," as Thomas Jefferson put it.[3] In a letter to William Stephens Smith, he wrote, "God forbid we should ever be twenty years without such a rebellion... What country can preserve its liberties if their rulers are not warned from time to time that their people preserve the spirit of resistance?"

And while the United States and other industrial nations have undergone many energy transitions in the past, this one must be different. It requires an evolution of our understanding of the biosphere and our part in it. In addition, the accelerating pace of climate change requires that the transition to clean energy be the most rapid in the history of industrial economies.[4]

No More Business as Usual

Most of us like order and predictability, but "business as usual" is no longer an operative concept in energy planning. Our energy economy in the twentieth century, including the public policies that influenced it and the public appetites that drove it, was formed by and for fossil fuels. Because fossil fuels are finite resources, it is an economy that by definition cannot be sustained. The transition to other fuels has always been a question of when, not if. Now we have the technology at our fingertips to expand energy productivity and the use of renewable fuels. Zero-carbon renewable electric generation and energy storage have plummeted in price in the past decade; their costs are expected to continue to decline. No industry in our economy would choose to return to the "business as usual" case of 20 years ago, yet that is where our utility sector remains mired.

While there appears to be no shortage of coal, oil, or natural gas in the world's underground reserves, their volatility, greenhouse gas emissions, impacts on public health, and costs to secure in unstable parts of the world threaten to bankrupt our economy. If we do nothing, the result will be progressively more severe crises in each of those areas, as well as in national and international stability. Our decision, to paraphrase Buckminster Fuller, is whether to be architects of our future or its victims. If we choose to be its architects, we will find that life in the new energy economy is better than the old in nearly every respect. Imagine a suite of services for consumers that puts them in control of their energy choices, a more resilient energy grid that provides more reliable power, and cleaner energy generation that helps preserve a hospitable and resource-rich natural environment for future generations.

We have demonstrated that we are capable of change, innovation, and better use of resources. If we can direct our creativity toward reducing the pollutants that are driving our changing climate, there is no doubt we can lead the world in a clean energy revolution just as we led the information revolution.

A series of events in recent history have raised our collective awareness of the responsibilities we bear as stewards of our environment.

The first photograph of the Earth from space was taken in 1946 by a camera strapped to a V-2 rocket that the United States appropriated from Germany after World War II. These views of the planet became more common after space exploration began in 1957, perhaps inspiring American statesman Adlai Stevenson to tell the United Nations in 1965:

> *We travel together, passengers on a little spaceship, dependent on its vulnerable reserves of air and soil; all committed, for our safety, to its security and peace; preserved from annihilation only by the care, the work, and the love we give our fragile craft.*[5]

A second critical event was the publication of Rachel Carson's book *Silent Spring* in 1962. In it, she described how pesticides were poisoning the environment (she called them "biocides"), killing birds and other wildlife. Her broader message was the profound impact human beings were having on the environment. The book was greeted with a publicity and legal counterattack from the chemical industry, but it became a seminal event in the early environmental movement.

Then in 1969, the heavily polluted Cuyahoga River in Cleveland, Ohio, caught fire. *Time* magazine covered the story, giving it national attention. The anti-intuitive visual proof that industrial emissions were bad enough to make a river burn created a political moment for the environment. The same year, US Senator Gaylord Nelson of Wisconsin witnessed a massive oil spill in California. It motivated him to found Earth Day, celebrated for the first time on April 22, 1970, by an estimated 20 million people.[6] As Earth Day organizers wrote, it was a "rare political alignment, enlisting support from Republicans and Democrats, rich and poor, city slickers and farmers, tycoons and labor leaders."[7] The year became even more significant for the environmental movement when the US Congress passed and the Republican president Richard Nixon signed the landmark Clean Air Act and the National Environmental Policy Act, two pieces of legislation that created the Environmental Protection Agency (EPA), and later, the Clean Water Act.

In December 1972, as the crew of *Apollo 17* traveled toward the moon, it snapped the first photograph of an entire sunlit side of the Earth. It showed the planet as a "little blue marble," our only home in black, inhospitable space. It became one of the most widely distributed photographs in history,[8] a potential planetary "aha moment" not only about the beauty and finite nature of the planet, but also about the common bond that everyone who inhabits it shares.

In those days, most environmental issues that received attention were local. So were the solutions. For example, Cleveland prevented more fires on the Cuyahoga River by cleaning up industrial pollution in the city. Air pollution could be reduced by local measures, such as cleaning up a factory's emissions or cutting down on car trips to reduce ozone levels.

Today our most serious environmental problems are global. Issues such as global warming are teaching us a lesson, if we choose to learn it. We are connected to, and indeed are part of, the biosphere – the planetary ecosystem and the life it supports. Greenhouse gas emissions in any country affect the well-being and future of us all. The photos taken from space today provide visual evidence of how air pollution migrates across international borders. The clear-cutting of forests in South America and

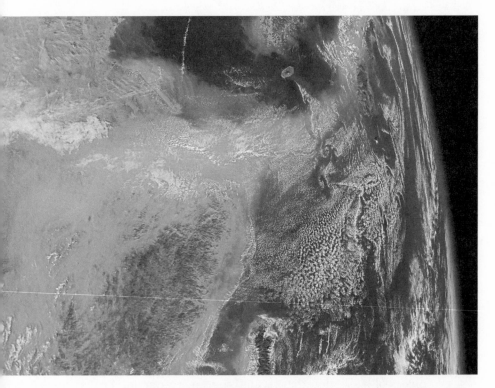

Industrial pollution from China migrates to Japan and then on to the Pacific Northwest, illustrating the international impact of air emissions. (Source: SeaWiFS Project, NASA/ Goddard Space Flight Center, and ORBIMAGE)

Indonesia undermine the ability of the Earth's natural systems to soak up and sequester carbon. The runoff that carries nitrogen pollution from farm fields and cities has created dead zones the size of Great Britain in our oceans.[9] Sixty percent of the coral formations essential to the ocean food chain are threatened by human activity. The World Bank reports that the global economy has lost more than $2 trillion over the last three decades because of the mismanagement of fisheries; 80 percent of ocean fish stocks are either depleted or in danger of depletion, threatening the primary source of protein for 1 billion of the world's people.[10]

We live in a global oil market, a global economy, and a world in which invasive species and deadly diseases travel from one country to another as easily as luggage on an airplane. Our numbers and collective footprint already exceed the planet's carrying capacity.[11] There have been five known large extinctions of species in the Earth's history, all caused by natural forces. Now, biodiversity loss is so extreme that scientists say we are experiencing the "Sixth Great Extinction," which is the most catastrophic of them all. Half of all plants and animals on the planet are expected to disappear by the end of this century, largely because of human activity.

Little Mystery Left

While we are not certain how rapidly the impacts of climate change will escalate, little mystery remains about what they will be. More than a century of research, including the largest scientific exercise ever undertaken – the Intergovernmental Panel on Climate Change (IPCC) – has foreseen a future of devastating drought, deadly heat, unprecedented floods, historic hurricanes, and wildfires so intense that they destroy the forests' ability to regenerate.[12] We are now observing evidence that confirms the predictions of past climate models: oceans are rising, species are migrating north and climbing to higher elevations to escape rising temperatures, and insects have turned vast forests in the American West and British Columbia into tinder where they stand. Pests and pestilence are appearing where they did not exist before. We have heard so many warnings from so many places about our ongoing disruption of the biosphere that we are in danger of becoming deaf to them.

These are crises largely of our own making, prolonged by political resistance and willful ignorance that stand in the way of national action to curb greenhouse gas emissions. Climate scientists are summoned to congressional hearings today to be accused of heresy by elected leaders who deny the reality of global warming. It is as though our politics have regressed four centuries to the time of Galileo.

We are better than this. And we can do better than this!

We need to find common ground on which to build a prosperity based on stewardship of natural capital and environmental systems, and on the knowledge that our well-being is intimately interconnected with those systems. While we want to grow our economy and markets for our products throughout the world, we must remain stubborn stewards of our environment, leaving the next generation a future worthy of all of our technological accomplishments.

We need a moral economy that recognizes our obligation to those who built and sacrificed to preserve our country in the past and to those who will inherit it in the future. The energy revolution requires that we reassert fundamental American values that transcend partisanship: conservation, independence, choice, freedom, self-sufficiency, transparency in government, duty to country, and the commitment that each generation will make life better for the generations that follow. There are selfish reasons, too. The need for a global energy revolution has been called the largest market opportunity in history. If we do not capture that opportunity, other nations will.

Good Karma Does Not Count

To repeat, the need for a radical transformation of our energy economy is not an indictment of fossil fuels, capitalism, industrialization, democracy, or the United States. The shift is necessary because of a historic irony: While fossil fuels have been our path to prosperity in the past, their emissions are now undermining the quality of life they helped create. It is not the industrial world's profligate energy consumption alone that drives the urgency for action; it is also the growing international competition for energy as people aspire to the middle class, including those 1.2 billion people who do not have access to modern electric power. In my view, other nations and future generations should judge those of us who live in the United States – and we should judge ourselves – not by what we did in the past, but by what we do now to help all nations build their economies with clean and sustainable energy.

We cannot count on good luck, good karma, cool new technologies, or serendipity to accomplish the disruptive shift we need in our energy and environmental policies. If we wait for climate impacts to become so destructive that all political resistance has been swept away, we will have allowed global warming to progress so far that many of its impacts will be irreversible. I do not know anyone who pretends that this transition will be easy; nor do I know any realists who believe it is not necessary. The good news is that trends and forces are at work today to make an energy revolution possible.

The bottom line is that we need to accelerate and complete a transformative energy revolution in the United States. It is not the only thing we must do to secure a better future, but we cannot achieve that future without it.

Given the formidable body of literature that already has been written about energy and environmental crises, I have wondered what new perspective I could bring to the conversation. Ideas abound. Helpful technologies are ready for market. New technical advances and policy developments happen almost daily. Global investments are increasing in clean and renewable energy. I cannot improve upon the eloquence of those who already have appealed to our consciences and common sense, and who have called for a new Apollo mission or a new national effort on par with our mobilization for World War II.

What I can contribute is the perspective of a governor who worked to find common ground between fossil energy and renewable energy industries and whose state became known nationally for its work to build a clean energy economy. My perspective has been enriched, too, by my work with governors of both political parties as the founder and director of the Center for a New Energy Economy at Colorado State University, where we work with energy decision makers at the state level. It has also been informed by a yearlong consultation my team and I conducted with more than 100 of the nation's top energy and climate thought leaders, an exercise we undertook at the request of the White House.[13]

My conclusion from these experiences is that there is hope. I believe we can find climate and energy solutions – indeed, we can embark on an energy revolution – that combines market forces with intelligent public policies that transcend partisan politics. And the time is now.

The Colorado Promise

1

The activist is not the man who says the river is dirty.
The activist is the man who cleans up the river.

– Ross Perot

Colorado has not been exempt from the weather disasters that are increasing in frequency and intensity around the world. These events can be attributed to complicated causes, but their impacts are profoundly personal.

Few Coloradans will forget the Hayman forest fire that burned southwest of Denver in 2002. It was so large and intense, it created its own weather system. More than 5,300 people had to evacuate their homes. Or the record Waldo Canyon fire near Pikes Peak in 2012 that killed two people and destroyed 346 homes. Or the 2013 Black Forest fire near Colorado Springs that set another record, destroying 511 homes and killing two more people. Or the West Fork fire the same year, which forced the evacuation of the entire community of South Fork.

Then, in the fall of 2013, 100 miles to the north of the West Fork fire, eight days of rains produced epic flooding across 17 Colorado counties and nearly 2,400 square miles – a disaster ranked as a 1,000-year rainfall event. The floods changed the course of rivers and the future of riverside communities.

Between 2006 and 2013, Coloradans were hit with nearly $4 billion in property damages and 70 fatalities due to severe weather; only eight other states had higher levels of deaths and damages.[14] State officials have tracked a temperature increase of approximately 2°F between 1977 and 2006, the blink of an eye in geophysical terms.

The rising temperatures have been accompanied by drought. In 2006, parts of Colorado were still recovering from a 2000–2003 drought that resulted in the driest conditions in the state's instrumented history.[15] The Colorado River, a vital source of water to 30 million people in seven states, fell to its lowest level since monitoring began in 1885.[16]

In a scene that has become all too familiar in the United States, the Black Forest fire rages near Colorado Springs in 2013. The fire consumed more than 14,000 acres, destroyed more than 500 homes, and killed two people. (Source: The United States Air Force)

Water Worries

In the meantime, Shell Oil was buying water rights for use in future oil shale gas production, raising concerns that the oil and gas industry would compete with agriculture, cities, tourism, and other industries for Colorado's limited water supplies. We can expect the impacts of climate change to get much worse. In 2006, for example, Colorado College issued a study showing that the state's ski industry could disappear by mid-century unless global warming and its adverse effects on snowpack were reversed.[17]

This was some of the backdrop when I contemplated running for governor in the 2006 election. Nevertheless, neither clean energy nor climate change were high on my list of interests. My personal history up to that point helps explain why. I was born in Denver and raised on a farm not far from the city, the middle child of twelve. At the age of 14, I began working summers in the construction industry to help support my family. I earned a bachelor's degree at Colorado State University and a law degree at the University of Colorado. The law, not environmental sciences, became my career path.

After college, I worked as a deputy district attorney for the City and County of Denver. Then in 1987, my wife Jeannie and I volunteered as lay missionaries in Zambia. This experience taught us a great deal about poverty, hunger, and aspiration in a less developed nation – the kind of nation, I would later understand, that has the most to lose from and the least ability to cope with climate change. When we returned to Denver three years later, I became a federal prosecutor. In 1993, then-governor Roy Romer appointed me as Denver's district attorney, and I served in that post for the next 12 years.

Deciding to Run

I began thinking about running for governor more than a year before the election. It is safe to say, I think, that most candidates who believe in public service are sincere in wanting to make their jurisdictions better places to

Only three months after the Black Forest fire, catastrophic floods took place along Colorado's Front Range. In and around Boulder, Colorado, the rainfall in just one of the flood days nearly equaled the area's average precipitation for an entire year. (Source: Federal Emergency Management Agency)

live and work, and that was the case for me. In the relative quiet before the fray of a statewide political campaign, I studied the issues that seemed most important to the future of our state. They extended beyond my experience as an attorney, missionary, and prosecutor. Colorado deserved a better education system, better transportation, better health care, a better way to deal with immigration, plans to ensure ample and clean water supplies, and, of course, a strong economy and new jobs.

After I decided to run for the governorship and assembled a campaign team, we bundled these goals into a platform we called the Colorado Promise, and our pledge was to help Colorado reach its full potential.[18] To be frank, the Colorado Promise was not only a statement of what my goals would be as governor, it was also an early campaign strategy to define myself as a candidate before my opponent could try to define me. A typical tactic for running against a former criminal prosecutor is to attack his or her record. In my case, the attacks would be about how my office used plea bargains rather than going to trial to prosecute criminals, and to resolve cases involving illegal immigrants. I would have no trouble defending myself against such attacks, but I wanted the campaign to be about bigger issues. The Promise theme put those issues on the table.

An important element in the Colorado Promise was to make the state a national leader in the use of clean energy. Energy was not my highest priority early in the campaign; it did not appear until page 24 in our 52-page booklet. It clearly was on the minds of Colorado's voters, however. In November 2004, after the state legislature rejected several consecutive proposals to establish a Renewable Energy Portfolio Standard (RPS) – a requirement that electric utilities generate a specific percentage of their power from renewable resources – citizens took matters into their own hands. Renewable energy advocates gathered enough signatures to put an RPS on the ballot of that year's election. Amendment 37 required the state's two investor-owned utilities to generate 10 percent of their electricity from renewable resources by 2015. It was approved with 54 percent of the vote. With that, Colorado became the seventeenth state in the nation to create an RPS, but it was the first and remains one of only a few to do so by citizen initiative.[19]

My advisors and supporters made me aware that other states were attracting a new generation of energy industries, including businesses that manufactured wind turbines and solar energy systems. I knew that the key to attracting these industries was state policies that created long-term market certainty for clean energy technologies – policies such as the RPS. As I campaigned across the state, I found that people in all parts of Colorado were receptive to clean energy development. Urban residents appreciated how clean energy would improve air quality. Rural residents in the more conservative parts of the state appreciated how ranchers and farmers could earn new income by leasing land for wind turbines. Rural counties and communities liked the idea of earning new tax revenues. Our substantial population of rugged individualists liked the idea of greater energy independence.

The New Energy Economy

One day one of my campaign advisors, Melody Harris – the wife of my communications director – pointed out that we were no longer simply talking about making Colorado a clean energy leader; we were talking about creating a "new energy economy." That idea and that phrase became a signature phrase of our campaign.

There was some disagreement among my advisors about this new plank in my platform. As the election approached, the state was enjoying a boom in natural gas production. There were nearly 23,000 producing gas wells in Colorado at that time and production was increasing. At the US Department of Energy (DOE), analysts concluded that Colorado was part of a region that would become *the* major source of the nation's fossil fuels in the years ahead, largely because of our unconventional gas deposits and new methods to reach them.[20]

Fossil energy production was ingrained in Colorado's history, so members of my team were concerned there would be political risks in promoting new energy resources that would compete with the old. Colorado companies had been producing coal, coke, oil, and natural gas since deposits were discovered in the 1800s.

We knew our state would not exhaust its fossil energy deposits for a very long time.[21] The US Government Accountability Office (GAO) estimates that if only half of the oil could be recovered from the shale rock in the Green River Formation under Colorado and Utah, it would be "about equal to the entire world's proven oil reserves."[22] Another key local deposit, the Piceance Basin, holds enough natural gas to fuel the nation for two full years.

But we also recognized the vulnerabilities for an economy that depends on fossil energy production. As the independent research organization Headwaters Economics put it, "The volatility of fossil fuel markets poses obstacles to the stability and long-term security of economic growth in energy-producing regions."[23]

It also concerned me that unless oil and gas were produced responsibly, their extraction and use could be detrimental to Colorado's citizens and to its indispensable tourism industry. An estimated 12 percent of America's outdoor industry companies reside in Colorado, accounting for more than 100,000 jobs and $10 billion in economic activity. But air pollution was already limiting visibility in Rocky Mountain National Park. By 2007, the bark beetle infestation had spread across nearly half of the forested lands in the entire state, leaving millions of acres vulnerable to fire and leaving wildlife without habitat. In other words, the growing impacts of global warming were casting a shadow on the Colorado Promise. All things considered, clean energy production seemed to be entirely compatible with a state known worldwide for its natural beauty.

Wind Farms and Wheat Fields

I told my team that I wanted my first campaign commercial to be filmed at a location in rural Colorado where wind turbines were generating electricity in a farm field. The commercial, which became known as "Wind Farms in Wheat Fields" among the campaign staff, began airing on September 5, 2006, showing me standing in front of turbines turning the wind into a new cash crop. "In Colorado," I said, "the future is building wind farms…" I believe that was the moment that separated me from my opponent. I never trailed in the race after the ad appeared. It was clear that clean energy development would be a top priority if I won the election.

I was elected on Tuesday, November 7, 2006. The next day, my staff and I began working on a transition plan. We created advisory teams to interview people for positions in my cabinet. I judged each candidate in part on whether he or she supported the goal of tying energy production and economic development to environmental sustainability. That criterion guided my selection of Colorado's new directors of Natural Resources, Labor, Local Affairs, Regulatory Affairs, Health and Environment, and the director of my Office of Energy Management and Conservation. My final appointment was Don Elliman as the director of Colorado's Office of Economic Development and International Trade – a person who understood the business community better than anyone I knew and who was clearly committed to a clean energy agenda.

Months before, while campaigning on Colorado's Western Slope and speaking to the Colorado Water Conservation Board – a conservative organization – I announced that if elected, I would create a cabinet-level position to work specifically on issues related to global warming. Some of the people on my campaign team were

When a New Energy Economy became a key plank in my campaign platform in 2006, I decided that my first TV spot would illustrate the potential of wind energy as a new cash crop for Colorado's ranchers and farmers. The spot became known as the "Wind Farms in Wheat Fields" video.
(Source: Ritter Gubernatorial Campaign)

not enthused because of the political risk involved in making climate change a priority in a state with a great history of fossil fuel production. Nevertheless, I made sure that one of my first hires was a member of my staff dedicated to developing a state climate action plan.

In my inaugural address on January 9, 2007, I returned to the theme that had resonated so strongly with Colorado's voters. "The Colorado Promise is simple," I said. "It's about making a better future. A better future for our children and our grandchildren. It's about hope. It's about finding the common ground for the common good."

"Let's start," I said, "by being bolder than any other state when it comes to renewable energy. Let's commit right now to making Colorado a national leader... a world leader... in renewable energy. Let's create a New Energy Economy right here in Colorado."

Weeks later, the Intergovernmental Panel on Climate Change (IPCC) issued its finding that global warming was unequivocal,[24] and its principal cause was the burning of fossil fuels.

2 | From Promises to Policies

Keep every promise you make and only make promises you can keep.

– Real estate executive Anthony Hitt

Within 48 hours of my election in 2006, I met with leaders of the Colorado House and Senate, who agreed that the new energy economy would be a priority in the upcoming session. First up was an expansion of the Renewable Energy Portfolio Standard (RPS) that citizens approved by referendum in 2004. It became apparent immediately that the politics of clean energy had changed dramatically since the referendum. By 2007, the two investor-owned utilities that were required by Amendment 37 to generate 10 percent of their electricity with renewable resources found they would meet the requirement more than five years before their 2015 deadline. Our biggest utility, Xcel Energy, turned from one of the most formidable opponents of the RPS to an advocate for its expansion.

My office worked with the legislature to increase the RPS for large utilities to 20 percent of their electric generation by 2020, double the requirement of Amendment 37, and to expand the RPS to the state's rural electric associations. The political impact of Amendment 37 became clear as the new RPS made its way through the legislature. From 2002 to 2004, before citizens took control, the legislature failed several times to approve an RPS. Now, the bill to double the requirement moved without strong debate through both houses of the legislature, with support from both Republicans and Democrats.

After the doubling of the RPS came bills to develop new transmission lines that would accommodate large-scale wind and solar projects, and to create a task force to map the state's solar, wind, geothermal, and other renewable energy resources. Another bill failed to pass the legislature the first year, but succeeded in the second. It created statewide net metering, a policy in which utilities give customers credit for electricity they produce with rooftop solar systems or wind turbines. (Investor-owned utilities already offered these credits as a result of the 2004 ballot initiative.) Yet another new law required electric and gas utilities to engage in demand-side management, also known as energy efficiency, by providing more incentives for customers to improve their equipment and buildings. These were all essential foundation blocks for the new energy economy, and I signed them into law during my first year in office.

I also took early action on Colorado's oil and gas production. Although I became an advocate of sustainable energy during my campaign, I never undervalued the importance of fossil energy production to Colorado's economy or to the nation.[25] I believed then and still do that natural gas, the cleanest of the fossil fuels, will be a valuable part of the nation's energy mix that includes high percentages of low-carbon inexhaustible resources combined with very high levels of energy efficiency.

But to maintain what the industry calls its "social license to operate," natural gas must be produced responsibly.[26] *Responsibly* means using a wide variety of management practices that protect nearby communities and environmental quality (see Chapter 15).

Responsible production was a growing concern in 2006 and 2007, with Colorado experiencing a boom in natural gas production. By 2007, the number of drilling applications submitted to state regulators grew to 6,400, double the number in 2004. One of my first decisions – and one of the most politically risky – was to reconstitute the Colorado Oil and Gas Conservation Commission (COGCC), the panel that oversees the regulation of oil and gas production in the state. In Colorado, the operative statute required the majority of COGCC members be from the oil and gas industry. This law ensured that representatives of the industry had long dominated the commission, which, as you might imagine, resulted in regulations that did not keep pace with dramatic technological improvements, primarily hydraulic fracturing and directional drilling.

During the 2007 legislative session, I advocated, and our legislators approved, two bills to reform the COGCC. One expanded it from seven to nine members so that we could add people who represented environmental and social issues related to oil and gas extraction. The other required the commission to give greater attention to how production affected wildlife, land, water, air quality, and communities.

These changes were a direct challenge to one of Colorado's most politically influential industries and a test case of whether my office and the legislature would stand our ground. Each new appointment to the commission required state senate confirmation. Several Republican senators and industry lobbyists argued that the new appointees would over-

Examples of New Energy Economy Legislation

HB07-1169: Statewide Net Metering

HB07-1281: 20 percent Renewable Portfolio Standard for Regulated Utilities

HB10-1365: Clean Air Clean Jobs Act

SB09-51: Renewable Energy Financing Act of 2009

HB07-1037: Natural Gas and Electric Demand Side Management for Regulated Utilities

SB07-100: Energy Transmission Development

HB10-1001: 30 percent Renewable Portfolio Standard and a 3 percent Distributed Generation Carve Out

For a full list of New Energy Economy Legislation, visit: **http://cnee.colostate. edu/graphics/uploads/BluePrintfortheNewEnergyEconomyColorado.pdf.**

Figure 2.1

regulate production, slow down exploration and drilling, and drive energy companies from Colorado. Despite these warnings, the senate confirmed the new commission members. The political rhetoric died down once the new commission went to work and it became clear that our emphasis on socially and environmentally responsible production was not driving oil and gas companies away from Colorado. In fact, the diversification of the commission became the first step in an ongoing collaboration with the industry to balance energy production with the protection of Colorado's natural beauty and quality of life. Over the next several years, including under my successor, Governor John Hickenlooper, Colorado set standards for oil and gas production that led the nation on issues such as wildlife protection, the disclosure of chemicals used in hydraulic fracturing, and, most recently, methane monitoring.

I learned an important lesson from this experience. When the government proposes policy changes or new regulations to protect the public interest, the industries affected by the changes push back hard. Many inside the industry see it as their job to resist government interventions in their businesses. Once the battle is over and the outcome decided, vested interests adapt and thrive with reasonable regulations. In fact, as I will explain in more detail later, oil and gas companies have told us that reasonable regulations are beneficial. They help weed out the "bad actors" that exist in every industry, they prevent competitors from engaging in unfair practices, and they increase public confidence in oil and gas production. As one oil and gas executive told me, good companies are smart and facile enough to adapt to almost any reasonable regulatory environment. The problem is not regulation; it is that government keeps changing the rules.

Those early steps were the beginning of four intensive years of clean energy legislation. Between 2007 and 2011, the Colorado legislature approved and I signed 57 new laws that reinvented the state's energy policies (Figure 2.1). Many of these originated from ideas within my administration's team. Among them was another increase in the RPS, this time requiring that investor-owned utilities generate 30 percent of their electricity with renewable resources by 2020 without raising their electric rates more than 2 percent.[27]

The new RPS gave Colorado one of the toughest renewable electric requirements in the nation, second only to California.[28] By 2014, the results were becoming clear. Although some lawmakers had argued that the 30 percent RPS would be unachievable, Xcel Energy supported the increase and was ahead of schedule to meet it. Because of a variety of factors, including the market certainty created by RPSs across the country, the costs of developing solar and wind energy and integrating them into the electric system have gone down.

The 30 percent RPS generated considerable opposition from the coal industry, large industrial customers, and many Republican lawmakers. They attacked the bill from several angles. They worried about the fact that renewable energy resources have an advantage over natural gas because, unlike gas, they do not experience price volatility. Two Republican members of the legislature's audit committee called for an investigation of two members of the state's Public Utility Commission, alleging that their participation in crafting the act was outside the scope of regulators. The Intermountain Rural Electric Association went to court to prevent one of the commissioners from ruling on Xcel Energy's compliance plan since he also participated in drafting the legislation. The court rejected that argument.

The RPS also generated controversy over its provision to require that some of the renewable energy requirement be met with distributed energy systems – for example, rooftop solar panels. The principal issue was how to allocate funding between small residential customers and utility-scale developers of distributed energy systems. As one of my staff put it, the discussion was ugly, but we resolved it in a way that has allowed both large and small distributed generation systems to flourish.

Another pioneering law, and arguably the capstone of our new energy economy initiatives, was the Clean Air Clean Jobs Act that I signed in 2010. It was a first-of-its-kind target to replace or refire 900 megawatts of coal-fired power – most of it located along Colorado's Front Range – with natural gas, renewable energy, and energy efficiency by 2017. Xcel Energy estimated the cost would be $1.3 billion, an amount that would add $1.16 to the average monthly electric bill of its customers. Since then, Xcel has found that the average monthly increase for its customers has been $.05 a month. The net result of this small increase to their bills was that consumers would receive a wide variety of indirect but important benefits, from new jobs to improvements in public health. One health expert estimated the act would result in health-care cost benefits totaling $590 million over 36 years.[29]

Despite encountering a few hurdles along the way, the act had an unusual coalition of supporters. Natural gas companies supported the legislation because it would expand their market share in the electricity sector. Environmental organizations joined with conservatives who believed it was better for the state to protect air quality than to rely on the US Environmental Protection Agency (EPA) to do it. In fact, the act was an elegant solution to several problems at once. It helped the Denver Metropolitan Area with its problem of nonattainment in limiting regional haze, it helped the state comply with EPA's other air quality standards, and it gave utilities a way to recover the costs of retiring coal plants before the end of their useful lives. The bill sped through the legislature in 17 days. At the signing ceremony, Republican senate minority leader Josh Penry told the press, "If I were in charge of writing this bill's name, I would have called it the Clean Air, Clean Jobs, More Drilling Act of 2010." He meant that as a compliment.

With the bill's passage, we completed a three-part strategy for making the oil and gas industry more accountable to the concerns of our communities. This strategy:

1. overhauled the state's oil and gas commission

2. improved environmental regulation of the industry

3. expanded the state's natural gas market.

We would not have supported Step 3 without Steps 1 and 2.

The argument we heard in the Colorado legislature – that the transition to clean and renewable energy would substantially increase consumer electric bills – has been a common criticism of RPS policies in other states. Several states have written caps on rate increases into their renewable energy standards, as we did.[30] Two of DOE's national laboratories issued an analysis in May 2014 of how RPSs had affected consumers' electric bills around the country.[31]

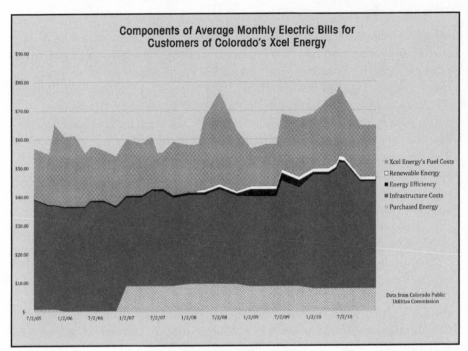

Figure 2.2

Opponents of energy efficiency and renewable energy policies often argue that the policies will drive up consumer energy prices. During my term as governor, we increased the use of renewable energy nearly tenfold, and improved energy efficiency throughout Colorado while keeping energy costs in line with the Consumer Price Index. Using Colorado's largest investor-owned utility, Xcel Energy, as an example, this chart shows that the real drivers of energy costs during my term were infrastructure and what the company paid for fossil fuels to run its power plants. The low and relatively steady costs of energy efficiency and renewables were a result in part of a 2 percent cap on retail rates incorporated into Colorado's RPS. (Source: Center for the Renewable Energy Economy with data from the Colorado Public Utilities Commission)

They found that the standards resulted in 46,000 megawatts of new renewable energy capacity through the end of 2012. The cost increase for consumers averaged less than 1 percent.[32] They also noted that while most states had not tried to quantify the indirect benefits of their RPSs, the upsides include the savings associated with avoided air emissions and job creation as well as improved public health.[33] Many of the benefits continue over the lifetime of renewable energy systems, the labs noted, while most of the costs of the systems are one-time expenditures to buy and install the hardware. In solar and wind energy systems, of course, the fuel is forever free (Figure 2.2).

Another objective at the start of my administration was to keep my promise to address the risks of climate change. We did not know how extensive those risks were or what the precise benefits of mitigating them would be, but it was a safe assumption that the benefits were enough to justify a search for common ground on clean energy. One of my first hires was a specialist on my staff who worked exclusively on developing a statewide climate action plan. Our statewide greenhouse gas emissions in 2005 were 35 percent higher than in 1990. The final plan was the result of a consultative process that involved leaders from the business, science, conservation, local government, and citizen sectors. It established the goal of cutting our greenhouse gas emissions 20 percent below 2005 levels by 2020 and laid out a roadmap to get there. We calculated that if the state continued business as usual, our emissions would grow to 81 percent above 1990 levels by the year 2020.

We announced the climate action plan in November 2007 at Denver's Coors Field, home of the Colorado Rockies baseball team, under the first solar photovoltaic system ever installed at a major league sporting venue.[34]

The results have exceeded our expectations. After passage of the increased renewable standard, energy efficiency requirements, and the Clean Air Clean Jobs Act, Xcel Energy estimated that its emissions in 2020 would be 35 percent below 2005 levels, exceeding our target of 20 percent.

The Low Cost of Clean Energy

A common assumption is that the clean energy revolution will be costly for utilities and consumers. However in 2015, Colorado had the second-lowest energy costs in the nation – $244 per month counting electricity, natural gas, motor fuel, and home heating oil.

Xcel Energy Inc., the state's largest electric utility, reports that the Colorado's Clean Air Clean Jobs legislation added only $.05 to its customers' monthly utility bills.

Xcel now considers wind to be a better long-term value than natural gas for generating electricity. The company is receiving bids of $25 per megawatt hour for wind power in 20-year power purchase agreements while it expects natural gas to cost $32 per megawatt hour over the same period.

Xcel, the largest provider of wind power in the United States, reports that on some of the windiest Colorado days, as much as 60% of its electricity is generated by wind.

Sources: Wallethub, Bloomberg Business, Xcel Energy Inc.

Independent Power Systems and Xcel Energy partnered to install the first solar power system to be built in a major league stadium. The 10-kilowatt system was designed to produce more energy than the stadium's scoreboard uses. (Source: Independent Power Systems, solarips.com)

During my time in the statehouse and in the years since, I have been asked what it was like to be governor. There were good days and bad, as in any vocation. But there was also an ever-present sense of responsibility, opportunity, and urgency. At times, I felt like a sprinter running through quicksand and minefields. I am sure that feeling is not unique to a Colorado governor. Day by day, my staff and I were involved in strategic decisions, political maneuvers, and frequent examinations of our policy compass to make sure we were on course during our four years in office to fulfill the energy and climate components of the Colorado Promise. At the same time, there were experiences that made it clear why the job was worth doing.

One of these great times involved a middle school in Oak Creek, Colorado. The school had been heated with coal boilers since the 1970s. During my second year in office, we learned that the system was leaking and children were breathing coal dust throughout the school day. The school also was having trouble retaining its maintenance workers because of the drudgery of stoking the boilers. Making an economic case for replacing the boilers with equipment that used a cleaner fuel was difficult because the school received its coal free from a nearby mine.

When we learned about this, the Governor's Energy Office, the Department of Education, and the Department of Local Affairs worked with an energy services company to design a solution. The company proposed replacing the coal boilers with a biomass boiler and a ground-source heat pump – a system that used subsurface ground temperatures to help heat buildings in winter and cool them in summer. State grants combined with school district bonding paid for the project. During this process, the Colorado Housing Finance Authority provided a loan to a small start-up business that planned to provide the school with wood chips from trees killed by pine beetles. This enterprise not only turned forest waste into a renewable fuel, it also increased forest health and reduced the risk of wildfires. Today, the company has expanded into the business of oil and gas bioremediation. It employs 48 people and plans to add 20 more. The school has healthier indoor air and has cut its carbon emissions by approximately 977 tons each year.[35]

The payoff in my mind came when the school district's business manager, Dina Murray, summed up the results. "In the process of implementing this project," she said, "it was clearer than ever how much coal dust is actually in the air of our schools. After the new boiler was installed, the classrooms are cleaner and I'm confident that our students and staff see and feel the benefits of breathing clean air during the eight hours per day, five days per week they are in the district buildings."

That was the Colorado Promise in action.

Throughout the legislative and regulatory battles during my time in office, our focus was on improving the quality of life, the economy, the environment, and the future of Colorado. But we knew that much bigger issues were at stake than those in any one state – or any one nation, for that matter. If I did not fully appreciate the global impacts of climate change before, my eyes were fully opened when I joined former President Jimmy Carter, media mogul Ted Turner, former Secretary of State Madeline Albright, Google CEO Larry Page, and other members of an eclectic group on a field trip to the Arctic in 2008.

The big global issues remain today. Our environmental challenges reach across the world and across generations. Pollution from untreated sewage, industrial wastes, oil spills, and fertilizers, along with warming and acidification due to climate change, threaten the Earth's oceans. These oceans cover 70 percent of the planet's surface, constitute one of the oldest ecosystems, and provide billions of people with their principal source of protein and livelihood. In 2009, a panel of 28 renowned scientists identified nine critical "planetary boundaries" we humans cannot cross without damaging the Earth's life support systems.[36] Climate change is only one of them. Others include the loss of biodiversity, freshwater supplies, and land-based ecosystems such as wetlands and forests, along with environmental degradation due to pollution from toxic chemicals, aerosols, nitrogen, and phosphorous.

I believe that confronting these big problems is a moral responsibility for government at all levels, as well as for voters and consumers. Neither governments nor citizens can solve these problems alone. And while planet-sized problems may seem larger than any individual, state, or nation can tackle, we must each do as much as we can with what we have.[37]

3 | The Emerging Energy Paradigm

Don't underestimate the power of your vision to change the world. Whether that world is your office, your community, an industry or a global movement, you need to have a core belief that what you contribute can fundamentally change (our) way of thinking about problems.

– Leroy Hood, American scientist

In July 2008, I traveled to Spain with my energy director, Tom Plant, and my economic development director, Don Elliman, to prospect for business opportunities for Colorado. We witnessed Spain's progress on concentrating solar power – a technology that uses mirrors or lenses to focus sunlight to produce steam, which drives turbines that generate electricity. After the trip, Tom and I established an audacious goal for Colorado: to be the site for installations that could generate one gigawatt of solar power. This goal led to the creation of a "carve out" – a requirement that a specific percentage of renewable energy come from solar – in the state's 30 percent Renewable Energy Portfolio Standard (RPS).

Another encounter persuaded me that our renewable energy mandate was an attractive element in the state's business climate. In 2007, Vestas, the world's leading manufacturer of wind turbines, opened a factory to produce turbine blades in Windsor, Colorado, creating 600 jobs. I asked the company's CEO if our RPS was the deciding factor. He told me he did not pick Colorado only because of the standard, but he would not have located in Colorado if we did not have one. It was the state's overall commitment to renewable energy that sealed the deal, he said. It was an affirmation that clean energy policies were an attractive feature for modern-day economic development.

In 2006, the year I was elected to the governorship, only 2 percent of Colorado's energy came from renewable resources. When I left the governorship in 2011, renewable resources provided 14 percent of Colorado's net electric generation – well above the national average, which was only 9 percent. Wind turbines and hydroelectric dams generated most

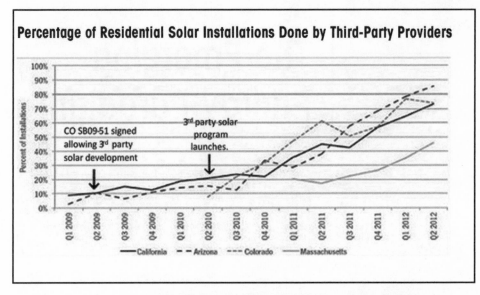

Percentage of Residential Solar Installations Done by Third-Party Providers

CO SB09-51 signed allowing 3rd party solar development

3rd party solar program launches.

California — — Arizona --- Colorado —— Massachusetts

With third-party financing, building owners can invest in residential solar energy systems without paying upfront costs. The costs are covered by a solar company that shares in the customer's energy savings. As this graph shows, this became a popular option for customers in Colorado after the legislature passed a bill exempting third-party solar development companies from regulation as a utility. (Source: Greentech Media)

of the state's renewable power, but solar generation was growing rapidly too. The growth continued after I left office. Solar power increased 20 percent from 2012 to 2013, moving Colorado into third place among the 10 states responsible for 87 percent of America's growth in solar energy production.

The Great Recession began in my first year as governor and continued throughout most of my tenure. Nevertheless, IBM opened a "green data center" in Boulder, creating another 100 jobs; Vestas opened three additional manufacturing plants that employed 1,800 workers; and a variety of other solar energy companies opened shop and created hundreds of new jobs. By 2009, Colorado was host to 1,500 renewable energy companies, including three factories that manufacture solar photovoltaic modules and four Vestas manufacturing plants. The components of completed wind turbines – blades, nacelles, and towers – were manufactured in-state at plants in the towns of Pueblo, Windsor, and Brighton. Overall, clean energy companies created more than 6,000 new jobs during the worst years of the recession, from 2007 to 2010.[38]

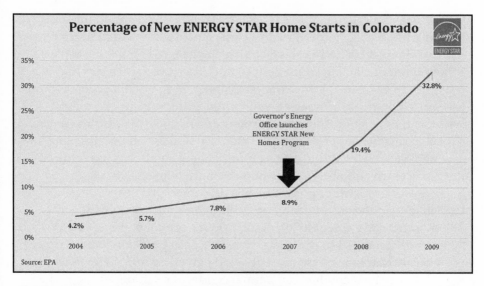

Percentage of New ENERGY STAR Home Starts in Colorado

Governor's Energy Office launches ENERGY STAR New Homes Program

4.2%
5.7%
7.8%
8.9%
19.4%
32.8%

2004　2005　2006　2007　2008　2009

Source: EPA

Public policies and programs can have significant impacts on energy markets. In 2007, the Governor's Energy Office began promoting consumer awareness and competitive financing for ENERGY STAR Certified homes. During the following two years, the number of new Energy Star homes increased by 250 percent. (Source: Tom Plant, Center for the New Energy Economy)

By 2013, Colorado's concentration of cleantech companies ranked fifth in the nation, directly employing 22,420 workers and averaging annual growth of 2.5 percent.[39] Clean Edge, the leading research and advisory firm for the cleantech sector, ranked Colorado fourth in the nation among the best places for clean technology businesses to locate.

During my term as governor, the work on creating a clean energy economy became a calling. After leaving the governorship, I did not go back to practicing law. I founded the Center for the New Energy Economy at Colorado State University to help governors, legislators, and utility regulators in other states work on their own clean energy programs.

The transition to a clean energy economy in Colorado continues, and the benefits are manifest throughout the state. In Lamar, Colorado, a wind farm of more than 100 turbines created 400 construction and installation jobs in 2003. The turbines have increased the Prowers County tax base by 25–30 percent. Renewable energy has taken hold at community scale, too. In Wray, a village on Colorado's eastern plains, the school district was spending $80,000 a year on electricity in 2006. When the school superintendent challenged the staff to find new ways to earn revenues, the district's vocational instructor, Jay Clapper, proposed installing a wind turbine to cut the district's energy bill while giving students a practical lesson in the benefits of renewable resources. In 2008, the district erected a turbine capable of powering more than 200 homes and began selling renewable energy credits to a private company. The turbine has reduced the district's greenhouse gas emissions by more than 53,000 tons.

My work with other governors has shown me that other states have made significant progress, too. Solar power attracted nearly $18 billion in new investment in 2014; solar power production increased 30 percent compared to the year before.[40] Industry officials expected the solar market to increase more than 30 percent in 2015. The Solar Foundation, which conducts an annual census of solar jobs in the United States, counted nearly 174,000 workers nationwide as of November 2014, with employment growing nearly 20 times faster than jobs in the overall economy.[41] By March 2015, solar power production in the United States was enough to provide electricity to 4.3 million homes.[42] Wind power capacity grew 8.3 percent in 2014, and was expected to grow 12.8 percent in 2015 and another 13 percent in 2016, according to the Energy Information Administration (EIA).[43]

A recent study by Environment America found that public policy is driving the energy revolution, particularly at the state level.[44] Government policies cannot do the job alone, but they can remove barriers, inspire technical innovation, and help create stable markets that attract private investment in clean energy technologies. As I will discuss in the following chapters, intelligent policies can correct market imperfections and inefficiencies to help energy technologies gain ground more rapidly. The top 10 states in solar energy growth during 2013 had several policies in common. Nearly all credited their customers at retail rates for the energy they supplied to the grid. They made it easy for customers to connect their solar systems to the utility grid. The leading states have RPS policies and offer either direct incentives to buy down installation costs or creative options for financing solar systems.[45]

Colorado has also made progress in achieving more responsible natural gas production. After the initial battles over the membership of the Colorado Oil and Gas Conservation Commission, industry and environmental advocates entered a period of greater collaboration. In 2007 and 2008, we worked with the oil and gas industry on a top-to-bottom modernization of the rules governing natural gas production. When the rules took effect in 2009, Colorado became the first state to update its oil and gas regulations. One was a new set of requirements related to hydraulic fracturing that took effect in 2012, followed by an agreement with oil and gas producers that they would begin disclosing the chemical family of each chemical they use in fracturing. It is a compromise that helps protect public health, builds greater public confidence in gas production, and protects the industry's trade secrets.

Hydraulic fracturing remains controversial in Colorado, particularly on the issue of whether communities have the authority to ban or restrict the practice within their jurisdictions. But collaboration continues between environmental leaders and the oil and gas industry. In February 2014, the state adopted the first requirements in the nation to cut methane emissions from oil and gas operations.[46] The new rules are based on recommendations from the Environmental Defense Fund (EDF) and Colorado's three largest producers: Anadarko Petroleum Corporation, the Encana Corporation, and Noble Energy. Officials expect the regulations to cut methane emissions by 100,000 tons. As a bonus, the rules will also help control volatile organic compounds, or VOCs, which are the chemicals that produce smog. Those pollutants are expected to decline in an amount equivalent to the emissions of all the cars and trucks in Colorado. As I write this, the Colorado rules are the most progressive of their kind in the United States.

In recounting this progress, I do not mean to imply that Colorado has discovered the magic formula for flawless energy policies, or to suggest that collaboration is easy between the fossil and renewable energy industries, or that clean energy development is simple, or that we are done. I do believe, however, that a rapid national transition to clean energy is possible among people of good will, and that it would be unconscionable not to try.

More extensive changes will be necessary if we hope to avoid irreparable damage to the biosphere, and I will detail several of these throughout the rest of this book.

4 | Lessons from the Biosphere

Humankind's greatest priority is to reintegrate with the natural world.

– Sir Jonathan Porritt,
environmentalist and author

The future we envision and build must be based on a deeper understanding of the biosphere and our role in it. I have come to this realization at several points in my life, starting perhaps with my childhood on our family farm. There are few livelihoods that require so close and collaborative a relationship with nature and natural resources.

Among other things, this collaboration teaches that what we do on the land can deplete the soils or replenish their fertility, pollute groundwater or protect it, and consume natural capital or conserve it. It teaches us that we have to work with the weather rather than trying to fight it. As I advocated clean energy as a critical goal of the Colorado Promise, I found a gratifying level of receptivity among Colorado's farmers and ranchers. For them, the idea of using the wind and sun to produce energy was not exotic; it was an extension of their appreciation for the need to work with nature.

The simple reality is that human beings and natural systems are interconnected and interdependent, especially now that human activity has already impacted, and has such enormous potential to further affect, the biosphere.[47] This fundamental fact is often obscured by our appetite for economic development combined with several conventional mindsets. One is the outdated idea that natural systems and other species can absorb whatever we choose to do, as they did when the human footprint was smaller. Another is that our rightful role in the biosphere is to dominate and consume it rather than to be its stewards. Yet another troublesome mindset is "reductionism" – the habit of thinking in parts rather than in systems. Environmental educator and author David Orr describes this last point very well:

The results (of reductionism) are dumbfounding. In record time, we have shredded whole ecosystems, acidified the oceans, killed off entire species, squandered topsoil, leveled forests, and changed the chemistry of the atmosphere... To anticipate and avoid such things requires a mindset capable of seeing connections, patterns, and systems structure, as well as a sightline far beyond the quarterly balance sheet or the next election. Wisdom begins with the awareness that we live amidst complexities that we can never fully comprehend let alone control.[48]

The consequences of uncontrolled carbon pollution, a practice some have compared to using the atmosphere as a waste dump, is only one of several ways in which human development has overstepped or is rapidly approaching thresholds that can push natural systems disastrously out of balance.[49] Some of those thresholds involve the ozone layer, others the oceans and freshwater resources, and still others the fertility of the soils we depend upon for food. And of course one threshold involves the historic extinction of other species.

Despite our extraordinary advances in knowledge and accomplishments in science and technology, we have lived for a very long time in denial of our physical codependence with natural systems. Accepting codependence does not require that we be subservient to nature, or that we anthropomorphize it, or deify it. It merely requires that we respect the symbiotic relationship. Suggesting that we try collaboration with natural systems is not Gaia-speak or pantheism; it is an acknowledgment that what we have been doing no longer works and that, in fact, we can learn a great deal from the natural systems that have developed over 4 billion years of evolutionary trial and error.

The Obligations of the Anthropocene Epoch

The point at which humans became numerous and powerful enough to have a major influence on the biosphere was the dawn of what some scientists call the Anthropocene Epoch.[50] Whenever it began, the Anthropocene has replaced the Holocene Epoch, a period of nearly 12,000 years, during which a relatively hospitable climate allowed life as we know it to flourish.[51]

There is plenty of evidence that our influence is largely negative. In addition to the damages I have already mentioned, there has been the clear-cutting of forests that serve as the lungs of the Earth; the over-

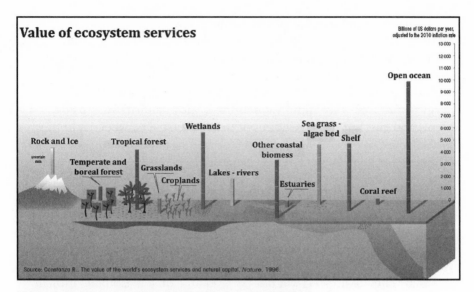

Value of ecosystem services

Billions of US dollars per year, adjusted to the 2010 inflation rate

Open ocean

Wetlands

Sea grass - algae bed

Shelf

Rock and Ice

Tropical forest

Other coastal biomess

uncertain data

Temperate and boreal forest

Grasslands

Croplands

Lakes - rivers

Estuaries

Coral reef

Source: Constanza R., The value of the world's ecosystem services and natural capital, Nature, 1996.

Many ecosystems provide valuable services for free, but many also have been degraded or destroyed by human development. (Robert Costanza, Riccardo Pravettoni, UNEP/GRID-Arendal. Data from "The value of the world's ecosystem services and natural capital," *Nature* 1998).

farming of crops that deplete soil fertility; the decline in freshwater supplies; and the destruction of many ecosystems that once provided essential services for free, from the wetlands that helped control flooding to the pollinators that make agriculture possible.[52]

Climate change, however, is arguably the most ubiquitous and long-lasting way we are altering the biosphere. When we burn fossil fuels, they emit carbon dioxide in amounts that overwhelm nature's carbon cycle – the production of carbon by plants and animals in balance with the ability of forests, soils, and oceans to absorb and store it. When carbon outputs exceed natural sequestration, the chemical ends up in the lowest level of the atmosphere – the troposphere – where it inhibits solar radiation that reaches the Earth from reflecting back into space. The result is the so-called greenhouse effect, which raises the temperature of the atmosphere and the Earth's surface. The surface temperature of the Earth has risen about 0.85°C since 1880.[53] Several other gases have similar effects, including methane (the principal component of natural gas), nitrous oxide (found among other places in emissions from coal-fired power plants and, to a lesser extent, gas-fired generation), and fluorinated gases (man-made and used in refrigeration, air-conditioning, manufacturing, and some of the equipment used to distribute electricity).

As the consequences of global warming have become more evident and destructive, one response has been to search for technical fixes – technologies that would allow us to continue behaving as we always have but with less damage. Technologies have done, and will continue to do, enormous good. In the context of mitigating carbon emissions, renewable energy technologies are rapidly emerging as clean alternatives to coal, oil, and natural gas. But there is an important difference between technologies that make use of natural systems and technologies that attempt to manipulate or alter them. The more exotic concepts of geo-engineering are in the latter category, including ideas about altering the atmosphere so it reflects more sunlight back into space, or seeding the ocean with iron salts to promote the growth of carbon-absorbing algal blooms. These strategies carry considerable risks of unintended consequences because they depend on an understanding of natural systems that climate change proves we do not have.[54]

Many climate impacts will not be reversible on a reasonable human timescale. The National Oceanic and Atmospheric Administration (NOAA) has concluded that some will be "largely irreversible for 1,000 years" even if we stopped emitting greenhouse gases today.[55] The complexity of these physical impacts, our evolving understanding of the forces at work, the permanence of the damages, and the political challenge of reaching national and international agreements to limit the use of fossil fuels all make climate change the most serious environmental issue of our time – and perhaps of all time.

But again, while the consequences of climate change are physical, the root cause is attitudinal. As author Janine Benyus says, "If we are to use our tools in the service of fitting in on Earth, our basic relationship to nature – even the story we tell ourselves about who we are in the universe – has to change."

The Moral Case for Action

Because the consequences of climate change are so pervasive, we can make the case for action in many different value systems. Climate action can prevent disruptions in the economy, the physical security of our homes and communities, public health, national security, global stability, and so on. But there is also a deeply moral case for action – a case articulated, for example, by Pope Francis in the encyclical he issued in June 2015.[56]

In the context of religion, the moral case for climate action is rooted in the obligation to care for God's creation and for the poor.[57] In secular communities, the moral obligation is rooted in humanitarianism – i.e., showing kindness, sympathy, and benevolence toward all human beings.

Many climate disruptions are taking place and will become far more severe in parts of the world where people are least able to cope, including regions already under environmental, social, political, and/or economic stresses. International agencies predict that as many as 200 million people may become "climate refugees" in the years ahead, fleeing desertification, famine, sea level rise, and weather disasters. The secondary consequences of the greenhouse effect include international instability, conflict, and even the failure of nation-states as vital ecosystems are disrupted, refugees cross national borders, and competition intensifies for critical resources. Military officials and intelligence experts in the United States now consider global warming to be a serious national security threat. Some consider it a greater danger than terrorism.[58] Preventing climate wars and humanitarian disasters are part of the moral dimensions of climate action.

As a Catholic and as a former missionary, I recognize the moral and spiritual dimensions of our role in the biosphere. There is a longstanding dialogue among Christians about whether God intended for us to dominate nature or be its stewards. Both sides in the conversation can cite biblical passages that seem to support their interpretations. But nature long predates the written word as God's way of communicating with humanity. I agree with the late Carl Sagan, who said, "The notion that science and spirituality are somehow mutually exclusive does a disservice to both."[59]

Pope Francis's encyclical drew objections from politicians and think tanks that argued that his job is to address moral issues, not political issues. As someone who has straddled the worlds of faith and public policy, however, I have rarely if ever encountered an issue of public policy that does not have a moral dimension. In regard to climate change, the distinction between the morality and the politics of climate action should be clear. The need to do something is without question a moral issue. It is about what the most privileged do for the least among us, including our responsibility to future generations. The goals necessary to abate climate change are a science issue. How we achieve those goals is a political issue. None of these should have become a partisan issue.

The challenge for religious and moral leaders is to lift the issue of climate change out of the partisan political purgatory into which it has sunk and back onto the high ground where it belongs. For many around the world, it is an existential risk that requires a good-faith response regardless of political party or religious affiliation.

For people of conscience, it should not take a pope to point out the problem. It is not that political leaders in the United States disagree how to address climate change, it is that some politicians question whether climate change is a problem at all. From the moral perspective, that is simply wrong.

There may come a point at which we find the keys to the universe and unlock its secrets. What we have already learned is that the interdependence of the human species with the rest of the biosphere must become part of the DNA of public policy and societal behaviors from now on. In practice, this means ongoing research to better understand the social, economic, and environmental costs and benefits of what we do. It means fully counting those costs and benefits in decisions about the nation's energy mix, including which energy resources – if any – should be promoted by government market interventions and policies. It means that we must elect leaders who understand the value of ecosystems and who educate the general public about the moral obligations as well as the practical necessities of stewardship. As one colleague put it, unless we do these things, we will forfeit the right to call ourselves the most intelligent species.

5 | A New American Vision

A vision without a task is but a dream; a task without a vision is drudgery; but a vision with a task is the hope of the world.

– Inscription on a church wall
in Sussex England, c. 1730

If we are going to create a new national conversation, how should it begin? A good place to start has to do with vision. What exactly is the twenty-first century America we should be building? What does it look like and how will it influence our lives? How will we give form to abstractions such as "a new energy economy"? What is the best way to communicate about it with one another?

If vision and visioning seem a bit too ethereal in the world of concrete public policy, then we should go back to an observation made in 1994 by the late environmental educator Donella Meadows:

Vision is the most vital step in the policy process… If we don't know where we want to go, it makes little difference that we make great progress. Yet vision is not only missing almost entirely from policy discussions; it is missing from our whole culture. We talk about our fears, frustrations, and doubts endlessly, but we talk only rarely and with embarrassment about our dreams.[60]

The first President Bush was criticized throughout his presidency for lacking a vision for America. One writer predicted that his lack of "the vision thing," as the president put it, would be the Achilles heel of his presidency. Others concluded that his inability to articulate a clear vision for the nation would limit the influence of his presidency. Historians predicted he would be remembered as a steward rather than a visionary leader.[61]

In my view, however, the role of a political leader is not only to create and communicate a vision of his or her own, it is also to facilitate a process that engages constituents in the visioning work. If people do not participate in creating an understanding of where they want to go, they will not own it. If they do not own it, they are less likely to work for it, defend it, or sustain their commitment to it.

While the principles and guarantees defined by the Founding Fathers – for example, our right to life, liberty, and the pursuit of happiness – are critical compass points, they are not a vision. As time passes, those principles remain constant but new knowledge, technologies, and influences appear, creating new opportunities and constraints. In each phase of the nation's life, it seems, Ronald Reagan's "shining city on the hill" must be remodeled without weakening its foundation.[62] One generation's vision was to create a society that could guarantee its peoples freedom from fear. Another generation's dream was a society free from slavery. Another's was to expand human understanding and enterprise beyond "the surly bonds of Earth."

It is clear in this century that we must envision and create a world in which societies prosper while living within their means. We should be able to accept limits without feeling deprived by them, to acknowledge and find opportunity as well as obligation in our codependence with other nations and the natural world, to end poverty just as we have banished certain diseases, and to create abundance in ways we can sustain.

We may be skeptical that the American people can agree on much of anything these days, let alone come to a consensus about what our future should be, but there are examples in our history where glimpses of the future transformed our society and eventually the world. Two of these took place at world's fairs in the United States. One inspired the greatest engineering achievement of the twentieth century; the second started the world's love affair with the automobile.

Power to the People

From space today, the planet looks like a Christmas decoration, with lights everywhere except in a few dark places. It did not look that way in the late 1800s, however, when electricity was a novelty. Buildings in those days were lit by smoky gas lamps that provided insufficient light. In cities, the fuel that gave us light was produced by local gasifiers and piped into homes. In 1882, the first electric power plant in the United States – the Pearl Street Station – went online in New York to light the lamps of 85 customers.[63] Within the next few years, the station was serving more than 500 customers in New York, and similar electric systems were operating in Pennsylvania

The White City was a stunning example of electrification at the Chicago World's Fair in 1893. One of every four Americans reportedly saw the exposition. It gave them a visual experience that almost certainly built public support for the development of the modern electric grid. (Source: Brooklyn Museum Archives, Goodyear Archival Collection. Visual materials [6.1.016]: World's Columbian Exposition lantern slides, 1893)

and Massachusetts, developed by Thomas Edison's Edison Illuminating Company.

The emerging electric system followed the model established by the gas industry at the time: central production facilities that distributed energy to customers located some distance away. The principal reason was economy of scale. It was less expensive to generate electricity in big power plants than in many small plants closer to customers.

In was not until 1893 that electric power became part of America's vision for modern society. Chicago hosted the world's fair that year and invited bids from companies interested in providing electricity to the exhibits.[64] The finalists were the General Electric Company, backed by Thomas Edison and J. P. Morgan; and Westinghouse, in collaboration with the brilliant engineer Nikola Tesla. The major difference between the two bids was that the General Electric Company provided DC power, while Westinghouse and Tesla favored AC power. Because AC power was less expensive, produced less waste heat, and was better suited to transmission over long distances, Westinghouse won the contract.

When the fair opened, its crown jewel was the White City, a life-size urban setting lit by electric streetlights, spotlights, and giant searchlights. Thanks to the White City, the fair reportedly used three times more electricity than the City of Chicago. It became the first large test of AC power, so impressive that one witness said the spectacle was "like getting a sudden vision of Heaven."[65]

Between 1900 and 1930, electricity was generated and sold by privately owned unregulated companies. They built generating plants where they could serve the largest number of people. Customers in cities had the luxury of choosing between several competing electric companies, while people in rural areas lived without modern electric power because it was too expensive for companies to run lines to small numbers of dispersed customers.

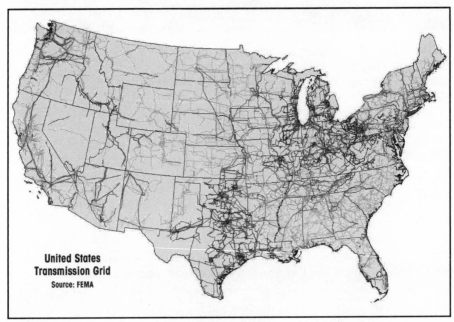

United States Transmission Grid
Source: FEMA

Figure 5.1

The US electric transmission grid has been called the greatest engineering achievement of the twentieth century. (Source: Federal Emergency Management Agency)

The desire to transmit electricity over longer distances led to interconnections between transmission systems to better manage power loads. In 1926, Congress passed the Electricity Act, which created a central board that established the first standardized and synchronized grid. Congress created the Tennessee Valley Authority in 1933 to bring modern power and economic development to a seven-state region hit especially hard by the Great Depression. Within five years after it was established in 1935, the Rural Electrification Administration[66] helped double the number of farm homes with access to electricity by providing loans to rural cooperatives that laid power lines and wired houses. By 1938, the national electric grid began operating, gradually evolving into today's complex system of large central power plants sending electrons over high voltage wires to substations where it is "stepped down" and distributed to customers through the grid's smaller treelike branches. This is all part of a highly synchronized and somewhat brittle system (Figure 5.1).

Estimates vary on the size of the power system today. The American Society of Civil Engineers (ASCE) counts nearly 400,000 miles of transmission lines in the United States, enough to circle the Earth 16 times.[67] The US electric grid is the largest interconnected machine on Earth and the greatest engineering achievement of the twentieth century, according to the National Academy of Engineering – a high compliment in a century in which we put men on the moon, roving laboratories on Mars, and mind-blowing computer power into the hands of billions of people.[68]

It is clear today, however, that our greatest engineering achievement of the last century needs to be reengineered. Many of its components are now old and less reliable. It is not uncommon for millions of electric customers to have their power interrupted due to everything from equipment failures to untrimmed tree branches touching power lines. The Department of Energy (DOE) says that the United States experiences more power interruptions than any other developed nation; these have increased 285 percent since data were first collected in 1984.[69] Severe weather, the most common cause of outages today, costs the economy as much as $33 billion every year, according to the DOE.[70] Between 2003 and 2012, severe weather caused an estimated 679 widespread power outages in the United States[71] – a problem expected to grow worse as climate change produces more violent and frequent weather events.[72]

Our centralized power system wastes roughly two-thirds of the primary energy that we put into the system. Conventional coal plants are only about 35 percent to 45 percent efficient. Another 6 percent of electric power is lost as it moves through transmission and distribution lines.[73] The power system has not kept up with rapidly emerging energy technologies such as generation from solar and wind technology. Utilities are struggling to accommodate the brave new world in which new power plants are appearing on rooftops and in farm fields. The Edison Electric Institute estimates that the nation will need to invest as much as $2 trillion by 2030 to repair, update, and expand the grid to serve growing electric consumption.[74]

Our oil and gas infrastructure is aging, too. More than 2.5 million miles of oil and natural gas lines crisscross the lower 48 states, many of them built long before modern safety standards were in place. ICF International estimates that companies will have to invest more than $640 billion in new oil and gas pipelines over the next two decades to keep up with the boom in domestic production.[75]

From the carbon emissions from coal plants to the water consumption required to cool them, the cost of producing electricity from fossil fuels is rising. The technical fixes that could feasibly mitigate the economic and environmental costs, including pollution and water consumption to cool thermoelectric equipment, will increase the cost of electricity from coal at the same time the cost of power from a variety of renewable resources is falling. It is within our reach today to provide much of the nation's electric energy with resources that produce no pollution, consume no water, emit no greenhouse gases, and are virtually free for the taking. National leaders have set goals for using these resources, but there is no consensus roadmap, no coherent plan to achieve the goals. We need a twenty-first century White City to fire the imaginations of the American people about the future we can and must create, because a secure and sustainable electric system today would look nothing like it did at the Chicago World's Fair. What has not changed, however, is the wisdom of an observation commonly attributed to Thomas Edison: "If we did all the things we are capable of doing, we would literally astound ourselves."

Our Love Affair with Cars

Another revolutionary influence rolled into the American Dream at the beginning of the twentieth century. Henry Ford introduced the Model T in 1908. Road building quickly followed and accelerated when Congress passed the Federal Aid Road Act in 1916.

Two decades later, there was a moment when the automobile graduated from a symbol of the good life to one of its requirements. It took place in 1939 at the New York World's Fair in Flushing Meadows. More precisely, it took place in a pavilion called Futurama sponsored by General Motors.[76] Futurama was the fair's most popular attraction, drawing 45 million visitors to an experience that was part museum exhibit, part amusement park ride. After surviving long lines, visitors sat in chairs on a conveyor belt that carried them for nearly 20 minutes through large-scale models of the United States as GM imagined it could be in 1960 (Figure 5.2).[77] When they emerged, visitors were given badges that read, "I have seen the future."

Norman Bel Geddes, the pavilion's designer, believed that the "free-flowing movement of people and goods across our nation is a requirement of modern living and prosperity." Futurama gave visitors an experience of what Geddes had in mind. He described it this way:

> *Futurama is a large-scale model representing almost every type of terrain in America and illustrating how a motorway system may be laid down over the entire country – across mountains, over rivers and lakes, through cities, and past towns – never deviating from a direct course and always adhering to the four basic principles of highway design: safety, comfort, speed, and economy.*

Figure 5.2

The Futurama pavilion at the New York World's Fair gave visitors General Motors' vision of a highly mobile society 20 years in the future. It became the prototype of the car-centered mobility that still dominates urban development and transportation investment today. (Source: GM Media Archive)

The GM/Geddes vision filled an acre of the fairgrounds with models of more than 500,000 individual buildings, 1 million trees, and 50,000 cars, 10,000 of which were speeding along a 14-lane superhighway. By all accounts it was mind-boggling for an audience still suffering the aftershocks of the Great Depression and hungry for hope that the future would be better. Futurama was a promise that American ingenuity would not only pull the country out of the Depression, it would also create a world of unprecedented personal freedom and mobility.

America entered World War II two years later. When millions of American soldiers came home, Futurama seemed to become the prototype for economic development. Within several decades, automobiles evolved into a symbol of progress for nations around the world. By 1950, the United States was producing 8 million automobiles a year, which equaled two-thirds of the world's total production.[78] By 2013, more than 65 million cars were produced worldwide, led not by the United States but by China, Japan, and Germany.

Whether it was Geddes' prescience, the allure of freedom on an open road, or an idea whose time had simply come, Futurama made such a deep impression that we and many other nations are still investing in Geddes' vision of the good life 75 years later. But like our twentieth-century electric system, there are signs that the standard for mobility is changing, along with the automobile itself.

Today, 42 percent of the nation's major urban highways are congested, resulting in more than $100 billion each year in wasted time and fuel.[79] Our dependence on automobiles is among the largest sources of US greenhouse gas emissions and the principal reason we have been dependent on foreign oil. The Federal Highway Administration estimates we will need to invest $170 billion each year if we want to make significant improvements in the highway system.

Meanwhile, both the demographics and the hardware of mobility are changing. Fewer young people want to own automobiles or even be licensed to drive them.[80] Millennials and baby boomers are moving to city centers and urban villages where they have greater access to the things they want, from entertainment to medical services.[81] The rise of the "shared economy" extends to vehicles with companies such as eGo Car share, Zipcar, and Car2Go providing mobility when people need it, rather than having vehicles sit unused in driveways and parking spaces.[82]

With the new Corporate Average Fuel Economy (CAFÉ) standards issued by the Obama administration, vehicles of all types are becoming more efficient. Electric, natural gas, biodiesel, ethanol, and even hydrogen-powered vehicles are on the road, and just around the corner, we are told, will be vehicles that drive themselves. While we ostensibly have national transportation policies trapped in multiyear funding reauthorization bills from Congress, our transportation policies are not keeping up with the changes in technologies and demographics.[83] We need a better vision and a better roadmap for America's transportation system in this new century. We need a new Futurama.

6 | What Is America Thinking?

The polls are an attempt to not reflect public opinion, but to shape it.

– Rush Limbaugh

If we were to engage in a national exercise to envision the future, what values and priorities would shape it? Public opinion research should give us insights into what the American people are thinking. Unfortunately, recent polls on national energy policy and climate change have produced results that are often confusing rather than enlightening.

When it is well designed and accurately interpreted, public opinion research offers the best available insights between elections into the moods, values, and views of the American people. Politicians, policy makers, pundits, and the press all rely on them. Unfortunately, not all of the research is well designed and accurately interpreted, even when it comes from some of our most prestigious polling organizations. And rather than providing us with objective insights into the "American mind," polls can be biased in favor of particular ideologies or political objectives. A few examples will illustrate this.

The Trouble with Ranking Polls

One of the more common types of research involves polls that ask respondents to prioritize a list of national issues based on their importance. The economy, jobs, the federal deficit, public health, and terrorism are among the issues that usually show up at the top of the list. The environment, energy, and global warming typically are at the bottom. The result is headlines such as these:

- CLIMATE CHANGE NOT A TOP WORRY IN THE US[84]

- ADDRESSING CLIMATE CHANGE IS THE DEAD LAST, LOWEST PRIORITY ISSUE FOR AMERICANS[85]

- OBAMA CLIMATE-CHANGE PUSH FACES A LUKEWARM PUBLIC: POLLS SHOW CLIMATE CHANGE RANKS LOW WHEN VOTERS ARE ASKED TO ASSESS PRIORITIES[86]

The flaw in ranking polls lies in their design. They force people to make artificial choices – artificial because in the real world, many of the issues on the list cannot be separated from one another. The low-ranked issues often have major influences on top-ranked issues. If you are concerned about the economy, for example, you cannot discount the importance of energy (the volatility of fossil fuel prices and their historic impact on recessions, for example) or climate (the impact of droughts on food prices and the agricultural industry) or public health (health-care costs resulting from heat waves, spreading disease vectors, and air pollution). If you are worried about federal spending, you cannot ignore the growing outlays for disaster prevention, response, and recovery; or infrastructure repairs; or humanitarian assistance to countries suffering from climate-related disruptions; or necessary spending on climate adaptation.[87] Public concern about terrorism often ranks high in these polls, especially when there has been an incident or a recent threat. But climate change, which usually ranks low, creates conditions that "enable terrorist activity and other forms of violence" around the world, according to the US Department of Defense's *Quadrennial Defense Review.*[88]

In contrast to ranking polls, surveys that ask people only about climate change usually show a high level of concern and strong support for government action. For example, when the Yale Project on Climate Change Communication conducted a poll centered on the topic of climate change in April 2014, 64 percent of the respondents said they supported strict limits on carbon dioxide emissions from existing coal plants to reduce climate change and improve public health, even if electricity would have to cost more (Figure 6.1).[89]

Similarly, while prominent political leaders in Washington and in some statehouses intended to "just say no" to the federal government's plans to limit carbon pollution from power plants, a survey by Resources for the Future and Stanford found that nearly 90 percent of Americans support government action to address climate change (Figure 6.2).[90] The interesting conclusion from these surveys and others like them is that the perceived rift between Republicans and Democrats outside of Washington, DC is small compared to the seemingly unbridgeable gulf between partisans in Congress.

The takeaway is this: Polls that require respondents to prioritize national issues cannot excuse policy makers from addressing issues that are lower on the lists. The issues are often interdependent. And government should be capable of multitasking.

Selective, Misleading, or Conflicting Conclusions

Few members of the general public are likely to pick through poll data in detail. Their first impression, and in many cases their last, comes from the headlines written by the media or by the pollsters themselves. Because communicators know that controversy and drama get the most attention from audiences, their headlines often highlight conflict, even if it is not the most significant part of a poll's results.

For example, even though the Gallup poll I cited earlier found that a likely majority of respondents worry to some degree about global warming – a significant finding – Gallup chose "Climate Change Not a Top Worry" for its headline.

In the same poll, Gallup found that "most Americans seem to accept that global warming is at least as serious a problem as news reports say it is," but its headline read, "Americans Most Likely to Say Global Warming Is Exaggerated."[91] And while its poll found that the largest segment of American adults, 39 percent, "attribute global warming to human actions and are worried about it," the headline read, "One in Four in US Are Solidly Skeptical of Global Warming."[92] It would seem that the more important result was that 75 percent of Americans are *not* solidly skeptical.

It is fair to ask whether even our most professional polling organizations are better at enlightening us or confusing us about what is, by scientific reckoning, the most important public policy obligation of our time.

Gallup is by no means the only pollster whose reports can be confusing; confusion sometimes comes from how the media and interest groups interpret results. When the Weather Channel reported on a survey by the Public Policy Polling group,[93] for example, its headline read, "Poll: 3 in 8 Americans Believe Global Warming Is a Hoax."[94] Yet the poll found that 51 percent of the registered voters who participated said they believe global warming is *not* a hoax and 12 percent were unsure.

There is less confusion about the message from polls that ask Americans what they think about energy. For the last 15 years, Gallup's polling has found that the American people prefer more energy conservation to more energy production. In what should have been a message to Congress, the Yale Project on Climate Change Communication

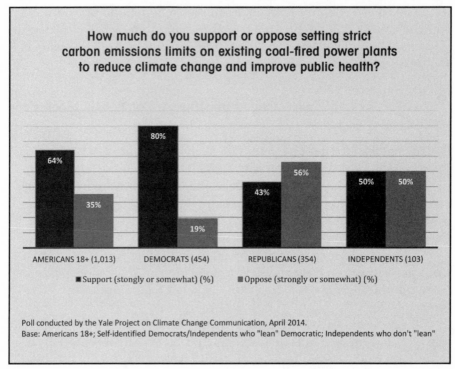

Figure 6.1

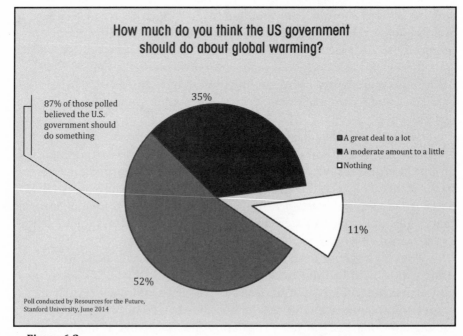

Figure 6.2

Although Americans tend to place climate and environ-
mental issues low in polls that ask them to rank national
issues, many polls like these by the Yale Project on Climate
Change Communications and by Resources for the Future/
Stanford University find overwhelming majorities in favor
of government action when people are asked only about
climate change. (Source: Charts by the Center for the
New Energy Economy; data from Yale Project on Climate
Change Communications and Resources for the Future/
Stanford University)

found at the end of 2013 that sizable majorities of Democrats and
Republicans (67 percent and 52 percent respectively)[95] support the
elimination of all fossil energy subsidies.

How Informed Are the Answers?

Another problem with many polls is that they do not tell us whether
respondents' answers are well informed. There has long been a suspicion
that many poll respondents give the answers they think pollsters want
rather than answers based on their own informed positions.

After conducting a roundup of other polls in 2013, Politico found
that "Americans are largely disengaged from the fierce energy debates
that embroil the capital and that many people know few details – or even
the larger trends – about where the United States gets its energy and
how much it costs."[96] Another poll, this one released in January 2015 and
reported in *Scientific American*, found a large split between what scientists
and the general public think about climate change.[97] Nearly 90 percent
of the scientists polled said that human activity is driving global warming,
while only half of nonscientists agreed. The CEO of the American
Association for the Advancement of Science, a cosponsor of the polls,
attributed the split to a failure by scientists to better communicate with
the public. Even the best communications, however, can fall victim to the
people's "rational ignorance" or the influence of peer groups, political
party affiliations, and the media they choose to follow.

Engaging in Deliberative Democracy

To ensure that poll responses are better informed, it would be useful for
public opinion researchers to use deliberative polling rather than, or in

False Choices: America's Level of Worry About National Problems

The economy 1

Federal spending and the budget deficit 2

The availability and affordability of health care 3

Unemployment 4

The size and power of the federal government 5

The Social Security system 6

Hunger and homelessness 7

Crime and violence 8

The possibility of terrorist attacks in the United States 9

The availability and affordability of energy 10

Drug use 11

The quality of the environment 12

Climate change **13**

Race relations 14

Poll conducted by Gallup, March 5–9, 2014

addition to, the types of surveys we usually see reported in the media. Most opinion polls detect what people think or believe at a particular time, regardless of whether they are interested in or informed about the questions the pollsters ask. In deliberative polling, researchers work with a statistically representative sample of a population on issues that require significant background information to have an informed opinion. Members of the group are polled after they engage in a discussion of an issue with other members or with objective experts. In other words, deliberative polling attempts to understand what public opinion would be if the public were well informed.[98]

For elected officials and policy makers who hope that opinion research will give them insights into the public's views on complicated issues such as climate change and energy security, deliberative polling seems tailor-made.

Pollsters and Press Have Standards

Whatever type of polling is used, it should conform to professional standards. Those who rely on polls, including the media, should be using these standards to judge the quality of surveys.

The National Council on Public Polls (NCPP) is one standard-setting organization. It has published "20 Questions a Journalist Should Ask about Poll Results, Third Edition," including the following:[99]

- **Who did the poll? Who paid for it?**
  "Polls are not conducted for the good of the world," the NCPP points out. "They are conducted for a reason – either to gain helpful information or to advance a particular cause." Knowing the sponsor helps us judge whether to trust the validity of the results.

- **Were a sufficient number of people interviewed to produce a scientifically valid result? What was the margin of error?**
  Generally, the more people interviewed, the better the chance the answers accurately reflect public opinion.

- **How were the respondents chosen?**
  "The key reason that some polls reflect public opinion accurately and other polls are unscientific junk is how people were chosen to be interviewed," the NCPP says. "In scientific polls, the pollster uses a specific statistical method for picking respondents."

- **Does the poll report the answers of everyone interviewed?**
  "One of the easiest ways to misrepresent the results of a poll is to report the answers of only a subgroup," the NCPP says. For example, "Reporting the opinions of only Democrats in a poll purported to be of all adults would substantially misrepresent the results."

- **What questions were asked?**
  The wording of poll questions can make major differences in the results. The questions should be fair and unbiased and should give respondents a balanced set of choices.

- **What other polls have been done on this topic? If the results are different, why?**

  One reason may have to do with timing. Different answers at different times might be evidence of swings in public opinion.

- **What was the context in which the poll was conducted?**

  Important events may influence responses for a time, but those influences may not last.

When to Lead and When to Follow

How policy makers use polls tells us something about how they view their jobs. Do they use polls to help guide their actions on issues? If their position is at odds with a poll's findings, should they make an effort to educate or persuade their constituents to take a different view? Or do they ignore polls because the opinions of interest groups and campaign donors are more important than the opinions of voters?

In many cases, education and persuasion are the better part of leadership. Most policy makers and elected officials have far more access to information and more help obtaining it than do the people who respond to polls. In my view, a public official's duties include helping constituents understand controversial issues. Sometimes, a public official's duty is to take courageous stands that are not consistent with what the polls say about the views of his or her constituents.

In any case, despite the many complexities involved in obtaining accurate insights into the American mind, a closer look across the multitude of surveys on climate and energy issues indicates there is far more common ground among voters than we often are led to believe by watching the political divide in Washington. This is something we should build upon, in part by closing the gap during the only polling exercise that really counts – the one at the ballot box every two years.

7 | Change the Conversation

If you don't like what's being said, change the conversation.

– Fictional Ad Executive
Don Draper (Mad Men)

In retrospect, one of the key decisions in my gubernatorial campaign was to produce the "Wind in the Wheat Field" television spot. It was important for me to present myself to the people of Colorado before my opponent tried to define me. As they say, you do not get a second chance to make a good first impression.

The fact is, the fate of a candidate often is determined by who frames him or her first and how they do it. The same is true for public policy. Those who define the argument usually win it.

That has been a hard lesson for the climate action movement. For nearly 30 years, the thousands of experts involved in the Intergovernmental Panel on Climate Change (IPCC) have assessed and published the most current science on global warming. Its work was important to the science community, certainly, but it went mostly unnoticed by the general public.

That changed when opponents of climate action began challenging the science, manufacturing controversy, and vilifying Al Gore, whose "Inconvenient Truth" lectures and movie were among the first attempts to make climate change and its impacts understandable to the lay public. The opposition's strategy closely followed the tobacco industry's efforts in the 1950s to discredit medical evidence that smoking causes cancer. I believe it is fair to say that the environmental community has been mostly playing defense ever since.

Unfortunately, the debate has been much easier for skeptics than for the self-described "climate hawks" who advocate action. There are multiple reasons. For one thing, the popular media thrives on controversy; its coverage of the national conversation and debate in Congress gave the impression that the science is more controversial than it is. Climate skeptics also have had inertia on their side. It is much easier to ask people to do nothing than to do something. Climate change is a topic tailor-made for procrastination. It is too easily dismissed as a problem far off in the future and far away in other lands, despite the fact that neither is true. To some, it falls squarely in the "important but not urgent" quadrant.

Another advantage for the denial industry has been the language barrier between scientists and the public. While the basic concept of the greenhouse effect is simple, few of us understand the physics and forces that will determine global warming's specific consequences. Few of us, in other words, can judge the credibility of the science for ourselves. When scientists have tried to explain it, their language was confusing. For example, when they have said they are 95 percent certain that climate change is under way, they mean we can take it to the bank. That is about as high as scientific certainty ever gets. To the lay public, however, it seems to mean that the scientists are not completely sure.

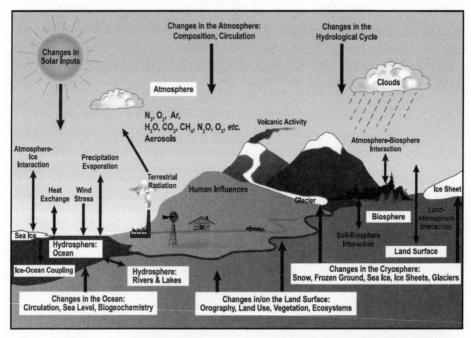

The interactions between the many components of the climate system are complex and not readily understood by the lay public. The complexity creates a language barrier between the public and climate scientists. (Source: *Climate Change 2007: The Physical Science Basis*. Working Group I Contribution to the *Fourth Assessment Report* of the Intergovernmental Panel on Climate Change, FAQ 1.2, Cambridge University Press)

The climate conversation actually began more than a century before it moved into the public arena. Scientists began researching and talking about it in the mid-1800s, when one of Napoleon's engineers, Jean Baptiste Joseph Fourier, recognized that some of the solar radiation that entered the Earth's atmosphere was not getting back out. A succession of discoveries related to climate change occurred in the decades that followed.[100]

When President Lyndon Johnson's science advisors warned him about climate change, they pulled no punches. "Through his worldwide industrial civilization, Man is unwittingly conducting a vast geophysical experiment," they wrote. "Within a few generations he is burning the fossil fuels that slowly accumulated in the earth over the past 500 million years." They predicted that by the year 2000, atmospheric concentrations of CO_2 would be "sufficient to produce measurable and perhaps marked changes in climate."[101] With remarkable prescience, they warned President Johnson about rising sea levels, melting ice caps, and warming oceans, all of which are evident in physical measurements and observation today. Despite President Johnson's subsequent warning to Congress and several new environmental laws,[102] carbon emissions continued growing in the United States and worldwide. There was no concerted effort to put a lid on greenhouse gas emissions.[103]

Twenty-three years later, the United Nations launched the IPCC. Political debate in the United States began in earnest around 1992 when President George H.W. Bush joined 153 other nations in signing the United Nations Framework Convention on Climate Change (UNFCCC), the document that has been the basis for international climate negotiations ever since.

With the United States a signatory to the UNFCCC and the IPCC issuing increasingly conclusive findings, organized opposition began in earnest. Coalitions of oil, coal, utility, automakers, and trade associations – including the US Chamber of Commerce, the National Mining Association, and the National Association of Manufacturers – formed lobbying groups such as the Global Climate Coalition and the Information Council on the Environment (ICE) to get involved in the climate policy debate. They originated the so-called climate "denial industry."[104]

In 2002, the leading consultant for Republicans at the time, Frank Luntz, warned the GOP that is was vulnerable on environmental issues. He wrote a strategy memo recommending that Republicans show concern for the environment, but uncertainty about climate change. "The environment is probably the single issue on which Republicans in general – and President (George W.) Bush in particular – are most vulnerable," he advised. "Should the public come to believe that the scientific issues are settled, their views about global warming will change accordingly. Therefore, you need to continue to make the lack of scientific certainty a primary issue in the debate."[105]

Then in 2013, a team of volunteers at the organization Skeptical Science assessed more than 12,000 peer-reviewed papers in the climate science literature and found that 97 percent of them concluded climate change is real and caused at least partly by human activity.[106] Since then, the denial industry has countered that:

- there is still considerable disagreement among scientists
- scientists who conclude that global warming is real do so to attract grants
- if the climate is changing, it is due to natural cycles
- climate hawks are alarmists
- global warming is a conspiracy to create big government
- switching to cleaner forms of energy would cripple the economy, kill jobs, and increase everybody's energy bills
- any US action on climate would be offset by China and India's growth in emissions.

The unfortunate result is that a scientific issue was turned into a political issue. Because prominent Republican leaders and the Republican Party have assisted the denial industry in sowing doubt,[107] the issue is widely considered one of conservatives against liberals and Republicans against Democrats.

In reality, the debate is not that simple. There are a number of Democrats, usually from states heavily dependent on fossil energy production, who oppose policies to cut greenhouse emissions. There are prominent Republicans who advocate action. In fact, many Republicans – among them several former presidential candidates – once were champions for climate action.

One of the most eloquent and personal statements I have seen from either party was written by then-governor and now congressman Mark Sanford, a Republican from South Carolina. It was published in the *Washington Post* in 2007.

> *For the past 20 years, I have seen the ever-so-gradual effects of rising sea levels at our farm on the South Carolina coast. I've had to watch once-thriving pine trees die in that fragile zone between uplands and salt*

marshes. I know the climate change debate isn't over, but I believe human activity is having a measurable effect on the environment. The real "inconvenient truth" about climate change is that some people are losing their rights and freedoms because of the actions of others – in either the quality of the air they breathe, the geography they hold dear, the insurance costs they bear, or the future environment of the children they love.[108]

During the 2008 presidential race, the Republican Party platform acknowledged climate change nine times, including this statement:

The same human economic activity that has brought freedom and opportunity to billions has also increased the amount of carbon in the atmosphere. While the scope and long-term consequences of this are the subject of ongoing scientific research, common sense dictates that the United States should take measured and reasonable steps today to reduce any impact on the environment. Those steps, if consistent with our global competitiveness, will also be good for our national security, our energy independence, and our economy.[109]

The platform went on to urge that the "power of scientific know-how and competitive markets" be mobilized to "decrease emissions, reduce excess greenhouse gases in the atmosphere, increase energy efficiency, mitigate the impact of climate change where it occurs, and maximize any ancillary benefits climate change might offer for the economy."[110]

After the 2008 campaign, the GOP's talking points changed. Climate change disappeared from the party platform in the 2012 presidential race, except to criticize President Obama for overreacting. The 2012 presidential candidates, Republican and Democrat, did not talk about it.

The growing impacts of climate change will eventually make it impossible for elected leaders in either party to avoid addressing it in national policy. When that moment comes, I believe it will be important to avoid further politicizing the issue by characterizing former skeptics as flip-floppers. In fact, climate hawks should offer rhetorical amnesty to skeptics who convert, acknowledge climate risks, and strive to doing something about them. Although those who have fought for sensible public policy for so long will choke on the idea, anyone of either party or from civic society who becomes a climate-action convert should be welcomed back to reason. For their part, the converts can point out that, as Ralph Waldo Emerson wrote, "a foolish consistency is the hobgoblin of little minds."

One might ask why, as a lifelong Democrat, I would encourage Republican leaders to realign themselves with climate science and the majority of the American people. Why, in other words, would I want Republicans to regain credibility? I believe that the American people and public policy are better served by creative tension and open dialogue between people with different views on how best to address big problems and threats. I found it to be true as governor that when we listen to one another, the diversity of views often produces better results. And frankly, many of the more conservative approaches to climate action and clean energy – including the mobilization of market forces – have merit. Finally, as one of the greatest challenges we face as a country, this is an effort that needs all parties pulling on the oars. No one segment of the political spectrum can solve these issues alone. Solving the climate crisis will take a sustained and committed effort. The question is, how do we get there?

Become Multilingual

There is moral and intellectual satisfaction when we convert someone to our point of view. But a more promising way to change the direction of a conversation is to engage the value system of the person to whom we are speaking. This requires insight, humility, empathy, and the ability to speak the languages of different values.

Several prominent Republican thought leaders in recent times have tried to persuade others in their party to think of climate action in the value system of conservatives. A prominent example is former Republican US Representative Bob Inglis, who lost his seat to a Tea Party candidate in South Carolina. In July 2012, he launched the Energy and Enterprise Initiative to show Republicans they could address global warming "guided by the conservative principles of free enterprise and economic growth, limited government, liberty, accountability, and reasonable risk avoidance to solve our nation's energy and climate challenges."[111]

In the fall of 2013, four former Environmental Protection Agency (EPA) administrators who served under Republican presidents published an op-ed in the *New York Times* titled *The Republican Case for Climate Action.* They wrote:

> *We served Republican presidents, but we have a message that transcends political affiliation: the United States must move now on substantive steps to curb climate change, at home and internationally... Rather than argue against (President Obama's) proposals, our leaders in Congress should endorse them and start the overdue debate about what bigger steps are needed and how to achieve them.*[112]

More recently, former Treasury Secretary Henry Paulson's column in the *New York Times* made the case for a carbon tax, a policy aligned with traditional conservative values because it would put markets rather than government regulations to work in the transition to clean energy.[113]

Some of the more recent advice on communicating with voters about energy issues comes from research on "what Americans really want," by Stephen Ansolabehere of Harvard University and David Konisky of Georgetown University:[114]

- In regard to preferences, people care less about partisanship and more about their perceptions of environmental harm and energy costs. When asked to make a choice between more expensive energy and greater environmental damage, people say they are willing to pay more for energy if it is cleaner.

- Energy preferences are not source-specific. "People don't like or dislike coal or wind because it is coal or wind," the researchers concluded. "Rather, it is the attributes that matter. People like coal because it is cheap, but they dislike that it's dirty. They like natural gas because it is relatively clean and has become relatively inexpensive. In this respect, Americans view energy sources as consumers view any good. Americans want energy to be less harmful to the environment and they want it to be less expensive."

- The American people don't think about these issues on a global scale. Their interest is engaged by policies that address problems they feel are proximate. Climate and energy issues should be discussed in terms of local benefits and impacts.

In March 2015, researchers from Yale, George Mason University, and Ohio State University conducted experiments to test ways to frame climate science so that lay people better understand it. They found that simple, clear messages using numeric data worked better than general statements to improve the public's understanding of the scientific consensus and their confidence in that consensus.[115] So, the best way to enlist the American people in a clean energy revolution may not be a frontal attack on the fossil energy industry, but rather a declaration of war against pollution and its impacts on public health, against volatile and unreliable energy prices and supplies, and against the proximate danger of weather disasters.

We can also note that the dangers of global warming have become all too proximate for many Americans. Nothing is as personal as a deadly heat wave, a paralyzing blizzard, or a devastating storm that takes lives and property. Clean energy and climate activists should help the public make the link between these events and global warming[116] in ways that avoid creating apocalypse fatigue.

One increasingly common framework for discussing climate change across ideological lines is risk management. In this conversation, there is no need to prolong the public debate over climate science. That debate should occur where it belongs – in the scientific community. As for the rest of us, including our elected leaders, the responsible course of action is to minimize the risk in believing that all those scientists are correct and climate change is real.

The risk conversation can be effective because the lay public can relate to it. We all practice risk management every day in multiple ways, from fastening our seat belts to obtaining hazard insurance, automobile insurance, health insurance, and life insurance. In each case, we do not believe something bad will happen and we hope it won't, but we protect ourselves against the possibility.

The financial risks of climate impacts are the focus of Risky Business, an ambitious project cochaired by former New York Mayor Michael Bloomberg, former Treasury Secretary Henry Paulson, and philanthropist Tom Steyer. Its first report breaks climate risks down into seven regions in the lower 48 states, in Alaska, and in Hawaii. Among its conclusions:

> Our findings show that, if we continue on our current path, many regions of the United States face the prospect of serious economic effects from climate change. However, if we choose a different path – if we act aggressively to both adapt to the changing climate and to mitigate future impacts by reducing carbon emissions – we can significantly reduce our exposure to the worst economic risks from climate change, and also demonstrate global leadership on climate.[117]

The American Association for the Advancement of Science (AAAS) has launched a campaign to explain climate science in risk-management terms:

> We are acting like people who take risks with their health (e.g., with behaviors such as smoking, poor food choices) but still hope to live long lives free of serious illness. To make decisions about managing a risk, we consider the likelihood that a particular event will happen, the consequences if it did, and the cost of effective actions to prevent it. These are the same steps that go into making decisions about climate change.[118]

America's most expert risk managers – the intelligence and defense communities – have long considered climate change and fossil energy dependence threats to national security.[119] The National Intelligence Council's studies on climate risks go back at least to 2008, when it declared that global warming would be an urgent and growing threat to national

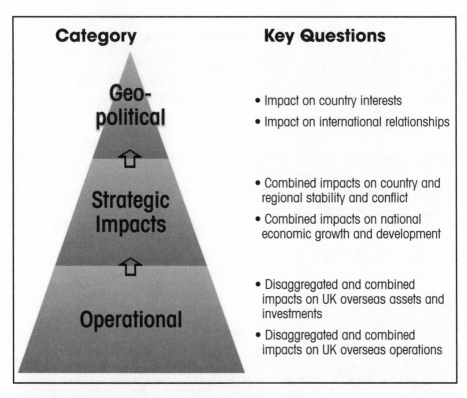

Category	Key Questions
Geo-political	• Impact on country interests • Impact on international relationships
Strategic Impacts	• Combined impacts on country and regional stability and conflict • Combined impacts on national economic growth and development
Operational	• Disaggregated and combined impacts on UK overseas assets and investments • Disaggregated and combined impacts on UK overseas operations

This chart, with information from Third Generation Environmentalism in London, shows some of the issues that should be considered in assessing climate risks. (Source: Degrees of Risk, Third Generation Environmentalism)

security over the next 20 years. The 2015 National Security Strategy lists climate change and disruptions in energy markets among our top security threats, alongside terrorist attacks and weapons of mass destruction.[120] The *Quadrennial Defense Review* from the Department of Defense warns that climate change will multiply threats around the world and put new pressures on the frequency, scale, and complexity of military missions.[121] These are conversations that national leaders and the American people should be having.

Dismantling the Echo Chamber

There are two other ways to change the climate conversation, although both are even more challenging. The first is to eliminate the echo-chamber effect in public discourse; the second is to strengthen journalism's ethics.

Managing Utility Risks

The utility industry is a perfect example of the need for major sectors of the economy to recognize and manage the risks associated with climate change and with the nation's energy transition. The chairman of the Colorado Public Service Commission during my administration, Ron Binz, has written a guide for regulators on "risk aware" oversight of utilities.

Binz points out that the power sector faces unprecedented challenges, including the need to double net invested capital in the electric system by 2030, building an infrastructure that may last 40 years or longer despite changing power demand, competition from distributed generation, uncertain economics of coal and gas, requirements to reduce greenhouse gas emissions, and similar factors.

"Ignoring risk is not a viable strategy," he writes. "Regulators (and utilities) cannot avoid risk by failing to make decisions or by relying on fate. Following a practice just because 'it's always been done that way,' instead of making a fresh assessment of risk and attempting to limit that risk, is asking for trouble."

"It falls to state electricity regulators to ensure that the large amount of capital invested by utilities over the next two decades is deployed wisely. Poor decisions could harm the US economy and its global competitiveness; cost ratepayers, investors, and taxpayers hundreds of billions of dollars; and have costly impacts on the environment and public health."

"Practicing Risk-Aware Electricity Regulation: What Every State Regulator Needs to Know," Ronald J. Binz et al., Ceres and the Regulatory Assistance Project, April 2012, http://www.ceres.org/resources/reports/practicing-risk-aware-electricity-regulation

The echo-chamber effect occurs when people seek out information only from others who share their views. In psychological terms, this is a form of "self-referencing" in which people tend to remember best and give most credibility to the ideas and opinions that agree with their own.

In a peer-reviewed article published by the *Journal of Communication*, researchers reported[122] that media viewers and listeners "insulate themselves in 'echo chambers' where they are exposed only to content consistent with their opinions while shielded from dissenting views." Echo chambers exist on both ends of the ideological spectrum.

The echo effect involves a type of perverse reciprocity between ideological or partisan media and their audiences. These media achieve popularity and profit by affirming the preconceived beliefs and perceptions of their viewers and listeners. Audiences become loyal to those stations, preferring them to media that conflict with or challenge their views. This symbiosis between ideological stations and their audiences is exacerbated when conservative media criticize "mainstream media" as liberal, biased, and untrustworthy.

If Thomas Jefferson was correct in concluding that a healthy democracy depends on an informed citizenry – and we know he was – then the echo chambers are bona fide threats to our form of government. Some recent evaluations of cable networks have shown that viewers are not only poorly informed, they are also misinformed by biased network content. The Union of Concerned Scientists (UCS) – itself a potential echo chamber for climate activists – assessed the coverage of climate change on three of the most widely watched cable news networks in the United States: CNN, Fox News, and MSNBC. It found that MSNBC offered the most accurate coverage, with 8 percent of its segments containing inaccurate or misleading statements. CNN was in the middle with about 30 percent of its segments containing inaccuracies or misleading information. The least accurate was Fox News – the channel whose motto is "Fair and Balanced" – with an astounding 72 percent of its climate change segments containing mistaken or misleading information.

Another study, this one in 2012, looked at how knowledgeable the viewers of different television stations were about political and economic events. It found that people who watched Fox News, CNN, and CNBC were less knowledgeable than the listeners/viewers of National Public Radio or Sunday morning talk shows. In fact, Fox News viewers scored "significantly worse than if they had reported watching no media at all."[123]

In the past, the government tried to prevent dogma from being disguised as news with a regulation called the Fairness Doctrine. Instituted in 1949, the doctrine required companies that held broadcast licenses to present "honest, equitable, and balanced" views on both sides of controversial issues of public importance. It did not require that opposing views be given equal time, but rather that both sides be presented. The requirement was considered an obligation for companies in exchange for using the public airwaves. The Federal Communications Commission (FCC) discontinued enforcing the doctrine in 1987 and allowed it to disappear altogether in 2011.

The FCC's reasoning, in part, was that with the great number of stations available today, viewers and listeners who want all sides of an issue can channel surf through a variety of echo chambers. But that is not what many people do. Instead, investigators at the University of Illinois, in a study published in the *Journal of Public Economics* concluded, "The fundamental reason for the inefficiency in electoral outcomes is that voters choose to listen to biased media."[124]

The investigators also confirmed that profit motivates broadcasters to cater to partisan audiences: "Profits of media firms depend on their audience ratings, and maximizing profits may involve catering to a partisan audience by suppressing information that the partisan audience does not like hearing."[125]

Even if it were possible to resurrect the Fairness Doctrine, a government mandate cannot force people to be intellectually curious and open-minded. We can lead people to information, but we cannot make them think. After studying the effects of media bias on political polarization and election outcomes, the University of Illinois researchers concluded, "The best option for society may be to foster a culture in which citizens appreciate learning about both sides of a political debate."[126] In other words, one way to begin changing the conversation is to promote every citizen's responsibility to be well informed by seeking out a variety of perspectives and views about the important issues of the day.

Putting Ethics Back into News

If seeking out a variety of views is the responsibility of informed citizens, what is the responsibility of the media? In the United States, the obligation of news media has always been to provide fair and accurate coverage and to be clear about the difference between news, opinion, and entertainment. The code of ethics promoted by the Society of Professional Journalists,[127] for example, encourages journalists to "take responsibility for the accuracy of their work," "be vigilant and courageous about holding those with power accountable," "recognize a special obligation to serve as watchdogs over public affairs and government," "label advocacy and commentary," and "acknowledge mistakes and correct them promptly and prominently." The study I cited earlier of accuracy in climate reporting by major television networks and their roles in the echo chamber make clear that these standards are not universally applied.

At the same time, journalists and editors must juggle a number of challenges when reporting the climate story. One practice that has drawn the ire of climate activists in recent years is how the news media defines "balance." In the past, balance meant giving roughly equal airtime or column inches to both sides of an issue. Applying the equal-time rule to coverage of an issue where 97 percent of experts agree and three percent do not gives the public the impression that both sides have equal credibility. Advocates say a fairer practice would be proportional rather than equal coverage – in other words, airtime and column inches that better reflect an issue's pro-con ratio.[128]

In October 2013, the *Los Angeles Times* faced a different ethical dilemma: whether it was obligated to publish all points of view in its letters to the editor section, even viewpoints that clearly were inaccurate. The issue was triggered by letters from readers who argued there is no scientific basis for the claim that humans have caused global warming. Letters Editor Paul Thornton decided he had no such obligation. He explained:

> As for letters on climate change, we do get plenty from those who deny global warming. And to say they "deny" it might be an understatement: many say climate change is a hoax, a scheme by liberals to curtail personal freedom...(but) scientists have provided ample evidence that human activity is indeed linked to climate change... Simply put, I do my best to keep errors of fact off the letters page; when one does run, a correction is published. Saying "there's no sign humans have caused climate change" is not stating an opinion, it's asserting a factual inaccuracy.[129]

We live in an age in which there is no penalty for misrepresenting facts; where the lines are unclear between news, entertainment, ideology, and propaganda; and where lies are considered protected speech under the Constitution.[130] I would argue that a profession protected by freedom of speech should protect the integrity of speech. Until that becomes the norm, the only recourse for an informed citizenry may be the old warning: In the information marketplace, let the buyer beware.

We seem to have a long way to go before we achieve a civil and constructive public conversation about climate and energy. We must get there, however, to ensure the political sustainability of energy and climate security. We cannot count on our elected leaders to guarantee consistent climate and energy policies. Policies to protect the biosphere are a permanent obligation in the hands of temporary leaders. The strong and persistent support of the American people is the only thing that can ensure the consistency of conscientious stewardship from election to election and for generations to come.

8 | Think Like a Revolutionary

Change is the law of life. And those who look only to the past or present are certain to miss the future.

– President John F. Kennedy

No one who knows me would classify me as a radical. But it has become clear to me, as it has to so many others, that our well-being and that of our children requires a radical change of direction in one of the most fundamental aspects of our lives: how we produce and consume energy. A first step is to challenge the conventional thinking of the carbon era.

Over 200 years of industrialization, the roots of carbon energy have grown deep. Our lives have been powered by it. Our policies promote it. Our aging infrastructure was built for it. Our retirement plans invest in it. The many elected leaders who rely on campaign support from the fossil energy sector vote to sustain it. To pull up these roots and make way for something new, we need to think like revolutionaries. We must be willing to reexamine ideas that have become a priori assumptions. Here are what I consider the Top Seven examples of old thinking that must be retired so that we can build the new energy economy.

1. Because we have abundant supplies of carbon fuels, we will use them for a long time to come.

New extraction methods ensure that we have sufficient fossil energy reserves in the United States and around the world to last well into the future. However the abundance of a resource is not a mandate to consume it, just as a dessert's presence on a menu does not obligate us to eat it. The threshold question about our energy choices is different today: It is not how much carbon we have in the ground, but how much we can put into the sky. The answer is not much. Simple math shows that to keep climate change from reaching catastrophic levels, most of the world's proved fossil energy reserves – as much as 80 percent – cannot be burned.[131] These underground resources account for trillions of dollars of the value of fossil energy companies today. Continued investment in these companies as though the constraints do not exist is producing a "carbon bubble," similar to but much larger than the credit bubble that brought down the economy in 2008.[132]

Some of the world's largest energy companies dismiss this risk. ExxonMobil predicts that global energy consumption will increase by 35 percent by 2040 compared to 2010, with renewable resources contributing only 5 percent.[133] One website that promotes coal boasts, "The United States as a whole has more recoverable coal resources than any other country on the planet – over 262 billion tons – enough to last over 200 years! Long after the rest of the world's coal, petroleum, and natural gas reserves have run out, America will still have enough coal to satisfy its energy needs."[134]

In contrast to his leadership on climate action, President Obama has boasted that the United States now has a 100-year supply of natural gas[135] and "more oil (is) produced at home than we buy from the rest of the world – the first time that's happened in nearly 20 years."[136] But that observation misses the point. The assumption that these reserves are part of the nation's future energy supply is dangerous old-think, given the carbon emissions they would create. But it also is an example of the "it exists, therefore we consume" mentality. We need not use up our carbon reserves before we transition to a clean energy economy. As one Saudi oil minister, Sheik Ahmed Zaki Yamani, once said, "The stone age didn't end because we ran out of stones." It ended because humans found better ways to meet their needs.[137]

2. Our reserves of fossil fuels will allow us to achieve energy independence.

Freedom from the bonds of foreign oil has been an ongoing quest since the embargoes of the 1970s. It is an objective that finally seems within reach now that the United States has become the world's biggest oil and gas producer. Unfortunately, fossil fuels cannot give us energy independence in our interconnected world. The United States does not control the price of oil, even when we produce it domestically. The world oil market determines petroleum prices and supplies. In 2014 and 2015, we were reminded of this when the Organization of Petroleum Exporting Countries (OPEC) decided not to curtail its oil production. With record production under way in the United States, global supplies grew, prices plummeted, and by the middle of March 2015, an estimated 75,000 US petroleum industry workers had lost their jobs.[138] So, as long as we use oil we will be vulnerable to vicissitudes in the world oil market.

Similarly, we live in a global economy. We could stop producing and consuming all oil tomorrow and we would still be vulnerable to the economic effects of oil prices and supply shocks elsewhere in the world. We were reminded by the credit crisis that began in 2007/2008 that other nations' economic problems can become ours, and ours can become theirs. "When America's housing market turned, a chain reaction exposed fragilities in the financial system," *The Economist* observed. "Complex chains of debt between counterparties were vulnerable to just one link breaking."[139] Comparing that crisis to climate change, Henry Paulson has written, "The nature of a crisis is its unpredictability. And as we all witnessed during the financial crisis, a chain reaction of cascading failures ensued from one intertwined part of the system to the next." When it comes to a dependence on finite resources for prosperity, one nation's addiction can be every nation's addiction.

This leads to a radical conclusion: The only way for America to achieve energy independence is to wean ourselves from finite energy resources and help all other nations do it, too.

This idea is neither as far off nor as far-fetched as it might seem. Small-scale distributed renewable energy systems are already the quickest, least expensive, and most versatile way to provide modern electricity to the 1.3 billion people in the world who do not have it. In the developed world, solar and wind energy already are competing economically with oil, coal, and natural gas. The financial advisory firm Lazard concludes that even without government subsidies and without counting externalized costs and benefits, the price of renewable resources places them squarely in competition with fossil resources in many areas of the United States.[140] Lazard reports that the levelized costs of energy (LCOE)[141] for solar and wind have dropped 82 percent and 61 percent respectively since 2009.[142] This is happening at the same time that mid- and long-term market forces are threatening to push up the cost of fossil fuels. Extraction is increasingly invasive and expensive as easy supplies disappear. More importantly, it is likely that nations will put a price on carbon either individually or collectively. Even the world's largest oil companies now advocate for it.[143]

Similar developments are under way in world markets. The International Renewable Energy Agency (IRENA) reports that the competitiveness of renewables reached "historic levels" in 2013 and

2014. "Biomass for power, hydropower, geothermal, and onshore wind can all provide electricity competitively against fossil fuel-fired power generation," IRENA stated. "Solar photovoltaic (PV) power has also become increasingly competitive, with its LCOE at utility scale falling by half in four years."[144]

The growth in solar and wind energy generation is pushed, too, by state goals and requirements. Today, 29 states have set mandatory standards and another eight have set goals for utilities to generate electricity from renewable energy.[145] The national regulation of greenhouse gas emissions from power plants is expected to encourage clean energy to penetrate America's markets even faster.

We need only look around our neighborhoods to see that a rooftop revolution is under way, testimony to the growing competitiveness of renewables.

3. **There is not enough capital to build clean energy economies at the level and speed necessary to prevent catastrophic climate change.**

The International Energy Agency (IEA) estimates that global investments in clean energy must total $1 trillion between now and 2030 to hold global warming to 2°C. In recent years, the worldwide recession and a shakeout in the solar industry caused capital investment in clean energy to falter. Nevertheless, Bloomberg New Energy Finance reports that clean energy investments grew fivefold between 2004 and 2014, reaching a record-breaking $310 billion in 2014 (Figure 8.1).[146]

Reaching the $1 trillion goal would provide enormous cobenefits beyond cutting global greenhouse gas emissions in half. Ceres, the nonprofit organization of investors, companies, and public interest groups, estimates that fuel savings would reach $100 trillion between 2010 and 2050 and create millions of new jobs.[147]

To provide capital for clean energy in developing nations, developed nations have agreed to contribute to a Green Climate Fund[148] established during climate negotiations in 2010. The fund's objective is to move $100 billion annually to developing economies by 2020 to help them develop clean energy systems and to adapt to climate change.

That merely scratches the surface of investment potential. Partly because of uncertainties created by the financial crisis, many investors reportedly remain on the sidelines. In fact, world markets are "structurally awash in capital" and in a state of "capital

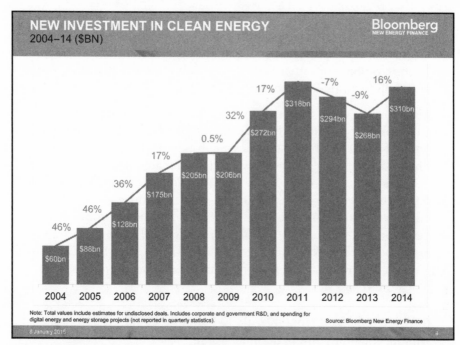

NEW INVESTMENT IN CLEAN ENERGY
2004–14 ($BN)

Bloomberg
NEW ENERGY FINANCE

46% $60bn
46% $88bn
36% $128bn
17% $175bn
0.5% $205bn $206bn
32% $272bn
17% $318bn
-7% $294bn
-9% $268bn
16% $310bn

2004 2005 2006 2007 2008 2009 2010 2011 2012 2013 2014

Note: Total values include estimates for undisclosed deals. Includes corporate and government R&D, and spending for digital energy and energy storage projects (not reported in quarterly statistics).

Source: Bloomberg New Energy Finance

8 January 2015

Figure 8.1

Global investment in clean energy increased significantly over the last decade, despite the lack of an international climate action agreement or a price on carbon. In the first half of 2015, global investments were $128 billion, according to Bloomberg New Energy Finance. The International Energy Agency (IEA) estimates that investments must average $1 trillion annually between now and 2050 to give the world an 80 percent chance of keeping global warming to 2°C. Potential sources of additional capital include a global price on carbon, a redirection of fossil energy subsidies, and greater certainty in national and international energy policies that would move private capital off the sidelines. (Source: Bloomberg New Energy Finance)

superabundance" today, according to a 2012 analysis by the management consulting firm Bain & Company.[149] Bain predicts that by 2020, global capital will reach $900 trillion. Fast-growing, emerging markets are a "natural destination" for capital investment, Bain says. The abundance of capital will "tip the balance of power from owners of capital to owners and creators of good ideas – wherever they can be found." In other words, the potential is enormous for capitalizing the transition to clean energy. The key to unlocking those investments is stable government policies.

Other sources of money could be available, too, if needed. Global or regional carbon pricing could produce substantial revenues. The international climate treaty or a parallel agreement could commit all nations to phase out their fossil energy subsidies, which total about $550 billion annually, according to the IEA.[150]

The termination of fossil energy subsidies would have significant cobenefits for societies. The International Monetary Fund (IMF) has estimated that fossil fuel subsidies amount to nearly $2 trillion annually when external costs are included, such as climate-related weather disasters and damages to public health.[151] The IMF is urging nations to reform fossil energy subsidies not only to help reduce global warming, but also to make more money available for education, economic development, public health, and so on. In a more rational world, there would be no argument over the fact that all of the benefits of moving public and private capital from fossil to renewable energy are simply too good to pass up.

4. New technologies will allow us to continue using carbon fuels without making climate change worse.

While we are justifiably optimistic in America about our ability to solve problems with new technologies, some can have detrimental social, economic, environmental, and national security impacts severe enough to outweigh their benefits. The result is problem *switching* rather than problem *solving*, often caused by the failure to look at a problem or a proposed solution from a systems perspective.[152]

One such example is the coal industry's ongoing effort to produce liquid fuels from coal, a process first used by Nazi Germany during World War II.[153] The industry argues that coal liquids will reduce America's dependence on imported oil, and for that reason, the federal government is giving the industry taxpayer funds to continue working on the process.[154] But making liquids from coal consumes a great deal of energy and water only to result in a fuel that can release as much as 80 percent more greenhouse gas pollution than the gasoline it replaces.

Some researchers advocate technical fixes known as geoengineering to continue burning fossil fuels without adding to climate change. Generally, geoengineering is the modification or manipulation of a natural system to produce a desired effect. That can be done benignly by managing forests and soils so they do a better job sequestering carbon. Its more exotic varieties cross the line into the land of unintended consequences.[155, 156]

One such idea is "solar radiation management," in which we would put a mirror the size of Greenland into space (or alternatively, as many as a trillion smaller mirrors) to reflect sunlight before it reaches the Earth's surface. Unfortunately, it would be a daunting challenge to keep the mirrors properly oriented and too little is understood about the effect that blocking sunlight would have on organic life, crop production, and photosynthesis. Other questionable ideas include spraying sulfuric acid into the atmosphere to scatter sunlight and fertilizing the oceans with iron to trigger phytoplankton blooms that absorb carbon dioxide.

Geoengineering is one part science fiction, one part engineering, one part overconfidence in our knowledge, and one part political expediency, because in theory, we could continue burning fossil fuels.

5. Switching to clean energy wastes the investments we have made in the conventional energy infrastructure.

It is true that a rapid transition to sustainable energy could force the retirement of pipelines, power plants, and other carbon-era infrastructure before the end of their useful lives and before investors have maximized their returns. This prospect has brought some new terms into the public conversation. They include "stranded assets," "sunk costs," and "committed carbon."

Infrastructure that can no longer be used or that is replaced ahead of its remaining useful life is called a stranded asset. Unrecovered investments become sunk costs. If we insist on operating a coal-fired power plant until the end of its design life, it becomes a de facto commitment to continue burning coal, aka "committed carbon."

These issues are important right now because we must make decisions about whether to live with, retire, retrofit, or replace America's aging energy systems. The American Society of Civil Engineers (ASCE) estimates we would need to invest $3.6 trillion to bring energy infrastructure to acceptable standards by 2020.[157] The Department of Energy (DOE) advises that a twenty-first century energy system must take several new factors into account – factors that were not an issue when pipelines, power lines, and other assets were constructed during the last century.[158] Among these are cyber-attack, extreme weather and other climate impacts, and the need to accommodate dispersed energy production, including energy produced by utility customers.

EPA limits on carbon emissions from existing power plants were expected to result in the early retirement of between 30 and 280 coal-fired generation plants, depending on who is counting. Many of these plants could still generate power, but the cost of complying with air quality standards would make them uneconomical.[159]

So, whether an industrialized nation plans to upgrade and expand its energy infrastructure or a developing country needs to provide modern power to its people, the question is where the investments are most wisely made. What should our plan be for new oil and gas pipelines and electric transmission lines if we are moving to a time when people are driving less, or drive vehicles that run on nonpetroleum fuels? How many miles of new transmission and distribution lines do we need in a nation whose fastest-growing sources of electricity are wind and solar power, some produced close to where it is consumed? Should public funds and private investments be used to build more highways or more public transportation options? Should our strategy for reducing flood disasters be to build more dams and levees or to restore natural flood control systems and to stop building in floodplains?

To a degree, stranded assets are an inevitable part of technical progress. Anyone who has a cell phone sitting unused in a drawer because smart phones came along knows what a stranded asset is. Even if the old cell phone still works, it has little if any economic or practical value. Our challenge is to minimize wasted investments in an old and no longer viable energy economy. That requires market certainty about our energy future, including the level and rate at which we intend to reduce greenhouse gas emissions. Market certainty requires that we have a clear bipartisan commitment to an energy revolution, effective public policies to bring it about, agreement on a trajectory, and a detailed national energy plan with goals, milestones, and performance measures. We have none of these in the United States today.

6. International treaties are a threat to national sovereignty.

I include this in my Top Seven because of the importance of international agreements to deal with climate change and to conduct the energy revolution. Some opponents of climate action fear that if the United States becomes party to an international treaty on greenhouse gas emissions, we will slide down the slippery slope to world government. Yet climate change cannot be brought under control by any one polluter or any one nation. All countries have to engage in the solution for there to be any solution at all.

The defense of sovereignty is one of the reasons that 38 treaties, many dealing with worthy and even moral issues, remain dormant in the United States today, some waiting decades for the required advice and consent of the Senate. They include treaties to ban land mines, guard the rights of children, eliminate discrimination against women, control biological weapons, ensure biological diversity, suppress the financing of terrorist organizations, establish the rights of refugees and indigenous people, protect the oceans from toxic wastes, and prohibit torture. In several cases, the United States is the only nation, or one of only a few, that has failed to ratify these agreements.

Concerns about sovereignty have been much in play during the more than 20 years that international negotiators have tried to reach a climate agreement. As negotiators prepared in 2009 to meet in Copenhagen, where expectations were high that a treaty finally would be achieved, the Heritage Foundation warned that, "The Obama administration should not sign any agreement reached in Copenhagen or thereafter that would deprive the United States of its sovereign right to determine the nature and extent of its treaty obligations and whether it has complied with those obligations."[160]

Sovereignty by definition is a nation's unlimited power over its own affairs and its freedom from external control. But this absolutely does not exist any longer for individuals or for nations in the contemporary world, if it ever did. Most of us in the United States have accepted – in some cases reluctantly – compromises in our "freedom from external control" as individuals. We are no longer sovereign smokers in most places. We are not self-governing drivers free of traffic laws. Some compromises of sovereignty are essential for the common good.

Yet whether it is one nation's virus turning into a global pandemic, or one country's economic problem becoming a worldwide recession, or one nation's drought raising global food prices, or one leader's irrational moment threatening the world with nuclear war, or everybody's carbon emissions impacting everyone's safety everywhere, it is in our own best interest to acknowledge that sovereignty is conditional today. On some issues it remains a valid principle; on others, it does not. One of the bigger challenges in regard to climate change is to find a proper balance.

That balance was found to the satisfaction of the 195 nations that adopted an international climate agreement in Paris at the end of 2015. It is an unprecedented achievement of diplomacy because of the critical nature of the issue, its promise of transformational change in the global economy, and the a remarkable consensus among so many nations with diverse interests and needs.

7. Business as usual remains an option.

"If you always do what you've always done, you'll always get what you've always got," Henry Ford once said. Today, however, it is no longer possible to do what we have always done. Technologies, economic conditions, environmental factors, demographics, and most other influences on our lives are not static, and the road to the future is not linear. We can try to maintain equilibrium in our personal and public affairs, but we cannot maintain the status quo. When we accept that reality, we will be more likely to help shape the future rather than try in vain to sustain the unsustainable present.

If we do nothing about carbon emissions, we will suffer radical change. If we choose to confront climate change, we will have to make radical changes in our views about the biosphere and in how we power our economies. Doing what we have always done is not on the table.

"Climate action was once perceived by many governments and many businesses as about sacrifice," writes Christiana Figueres, the executive secretary of the United Nations Climate Change Secretariat. "Today, the value proposition is very different. Today, it is the sacrifice economies and communities will increasingly have to make if the world fails to address climate change and the buildup of greenhouse gases."[161]

In other words, building a new energy economy is not a sacrificial act; it is the process of seizing opportunity.

These are just a few examples of stultifying old-think. They illustrate that the clean energy revolution is as much about our thinking as it is about our technologies.

John Kenneth Galbraith once said, "The conventional view serves to protect us from the painful job of thinking." Buddha is quoted as saying, "With our thoughts we make the world." Put together, these two bits of wisdom tell us that challenging convention may be painful, but we cannot make a new world without new thoughts. That is where the energy revolution begins.

9 | Everything Counts

There are three types of accountants: Those who can count and those who can't.

– Anon.

Let me be clear about fossil fuels. The American economy became the strongest in the world after the Industrial Revolution, in part because of the fossil fuels we had access to, particularly coal and oil. We built a coal-fired manufacturing economy that in turn built and buttressed other economic sectors. It is fair to say that the middle class in the United States owes its livelihood to fossil fuels. The problem is that we were not paying the full costs of our fossil fuel use. Instead, we treated the real costs of using fossil fuels like a shell game.

Most of us are familiar with the shell game – an old army pastime that involves three walnut shells and a small pea. The game's operator places the pea under one of the shells and moves them around rapidly. Players bet that they can pick the shell with the pea underneath. Rather than a game of skill, however, the shell game is usually a swindle in which the person moving the cups uses sleight of hand to fool the bettor.

The shell game is a suitable metaphor for the old energy economy. As I have pointed out, many of the actual costs we pay for energy are hidden. The price of gasoline at the pump, to cite just one example, does not include the medical costs associated with asthma from air pollution, or the cost of maintaining the Strategic Petroleum Reserve to protect against interruptions in oil supplies, or the military cost of keeping oil shipping lanes open in the Persian Gulf, or even the full cost to maintain our roads. It does not reflect the fact that we spend money to protect ourselves from terrorism at the same time part of the money we pay for gasoline is ending up in oil-producing countries that support terrorist organizations.

These hidden costs are said to be "externalized," meaning that someone other than purchaser of the fuel pays them. For example, the external costs may be borne by taxpayers, or people in need of health care from respiratory illnesses due to air pollution, or higher insurance rates, or the victims of weather disasters. Businesses benefit from externalizing costs by keeping the market price of their products lower and more competitive. In other cases, the real cost of a product or a unit of energy is not fully reflected in the price because we do not know how to place a monetary value on some costs and benefits. For example, air pollution from fossil fuels is the principal cause of global warming, which in turn produces drought, which results in wildfires that destroy wildlife habitat. We simply are not good at monetizing that level of disruption to the ecosystem.

Quantifying the monetary value of many indirect costs and benefits of an energy resource is an evolving science. It is likely we will never be able to assign a defensible economic value to some less tangible costs and benefits. But in the new energy economy, we need to do a much better job than we do now by counting all of the costs and benefits we can and considering important factors that cannot be monetized. This is known as full-cost accounting, the practice of reflecting as many costs and benefits as possible, both direct and indirect, in policy making and market pricing (Figure 9.1). As I will discuss further in Chapter 10, full-cost accounting allows energy markets to work more efficiently because it gives consumers more accurate price signals about their choices.[162]

For now, I will point out a key reason we must begin using full-cost analysis in energy and climate policies: It gives us an objective method for identifying the options with the greatest economic, social, and environmental value at least cost. When the numbers do the talking, fewer decisions will be made because of political pressure from special interests. If policy makers believe it is necessary to support an energy resource even though it has higher costs or fewer benefits than other options, the burden would be on them to explain why.

In one way of looking at it, America's evolution to a twenty-first century energy economy is a big math problem – two math problems, actually. The first is to count costs and benefits we have not counted before. The second is to learn to consider the intangible costs and benefits for which no monetary value can easily be assigned.

Pricing Nature

Ecosystem services are among the significant benefits we have not traditionally counted in making decisions about public policy, or about economic development. At the Museum of Science and Industry in Portland, Oregon, there is an elegant example. The museum and its 800-vehicle parking lot are adjacent to the Willamette River. The surface of the parking lot is pitched so that when rainfall picks up oil, antifreeze,

Penny-Wise and Pound-Foolish

It is not uncommon for policy makers, businesses, and consumers to pay more attention to the initial costs of a product or policy than to consider long-term benefits and costs. First-cost accounting is penny-wise and pound-foolish as the old saying goes. For example, someone purchasing a car should look past its sticker price to calculate its operating, insurance, and maintenance costs over the period of time the buyer plans to own it. The buyer may find that if he pays a little more upfront for extra fuel efficiency, he will spend and pollute a lot less in the long term.

The alternative to first-cost accounting is full-cost accounting, also called true cost accounting. It considers and attempts to quantify actual costs rather than simple cash outlays. The actual costs include factors such as hidden costs and externalities, overhead and indirect costs, past and future outlays, and costs throughout the life cycle of the action or product. Typically, the counting includes economic, environmental, and social costs.

Environmental accounting is a close cousin to full cost accounting, although its focus is less on social costs than on environmental and economic costs. It considers long-term environmental impacts and remediation costs, for example. Another close cousin is life-cycle costing, which considers the benefits and costs of a product or policy from "cradle to grave."

At the Center for the New Energy Economy, we recommend counting the costs and benefits of a policy in all respects – social, environmental, and economic – throughout the policy's life. In their role as custodians of taxpayer money, governments should support ongoing work to better quantify and build consensus on costs and benefits that traditionally have been considered uncountable.

Figure 9.1

or other pollutants from parked cars, the runoff spills into several planting beds. The city calls them "bio-swales." The bio-swales contain hyperaccumulators – plants that thrive on absorbing toxic metals and storing them in their tissues. They soak up the pollutants, serving as a filter that keeps the toxins from entering the river.

When plants are used to treat environmental problems, the process is called phytoremediation. Multiply Portland's bio-swales by several acres and you have a "constructed wetland" in which plants and biota rather than chemicals treat wastewater. Put the constructed wetland under glass or inside a building, add some beneficial bacteria, and you have an "engineered ecosystem" that environmental pioneer John Todd calls an

Eco-Machine. Wastewater goes in one end; usable water comes out the other, purified without chemicals.[163]

Whether we mimic natural systems or employ them, they are essential to our quality of life as well as to our economy. For example, one of every three bites of food we eat depends on pollination. By one estimate, pollinators such as bees and butterflies provide about $20 billion worth of benefits to American agriculture each year.[164] Soils filter and purify rainwater. Vegetation on hillsides helps prevent floods by absorbing rainfall. It also holds soil in place, keeping it from filling riverbeds with silt – a problem that reduces a river's capacity to keep water within its banks. Wetlands also reduce flooding, by holding and storing water. Wetlands multitask by providing wildlife habitat and recharging groundwater. Coastal wetlands buffer oceanside communities from storm surges. Trees sequester carbon while giving shade that provides natural cooling, which in turn reduces energy consumption and greenhouse gas emissions at the power plant, and even lowers the risk of heat-related illnesses in cities. Urban green spaces also reduce the heat-island effect,[165] while their permeable surfaces minimize storm water runoff and help recharge water tables.

These all are gifts. Unfortunately, many communities leave them unopened or destroy them completely for the sake of development. It happens because communities do not know about ecosystem services, do not fully understand them, or do not appreciate their value.

Experts in the field of ecological economics are working to fix that. In 1997, Dr. Robert Costanza and several of his colleagues attempted to calculate the monetary value of ecosystem services worldwide.[166] As one writer for the National Academy of Sciences noted, it was "the most ambitious attempt at valuation of ecosystem services to date… nothing less than the value of ecosystem services for the entire planet (i.e., 'the value of everything')."[167] The result led to considerable debate. Costanza and his team estimated that natural systems were providing as much as $33 trillion in services each year (1995 $US), considerably higher than the global gross domestic product at the time ($18 trillion).[168] In 2014, Costanza led another team that updated the earlier work. It estimated that global ecosystem services in 2011 were worth at least $145 trillion yearly, roughly double the global GDP that year. From 1997 to 2011, as much as $20 trillion in ecosystems services were lost each year due to land use changes alone.[169]

True-Cost Energy Policy

Because true-cost accounting has not been common practice in energy markets, the markets suffer from inaccurate "price signals" – the price tags that are supposed to help inform consumer choice. Government policies often distort price signals by encouraging the use of energy resources that impose high costs on society. Fossil energy subsidies are the most obvious example today because they encourage and even reward greenhouse gas pollution and, as a result, global climate change. These self-inflicted costs have led to proposals, as yet unsuccessful in Congress, to reduce or eliminate carbon subsidies and to use a carbon tax to internalize the costs of climate change in fossil energy prices.

Different agencies within or associated with the federal government have attempted to calculate the true costs, or at least a truer cost, of carbon fuels in recent years. In 2009, for example, the National Research Council (NRC), part of the National Academy of Sciences,[170] issued a study on the hidden life-cycle costs of coal, oil, other fossil fuels, and the electricity produced from them.[171] The NRC estimated that these fuels caused externalized damages of $120 billion in the United States during 2005, the most current year for which data were available. The estimate reflected health damages from vehicle and power plant pollution, as well as damages that air pollution caused to crops, timber yields, buildings, and recreation. The NRC did not try to determine the costs of several other important detrimental impacts, including climate disruption, the degradation of ecosystems, and risks to national security. Nevertheless, in what might rank as the most obvious observation in any government study before or since, the NRC concluded that in electric generation, "life cycle CO_2 emissions from nuclear, wind, biomass, and solar power appear to be negligible when compared with fossil fuels."

In 2010, the Environmental Protection Agency (EPA) began advocating that when federal agencies propose new rules, they should calculate the "social cost of carbon," or SCC, using a formula that the EPA developed.[172] The formula is a step toward full-cost accounting although it is not perfect. The EPA explains it this way:

> The SCC is meant to be a comprehensive estimate of climate change damages and includes changes in net agricultural productivity, human health, and property damages from increased flood risk. However, it does not include all important damages... The models used to develop SCC estimates do not assign value to all of the important physical, ecological, and economic impacts of climate change recognized in the climate change literature because of a lack of precise information on the nature of damages and because the science incorporated into these models lags behind the most recent research.[173]

Despite these shortcomings, the EPA regards the SCC as a "useful measure to assess the benefits of CO_2 reductions."[174]

In 2014, the Obama administration took a further step toward making climate impacts more transparent. Under the National Environmental Policy Act of 1970, federal agencies are required to assess the environmental impacts of what they do and what they fund. The White House Council on Environmental Quality (CEQ) has told agencies they must now assess the climate impacts of federally funded projects as well as the climate's impacts on those projects.[175]

Full-cost accounting has also been the focus of research outside the federal government. In 2011, the Center for Health and the Global Environment at the Harvard Medical School estimated the life-cycle costs of coal,[176] including its impacts on land, public health, fatalities in coal production, air and mercury emissions, and climate change. The center calculated that the true costs of coal-fired power amounted to nearly 27 cents a kilowatt-hour, more than twice the national average of 11.72 cents that retail residential customers were paying for electricity that year.[177] The Harvard report continued:

> *We estimate that the life cycle impacts of coal and the waste stream generation are costing the US public a third to over one half a trillion dollars annually. Accounting for the damages conservatively doubles to triples the price of electricity from coal per kWh generated, making wind, solar, and other forms of non-fossil fuel power generation, along with investments in efficiency and electricity conservation methods, economically competitive. Beyond dollar evaluations, qualitative impacts include harm to air quality, watersheds, land, plants, animals, families, and communities.*[178]

At the international level, environmental ministers from 13 nations conceived an initiative called The Economics of Ecosystems and Biodiversity (TEEB) to follow up on the Costanza studies.[179] TEEB organized ecosystem services into four areas: **provisioning services** such as food, water, raw materials, and medicines; **regulating services** such as air quality, carbon sequestration, and the moderation of extreme weather events; **supporting services** such as species habitats and genetic diversity; and **cultural services** such as recreation, tourism, and even the beneficial psychological impacts of mountains, forests, wildlife, and other natural features.

The TEEB project called the monetization of these services an effort to "mainstream the economics of nature." The project's leaders explained why they considered this important:

> *Applying economic thinking to the use of biodiversity and ecosystem services can help clarify two critical points: why prosperity and poverty reduction depend on maintaining the flow of benefits from ecosystems; and why successful environmental protection needs to be grounded in*

sound economics, including explicit recognition, efficient allocation, and fair distribution of the costs and benefits of conservation and sustainable use of natural resources.[180]

In its attempt to estimate the life-cycle costs of energy production and consumption in the United States, the NRC repeatedly noted that the exercise is "extremely difficult" due to the lack of adequate methods and information. Nevertheless, the exercise is worth the trouble. In addition to the benefits I have already mentioned, full-cost accounting:

- helps avoid unintended economic consequences, including expenses and damages we otherwise might not anticipate.

- provides a more accurate indication of financial risks – for example, the risks that extreme weather events and disasters pose to the federal budget, taxpayers, and the solvency of government disaster programs.

- reveals which energy options are more sustainable than others in reaching a given objective such as reducing greenhouse gas emissions.

- discourages the "first cost" mentality in which we pay attention only to the costs on the front end rather than over time.

- helps fix the inequities of cross subsidization, in which the people who suffer the consequences of pollution are not the people who create it.[181]

Whether the motive is market efficiency, bang for the taxpayer buck, fewer greenhouse gas emissions, or a "do no harm" energy mix, true-cost accounting should be adopted, used, and continuously improved at all levels of the economy.

One of the common benefit-cost assessments that must be heeded in a clean energy economy is Energy Return on Investment (EROI). It takes energy to make energy. EROI is the ratio of energy spent to produce a fuel and the energy we get from it.

When new technologies such as horizontal drilling and hydraulic fracturing make oil and gas easier and less expensive to extract, their EROI becomes even better. But, as with many other signals in energy markets, the conventional EROI calculation is skewed because it does not reflect all the indirect and externalized environmental, economic, and social costs of fossil energy.[182] Going forward, energy policy makers and investors should make sure that EROI analyses include full costs and benefits that have not been counted before but that reflect important national priorities. Because freshwater resources are a growing concern, for example, EROI analyses should include water returns on investment. Because mitigating climate change is a major concern, EROI should include carbon return on investment.

One simple message should stand out in the midst of these complexities: No business could succeed if its managers hid expenditures, failed to fully consider costs and benefits, or invested capital in ways that were detrimental to the enterprise's long-term health. The biggest business in the United States is the federal government, with annual outlays that exceed $1 trillion. Every man, woman, and child in America is a shareholder in that enterprise. We should not allow the people who manage the government – or private companies in which we are invested – to use bad math. Any manager who practiced inaccurate accounting would be fired at his or her next performance review. In the public sector, those performance reviews occur every two years at election time.

Measuring Genuine Progress

Another type of true-cost accounting has less to do with money and more to do with happiness. It measures things such as quality of life and "genuine progress."[183]

Most of us probably can agree that if we share a common purpose, it is to improve the quality of our lives. That objective is recognized in the US Declaration of Independence as our God-given right to "life, liberty, and the pursuit of happiness." When we get right down to it, improving and protecting the quality of our lives is a fundamental mission of government and many of the institutions of civil society. And just as it is important to undergo regular physical checkups, society needs regular checkups to make sure everything is functioning as it should for our health and well-being.

Since the middle of the last century, we have checked national well-being with a specialized tool – the Gross Domestic Product or GDP. However, the GDP only measures economic activity, which is but one factor in our quality of life. The GDP was designed for the specific job of keeping tabs on "all final goods and services that are produced and traded for money within a given period of time."[184] But the movement of money in the economy is not the same as well-being.

The analogy of a car accident has been used to explain this better. An automobile accident is a good way for a citizen to contribute to the GDP. It creates jobs for tow truck operators and auto body shops. We have to spend money on doctors, hospitals, and physical therapists. Our insurance premiums rise, which pumps more of our money into the economy. The more severe the accident and the worse our injuries, the better it is for the GDP. A more elegant critique of GDP came from Robert Kennedy in 1968:[185]

Too much and for too long, we seemed to have surrendered personal excellence and community values in the mere accumulation of material things. Our Gross National Product... counts air pollution and cigarette advertising, and ambulances to clear our highways of carnage. It counts special locks for our doors and the jails for the people who break them. It

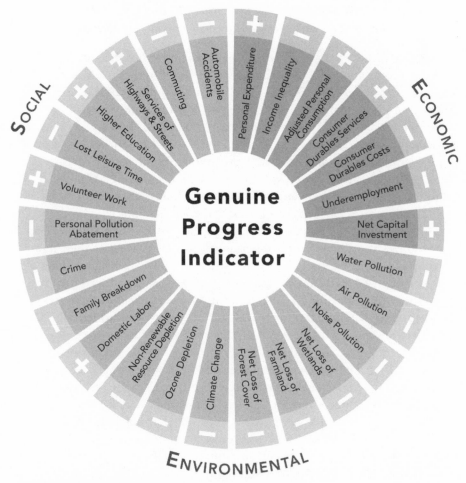

One alternative to the GDP is a Genuine Progress Indicator (GPI). In this example, developed by the Donella Meadows Institute, the GPI is based on 26 social, environmental, and economic indicators. (Source: Donella Meadows Institute)

Figure 9.2

counts the destruction of the redwood and the loss of our natural wonder in chaotic sprawl. It counts napalm and counts nuclear warheads and armored cars for the police to fight the riots in our cities. It counts Whitman's rifle and Speck's knife, and the television programs which glorify violence in order to sell toys to our children. Yet the Gross National Product does not allow for the health of our children, the quality of their education, or the joy of their play. It does not include the beauty of our poetry or the strength of our marriages, the intelligence of our public debate or the integrity of our public officials. It measures neither our wit nor our courage, neither our wisdom nor our learning, neither our compassion nor our devotion to our country. It measures everything in short, except that which makes life worthwhile. And it can tell us everything about America except why we are proud that we are Americans.

Much of the data already exist to give us better insights into these nonmonetary elements of health and well-being, but they are scattered and rarely considered as a whole. To continue with the medical analogy, it is as though the nation's health were periodically checked by a wide variety of specialists who work in separate exam rooms and do not share information with one another. In effort to bring the diagnoses together, a number of alternatives to the GDP are gaining popularity.[186] Among them are the Genuine Progress Indicator (GPI) (Figure 9.2), the World Happiness Report,[187] the Happy Planet Index[188] of the New Economics Foundation, the Social Progress Index,[189] the Millennium Development Goal Progress Index,[190] and the Better Life Index of the Organization for Economic Development and Cooperation (OECD).[191] Despite their names, these systems are not designed to turn the world into Disneyland. They measure many of the fundamental components of the quality of our lives.

Bhutan has become a pioneer of national performance measures with its Gross National Happiness Index.[192] It looks at psychological well-being, standard of living, good governance, health, education, community vitality, cultural diversity and resilience, the use of time, and ecological diversity. GPI[193] and similar systems are similarly gaining traction in the United States.[194] Maryland implemented GPI in 2010 as the result of an administrative action by former Governor Martin O'Malley. Vermont was the first state to implement GPI by law in 2012. By September 2014, press reports indicated that 20 US states were using the system.[195] In 2012, O'Malley hosted the first-ever GPI summit attended by delegations from 20 states. Explaining his decision in Maryland, Governor O'Malley said:

To make genuine progress, we must be willing to adopt a more holistic definition of progress itself. To seek an honest assessment of whether our graphs are moving in the right direction – or in the wrong one. A system without feedback eventually fails. And our country, our states, our cities – they are all systems. Life creates the conditions that are conducive to life. Period. Full stop. Perhaps, there is no better description of the intent of GPI. Its purpose is to further the conditions that are conducive to life.[196]

International progress indicators quickly discredit the idea that wealth ensures well-being or a high quality of life, with the United States as a prime example. The Social Progress Index, a tool created by a team at Harvard, defines social progress as "the capacity of a society to meet the basic human needs of its citizens, establish the building blocks that allow citizens and communities to enhance and sustain the quality of their lives, and create the conditions for all individuals to reach their full potential." The index uses more than 50 indicators in each of the following three categories: basic human needs, foundations of well-being, and opportunity. In the 2014 rankings of 132 countries, the United States had the second-highest GDP, but ranked only 70th in health, 69th in ecosystem sustainability, 39th in basic education, and 34th in access to water. (The countries with the highest overall ranking were New Zealand, Switzerland, Iceland, and the Netherlands. The United States ranked number 16.)[197]

Genuine progress indicators can reveal some useful if troubling facts. A study published in the *Journal of Economic Literature* in 2011 showed, for example, that families in the United States had higher incomes than families in France from 1975 to 2006. But when families in the top 1 percent of earnings were taken out of the calculation, it turned out that 99 percent of the families in France did better than 99 percent of families in the United States. The difference between the two results was further evidence of the large income gap in the United States between the top 1 percent of earners and the rest of the population.[198]

Tools such as these allow us to examine whether public policies are moving us where we actually want and need to go. When properly designed, they consider a wide variety of indicators, and do so holistically.

The Value of Systems Thinking

Learning to count everything requires that we engage in what engineers call "systems thinking" or "systems engineering," and what environmentalists call "holistic thinking." Business managers allude to it when they say we can't manage what we do not count. Urban planners know it as "sustainable development."

Environmental educator and author David Orr notes that systems analysis was the rage in the decades immediately after World War II, but our failure to use it regularly since then has caused a variety of serious problems:

Despite the inherent logic of systems thinking, governments, corporations,
foundations, universities, and nonprofit organizations still work
mostly by breaking issues and problems into their separate parts and
dealing with each in isolation. Separate agencies, departments, and
organizations specialize in energy, land, food, air, water, wildlife,
economy, finance, building regulations, urban policy, technology, health,
and transportation – as if each were unrelated to the others... The
results are often counter-productive, overly expensive, risky, sometimes
disastrous, and most always ironic. Systems modeling, for example,
allowed us to anticipate and understand the looming catastrophe
of rapid climate change, while systemic failures in government,
policymaking, and economics have heretofore crippled our ability to do
much about it.[199]

So, how should our policy makers go about counting everything?
Here are a few suggestions:

- The federal government should finish developing
  "sustainability indicators" for the United States. Work on
  these metrics began more than a decade ago but has never
  been completed. State and local governments can follow
  up by shaping the indicators to reflect local conditions and
  aspirations.

- Future presidents should include a genuine progress report
  in their State of the Union addresses to Congress. Jobs,
  economic growth, and other traditional measures are no
  longer enough for a report that truly reflects the state of the
  nation.

- Colleges, universities, national laboratories, and other
  research institutions should make it a high priority to quantify
  the monetary and nonmonetary value of ecosystem services.

- Educational institutions should teach systems thinking,
  including the practices of ecological engineering and
  environmental accounting.

- Communities, whether led by civic organizations or local
  governments, should periodically inventory the condition of
  the ecosystems that provide valuable services, with a priority
  on those that help mitigate and adapt to the impacts of global
  warming.

To sum up, our traditional metrics for understanding the nation's energy profile tell only a small part of the story about how we use energy. We cannot know the full story until we learn to count the true costs and benefits of our energy options. In this as well as in other areas of public policy, it is a good idea to count everything because some place or some time, one way or another, everything usually counts.

Why Governments
10 Must Intervene in
Markets

Climate change is a result of the greatest market failure
the world has seen.

– Lord Nicholas Stern[200]

It would be comforting to know that all of the ways the federal government gathers and disperses money – collectively called "fiscal policy" – were working together to give us a secure, reliable, clean, and affordable energy system in the United States. Unfortunately, that is not the case. To put it bluntly, we have neither defined nor embarked on a path that would lead us to that goal.

If we want to more fully understand the role of government in the energy revolution, we must dive deeper into the role of government in the economy.

The first thing to know is that our de facto national energy policy consists of a hodgepodge of government market interventions, many of which were created for the benefit of influential special interests. The most recent inventory I have found, conducted in 2005 by the US Government Accountability Office (GAO), counted more than 150 energy programs scattered across at least 18 agencies.[201]

Further, there is little political consensus on what our energy challenges are, let alone on how to confront them. And, as I will explain later, there is no roadmap to guide us into the future.

To paraphrase one famous American's comment about the weather, everybody talks about reforming fiscal policy – especially the tax code – but no one does anything about it.[202] Interfering with tax breaks and other types of favorable treatment for one constituency or another is a political minefield that most elected officials refuse to enter. Nevertheless, there are several reasons we should insist that our leaders clean up and retool the government's energy policies for the twenty-first century:

- The public policies that influence how we obtain and use energy in the United States were shaped largely by and for a carbon economy. Many are obsolete. Many others should be modified to eliminate biases and barriers against clean energy technologies.

- Our energy policies are inconsistent. In fact, some are at war with each other. Some encourage the production and consumption of fossil fuels, for example, while others are meant to reduce the nation's carbon emissions.

- The playing field is not level in fiscal policy. Several policies that give favorable tax treatment and investment avenues to fossil energy companies are not available to renewable energy companies. The tax benefits available from a mechanism called Master Limited Partnerships are just one example.

- Provisions in the tax code that are meant to influence the nation's energy mix are poorly designed and minimally effective in carrying out their intended objectives. I elaborate on this in Chapter 11.

- The federal government's authority to intervene in energy markets is fragmented. Some responsibilities are delegated to the president, others to federal agencies that have been given regulatory authority by Congress. Congress also intervenes by passing laws that influence energy choices and by funding or defunding government programs. These responsibilities could be harmonized by a clear national energy strategy, but again, no such strategy exists.[203]

The Free Market Myth

Any discussion about federal energy policies runs head-on into the argument that we should have a free market unfettered by government interference.

Free-market advocates characterize government support for an industry as "corporate welfare." They warn that the government should not "pick winners" in the competition between energy resources. As the Cato Institute puts it, solving energy and environmental problems should be left "to the market rather than government planners."[204] The Republican Party platform during the 2012 presidential election took the same view. "Unlike the current administration," it said, "we will not pick winners and losers in the energy marketplace. Instead, we will let the free market and the public's preferences determine the industry outcomes."[205]

At the other end of the spectrum are the proponents of proactive market interventions. Former Secretary of Labor Robert Reich argues, "Governments don't 'intrude' on free markets; governments organize and maintain them. Markets aren't 'free' of rules; the rules define them." Yet too much government intervention provokes fears of Big Government and socialism.

There is a middle ground. If we find it, we can make smoother and more rapid progress in the energy revolution. What is required is the acknowledgment that a healthy and secure energy economy will not result from market forces alone or government interventions alone, but from both working together.

The Theoretical Invisible Hand

As I noted earlier, a functional free-energy market exists only in theory in the United States. Imperfections and barriers sabotage its magic. The most consequential imperfection is that the price we pay for energy does not reflect its real costs to society and the environment.

The market price for a gallon of gasoline, for instance, does not include the medical bills forced upon people who develop respiratory diseases because of energy-related air pollution. It does not reflect the cost of defending shipping lanes in the Middle East, or of fighting terrorists whose money comes from our purchases of gasoline from oil-producing countries.[206]

Market barriers include the fact that many consumers are not fully informed about how to save energy or why they should. People who want to invest in clean energy may be unaware of where to find suitable financing. In the real estate market, home prices provide little or no clue about operating costs; if they did, buyers would have greater incentives to purchase energy-efficient residences. One role for government intervention is to fix these imperfections, when fixes are possible.

In recent times, we have seen what unfettered electricity markets can do to consumers. The California Energy Crisis is an example. The state's experiment with deregulation in 2000–2001 ultimately led to a false shortage of the supply of electricity due to criminal market manipulation detailed in the documentary *Enron: The Smartest Guys in the Room*. The memory of the Enron debacle is still fresh in the minds of state and federal utility regulators.[207]

In other cases, government intervention is appropriate because market forces alone are unable to address an urgent national priority or to do so quickly enough. The classic example is President Franklin Delano

Roosevelt's historic intervention to rapidly turn American industries into arsenals of democracy during World War II. Today's parallel is federal renewable energy tax credits and state renewable energy portfolio standards that have accelerated the market penetration of wind and solar energy systems, in part to help avert a climate crisis.

So the appropriate question is not whether governments *should* have a role in markets; it is whether an intervention is smart, well designed, competently managed, and truly in the national interest. That is where the discussion about government's role in markets should be focused today.

The History of Energy Subsidies

It also is important to know that the federal government has always sought to influence the nation's energy choices, and so far has avoided turning America into a socialist state. In their paper "What Would Jefferson Do?" investment advisor Nancy Pfund and researcher Ben Healey point out:

From land grants for timber and coal in the 1800s to tax expenditures for oil and gas in the early twentieth century, from federal investment in hydroelectric power to research and development funding for nuclear energy to today's incentives for alternative energy sources, America's support for energy innovation has helped drive our country's growth for more than 200 years. [208]

The federal government has subsidized fossil fuels with tax benefits and spending programs since 1916. During most of the last century and until 2005, federal interventions in energy markets focused mostly on increasing domestic oil and gas production. Subsidies for renewable fuels and energy efficiency began to increase in 2006. While there are disagreements about how to accurately compare subsidies for fossil energy with subsidies for renewable energy, the Congressional Budget Office (CBO) estimates that by 2011, energy efficiency and renewable energy technologies accounted for 78 percent of the government's energy tax benefits. [209]

What's in the Mix?

In Chapters 14 and 15, I focus on whether fossil fuels have a future in the nation's energy mix. Other energy options are part of the discussion, too, including nuclear power and biofuels. Both illustrate the competition between different resources for a place in America's energy portfolio as well as the complexities of deciding what belongs there.

Your Local Monopoly

One of the major players in the energy economy was never meant to be a market-driven entity. In the early part of the last century, American planners focused on electrifying the country, and government officials made what is known as a "monopoly compact" with utility companies.

The agreement was this: If the companies would build generation and transmission capabilities and provide reliable electricity for all residents, the government would ensure they had no competition; the companies could establish their exclusive right to serve their territories, or "meets and bounds." The government would protect them from competition by establishing a monopoly – one provider of services to a captive customer base. The utilities were also granted *monopsony* power, the exclusive buyer of electricity from third-party providers.

A monopoly/monopsony environment is as far as one can possibly get from a free market. This is one of the reasons that America has seen relatively little innovation in the utility sector over the last century. Innovation is not built into the utility regulatory compact. While the rest of the marketplace has increased customer choice, adopting individualized service models driven by customer involvement (think cell phones), most electric consumers are served by utilities that still operate under a "one size fits all" mentality, where the concepts of what consumers want are dictated by a three- or five-member elected or appointed state commission.

In some states, the monopoly/monopsony agreement has been modified to allow customers to choose their electric services through different providers. In much of the country, however, customers have no choice. In some other countries, third party providers of energy services can aggregate customers and offer customized demand-side services using intelligent data management through smart grids, but the United States continues to lag in this respect even though our domestic clean energy industry leads the world in product innovation.

Nuclear Energy: As of January 2015, there were 61 commercial nuclear power plants operating across 30 states in the United States. In 2014, the plants provided 19 percent of the nation's electricity. However, the fleet is aging and showing it.[210] Most of the plants were built in the 1960s and 1970s and were designed to operate for 40 years. The industry would like to relicense many of them and operate them for another 20 years or more.

Many environmental leaders who opposed it in the past now believe the nation – and the world – cannot achieve the necessary carbon reduction goals without nuclear energy. The reason: Nuclear plants do not emit carbon pollution when they generate electricity. The industry's advocates argue that nuclear power should be defined as clean energy.

But the industry has a variety of problems. One is that it has never existed without substantial government subsidies and it probably never will.[211] The first nuclear power plant in the United States began operating on December 20, 1951. To date, the industry has never produced a kilowatt of energy without taxpayer subsidies. To cite just one example of this in action, taxpayers rather than the nuclear industry are responsible for paying damage claims of over $13 billion if there is a power plant "incident."[212]

To true up the real cost of nuclear power, the price we pay for it would reflect its full life-cycle costs – a rule that should apply to all forms of energy, including renewable fuels. In the nuclear power industry, full costs include the pollution emitted when the fuel is mined, processed, and transported; the cost and liabilities of storing nuclear wastes; the cost of water needed to cool reactors; investments to adequately protect power plants from terrorism or sabotage; and the cost of government efforts to prevent the proliferation of nuclear materials that could be used by other countries to create nuclear weapons or by terrorists to create dirty bombs.

Biofuels: Full-cost accounting should be applied even when we assume that a fuel is clean and sustainable. Not all renewable resources meet the test. For example, fuels made from plant materials are renewable but they may not be clean or sustainable.

Since 2007, gasoline sold in the United States has been required to contain a percentage of ethanol, a liquid fuel most often made from corn. The purpose of this is to reduce carbon emissions and America's dependence on foreign oil. The value of corn ethanol has been questioned, however, because the amount of energy and water necessary to produce corn may outweigh the fuel's carbon-reduction and environmental value. Some critics suggest that it does not pass even Energy Return on Investment (EROI) analysis, let alone other environmental factors.

Critics claim the ethanol mandate, part of a national renewable fuel standard, is actually intended to help farmers and a food-processing/ commodities-trading corporation called Archers Daniel Midland (ADM) find a profitable use for excess corn. "Since the era of the Civil War, farm lobbyists have called for government subsidies to convert crop surpluses into fuels and thereby make the surpluses disappear and drive up crop prices forever," the Cato Institute has written.[213] There are more effective options including more advanced types of biofuel that can power vehicles.[214]

As we can see, constructing a clean energy mix involves many variables and some difficult decisions. Economic, environmental, market, technical, and political forces are among the factors. Under the pressures of reducing greenhouse gas emissions, modernizing America's energy systems, and achieving greater energy stability and independence, there has never been a more important time to evaluate our options objectively, with minimal political interference.

Republicans and Democrats alike have advocated an "all of the above" approach to energy, but that is not an energy policy. It is a pretext to avoid the tough decisions that must be made about which energy resources are suitable and which are not. A real national policy would identify and support "the best of the above," not all of the above. A national energy strategy would consist of clear goals, timetables, milestones, and performance measures, and challenge the market to innovate toward those outcomes.

The social, economic, environmental, and security benefits of a well-designed roadmap would be significant. The market certainty it created would move private capital off the sidelines and into clean energy investment. The result would be new industries, businesses, and jobs. The money that industry, universities, and governments spend on research and development would be better focused. The map would provide a context for designing and prioritizing government programs and the federal budget process. It would let traditional energy industries, and the workers and communities that depend on them, anticipate and adjust to the disruptive changes that are an inevitable part of a major economic transition.

The good news is that Congress already requires the development of a coherent national energy plan. When it created the Department of Energy (DOE) in 1977, it included a requirement that each president prepare a National Energy Policy Plan every two years.[215] The law requires that the plan look forward in increments of five and 10 years to describe the energy production, consumption, and conservation needed to "meet the general welfare of the people of the United States and the commercial and industrial life of the nation, paying particular attention to the needs for full employment, price stability, energy security, economic growth, environmental protection, nuclear non-proliferation, special regional needs, and the efficient utilization of public and private resources."[216] In addition, each president is supposed to identify the strategies, policies, legislation, and resources needed to meet the plans' objectives, including executive actions, legislation, tax provisions, and so on.

The bad news is that no one is paying attention to the law. It has been many years, perhaps as far back as the Reagan administration, since a president has presented Congress with a plan that meets the law's requirements. Past presidents do not deserve all the blame. Energy policy is a hodgepodge of programs, laws, and regulations throughout government. It includes more than 150 programs cited by the GAO, and at least 112 relevant federal statutes in which Congress has delegated powers to the Executive Branch related to energy or the environment. Of these 112, 96 specifically address global warming, climate change, or greenhouse gas emissions.[217] In addition, each administration receives a steady stream of policy recommendations and energy plans from think tanks, nongovernment organizations, academia, lobbyists, and civilian policy experts.[218]

The Clinton administration conducted a multiyear exercise called the President's Council on Sustainable Development to come up with proposals that met the nation's environmental, economic, and social needs. President Clinton also initiated a variety of climate programs. The administration of President George W. Bush developed an energy plan that triggered lawsuits going all the way to the US Supreme Court because of the involvement of unnamed leaders from fossil energy companies. President Obama has issued a climate action plan and an executive order on sustainability among federal agencies, and has initiated a Quadrennial Energy Review. But none of these meets the detailed requirements that Congress codified nearly 30 years ago.

Because climate change already is under way, developing a roadmap to the twenty-first century energy economy would be like planning a road trip after much of it has already occurred. But it is not too late. Research shows that the American people are in general agreement about what our energy mix should be.

The climate agreement achieved in Paris establishes the international objective: limiting global warming to 1.5°C above preindustrial levels. The Obama administration has defined the US role: greenhouse gas reductions of 17 percent by 2020, 26–28 percent by 2025, and 80 percent by 2050. So the critical milestones are in place – if the American people insist that there be no backsliding by future presidents. Now we need a map that shows in detail how we will meet each of those milestones. As far as government interventions in markets go, a national energy plan would be the most important of all.

11 | Good Subsidies and Bad Subsidies

Far too many well-connected businesses are feeding at the federal trough.

– Charles Koch

Imagine that Congress finally understood the urgency of climate action and decided to "decarbonize" federal fiscal policy – in other words, to remove all of the inducements the government provides for the use of carbon fuels. Who would take the hit?

Nearly all of us, as it turns out. The federal government promotes greenhouse gas emissions in one way or another, including in the tax code and through grants and loans, technical assistance and research, oil and gas leases, and other benefits. Carbon pollution is subsidized in many ways, both direct and indirect, and it is not only big oil companies that benefit.

In 2007, former US Representative John Dingell (D–Michigan), then the chairman of the House Energy and Commerce Committee, tried to illustrate how close to home decarbonization might hit. He introduced a bill to eliminate the mortgage interest deduction for homes larger than 3,000 square feet.[219] He argued that the deduction encourages people to build bigger homes that use more energy and contribute to urban sprawl and therefore increase greenhouse gas emissions.

The link between the mortgage interest deduction and climate change was a stretch, but Representative Dingell apparently wanted to make a point: Taken to its logical conclusion, the reform of carbon subsidies could touch some very popular programs. Dingell wondered whether the American people were really willing to pay the price. Today, polls show the majority of Americans are willing to pay a somewhat higher price for clean energy, water, and a new electric grid.[220] But chances are that voters would not be enthusiastic about losing one of their sacred cows.

Nor is the carbon industry when anybody starts talking about taking away its tax breaks.

Before going further into this topic, I want to make clear that when I talk about "good" and "bad" energy subsidies, I am not suggesting that all fossil energy subsidies are bad and all clean energy subsidies are good. Some policy makers contend that the best way to reform energy subsidies is to eliminate all of them. But if we accept that some government interventions are necessary in energy markets, especially in view of the close link between climate change and the combustion of fossil fuels, the threshold question is whether a given energy resource offers benefits that significantly outweigh its costs to the economy, society, and the environment. If the answer is yes, then the next question is whether the resource requires government intervention to ensure that we capture its benefits. Then comes the question of what kind of intervention is warranted and most effective. If it is a subsidy, the criteria for *good* and *bad* are whether it is intelligently designed, effective in carrying out its purpose, limited in its duration, and consistent with the other requirements I will describe in this chapter.

America's De Facto Energy Policy

Government subsidies for energy – or "forgone revenues" as tax breaks are officially known – are the most familiar type of federal interventions in energy markets. In the context of preventing climate change, subsidies that encourage the use of fossil energy are considered perverse, while those that discourage carbon emissions are considered constructive. Either way, energy subsidies are important because, as writer Jeff Goodell notes, they are "America's de facto energy policy."[221] They serve as an imperfect substitute for the national energy policy we do not have.

Unfortunately, it appears that even the "good" subsidies in federal policy today are ineffective at reducing greenhouse gas emissions. In 2011, US Representative Earl Blumenauer (D–Oregon) became curious about how current tax policies influence carbon emissions. He succeeded in passing legislation that directed the National Academy of Sciences to conduct a "carbon audit" of the tax code.[222]

The academy complied by creating a 12-person committee chaired by Yale economist William Nordhaus. After two years of study, it concluded that as the tax code is structured today, it does not have a major influence one way or the other on greenhouse gas emissions.[223]

The Nordhaus committee acknowledged that it was able to study only some of the energy-related provisions in the encyclopedic code because even two years and $1.5 million were not sufficient to be more thorough. It

Wind on a Roller Coaster

In one example of bad subsidy design, the Production Tax Credit (PTC) has actually impeded the growth of wind power, according to Lawrence Berkeley National Laboratory (LBNL).

After each expiration of the credit, the number of new wind installations dropped 73–93 percent with associated job losses. In its analysis, LBNL concluded, "The frequent expiration/extension cycle that we have seen since 1999 has had several negative consequences for the growth of the wind sector. Due to the series of one- to two-year PTC extensions, growing demand for wind power has been compressed into tight and frenzied windows of development."

LBNL continued: "This has led to boom-and-bust cycles in renewable energy development, under-investment in wind turbine manufacturing capacity in the United States, and variability in equipment and supply costs, making the PTC less effective in stimulating low-cost wind development than might be the case if a longer-term and more stable policy were established."

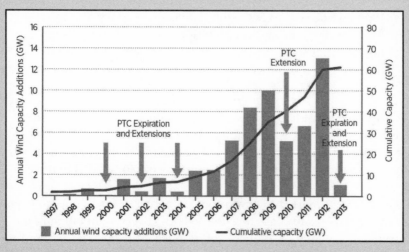

Inconsistent subsidies have hurt the growth of the wind industry in the United States. Each time the PTC has expired, the construction of new wind capacity has nosedived.

Sources: *AWEA US Wind Industry Annual Market Report*, Year Ending 2014, http://www.energy.gov/eere/wind/maps/wind-vision; Ryan H. Wiser, Mark Bolinger, and Galen L. Barbose, "Using the Federal Production Tax Credit to Build a Durable Market for Wind Development in the United States," *The Electricity Journal* (November 2007): 17, http://emp.lbl.gov/publications/using-federal-production-tax-credit-build-durable-market-wind-power-united-states

Figure 11.1

also acknowledged that it could not be precise about the code's impact on carbon emissions because of the complicated ecology of regulations that directly or indirectly affect energy use. Nevertheless, it did venture a few notable conclusions:

- The current code affects less than 1 percent of total US greenhouse gas emissions. "The national and global emissions reductions necessary to meet internationally agreed-upon climate objectives are many times larger than those resulting from current tax subsidies," the committee found.

- Some government incentives to encourage the development and use of clean energy are more effective than others. For example, ethanol subsidies that result in more use of fossil fuels in agriculture can cause more emissions than they prevent. On the other hand, the Production Tax Credit (PTC) Congress created to encourage the development of wind power appeared to reduce greenhouse gas emissions but it has been too small and erratic to be fully effective (Figure 11.1).

- When we design taxes to stimulate economic activity, we are likely to stimulate carbon pollution, too. One option is to use tax revenues from the new economic growth for programs that cut greenhouse gas pollution.[224]

Other analysts have pointed out additional shortcomings in energy subsidies. Some subsidies have remained on the books long past their defensible lives, usually as a result of pressure from special interests. Some subsidies for oil, for example, have been in federal law for nearly a century, even though the petroleum industry has long been mature and profitable.

Government market interventions on behalf of fossil fuels go beyond the tax code. One example is how the federal government encourages the production of energy resources on public lands. The Department of Interior (DOI) leases federal land for private companies to produce oil, gas, and coal. It charges the producers royalties on the sale of the fuels. DOI's job is to make sure that the American people get a fair return from the sale of these public assets.

In the past, however, the DOI has not done the job well. In 2007, the Government Accountability Office (GAO) reported that the US government charges one of the lowest royalty rates in the world.[225] In 2008, the GAO found that the DOI had not evaluated its lease fees in more than 25 years. In December 2013, GAO reported that the DOI still had no procedure for periodically evaluating its royalty rates and it still had not

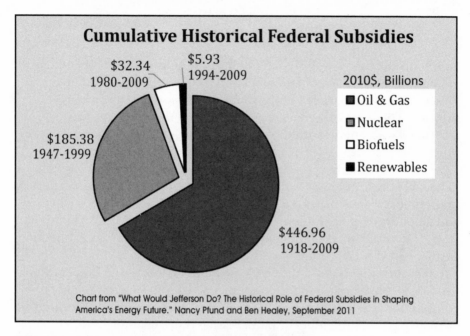

Cumulative Historical Federal Subsidies

$32.34
1980-2009

$5.93
1994-2009

2010$, Billions
- ■ Oil & Gas
- ▣ Nuclear
- ☐ Biofuels
- ■ Renewables

$185.38
1947-1999

$446.96
1918-2009

Chart from "What Would Jefferson Do? The Historical Role of Federal Subsidies in Shaping America's Energy Future." Nancy Pfund and Ben Healey, September 2011

While renewable energy technologies receive more federal subsidies than fossil fuels do today, support for oil and gas, nuclear power, and biofuels has greatly exceeded that for renewable resources over time. (Source: Pfund and Healey)

raised its rates for onshore oil and gas production.[226] The result has been an ongoing discount for oil companies and lost revenues for taxpayers.[227]

Another indirect subsidy involves the practice of venting and flaring natural gas. Oil producers consider the gas a waste product. The gas that is flared is not sold, which means fewer royalty revenues for taxpayers. In addition, the vented gas is a highly potent greenhouse pollutant. In 2010, the GAO calculated that if oil companies captured and sold the gas rather than venting it, the government would receive an additional $23 million in royalty payments each year and would reduce greenhouse gas emissions equal to taking 3.1 million cars off the road.[228]

After 180 pages of discussion and findings, the Nordhaus committee's bottom line was this:

Tax policy can make a substantial contribution to meeting the nation's climate-change objectives, but the current approaches will not accomplish that... If tax expenditures are to be made an effective tool for reducing GHG (greenhouse gas) emissions, much more care will need to be applied to designing the provisions to avoid inefficiencies and perverse offsetting effects.[229]

So what is the best way for federal policies to help mitigate greenhouse gas emissions? The Nordhaus panel and the Congressional Budget Office (CBO) have arrived at the same conclusion: Put a price on carbon. "The most cost-effective way to reduce the external costs associated with energy would be to enact policies, such as taxes, that would increase the prices of various types of energy to reflect the external costs that their production and use entail," the CBO has said. "That approach would provide a financial incentive for businesses and households to consider those external costs when deciding on the types and amounts of energy to use."[230] The International Monetary Fund (IMF) calls carbon taxes "the most effective instruments for encouraging cleaner fuels and less energy use."

On the other hand, a tax break meant to discourage carbon emissions – for example, a deduction for power plants that reduce their pollution – "adds to the deficit or requires that the government pay for those subsidies by reducing other spending or by increasing other taxes."[231]

If Congress ever gets around to reforming the tax code, it should consider these recommendations in regard to energy:

Impose Time Limits: Public subsidies should be time- or condition-limited based on a businesslike assessment of how long they are needed to achieve their intended objectives. For example, if we want to accelerate the market penetration of a new clean energy technology even faster than carbon pricing would, Congress should create an incentive that continues until the technology reaches a specific goal. That goal might be a price point or level of market penetration that allows the technology to mature enough to compete in the marketplace.

Anticipate Impacts: Doug Koplow, one of the nation's leading experts on energy subsidies,[232] points out that government regulations typically undergo intense scrutiny before they are finalized, including periods of public comment. Energy subsidies do not get that level of scrutiny. He recommends that policy makers conduct detailed analyses of proposed subsidies of more than $100 million to make sure they do not work at cross-purposes with other energy, social, or environmental goals.[233]

Define and Track Policy Objectives: Federal officials should track the performance of market interventions to make sure they are producing their intended results. The intervention's performance should be judged on the basis of specific measurable policy objectives. For example, "reduce demand for imported oil by 75 percent" is a better performance measure than "allow percentage depletion on domestic oil production." An objective rather than a prescribed action invites competition among options and allows policy makers to identify which interventions deliver the most benefit at least cost.

Make Subsidies Transparent

Finally, market interventions should be transparent. There are more than 74,600 pages in the tax code today – 187 times longer than it was a century ago. It is easy for energy subsidies to burrow deep and hide there. Out of sight and mind, their costs can grow beyond what was intended. In other cases, new economic or technical developments can make subsidies obsolete. And in many cases, the beneficiaries of a subsidy that has been on the books a long time ends up considering it an entitlement.

Keeping subsidies in full view can reveal flaws and unintended consequences. A study sponsored by Pew Charitable Trusts in 2012, for example, found that between 2005 and 2009, there were 60 different federal subsidies designed to increase energy production and consumption.[234] By 2009, more than $15 billion in subsidies had the effect of increasing US carbon emissions, while $18.5 billion in other subsidies were meant to reduce carbon emissions, generally by supporting renewable energy production and energy efficiency.[235] The tax code was, and still is, at war with itself.

Koplow acknowledges that making sense of energy subsidies is not easy. "Assembling an integrated picture of the size and distribution of federal subsidies to energy is a challenging undertaking," he says. "Many of the non-cash interventions are difficult to quantify, and requisite data needed to do so is often lacking... The government itself currently faces no requirements to compile this information internally."[236]

The same issues and reforms also apply to subsidies at the state and local levels, albeit at a smaller scale. In the interest of transparency, governments at every level should itemize their energy subsidies and costs and make them public as part of their annual or biennial budget processes. That is not common practice today.

A Global Subsidy Shift

Energy subsidy reform is important in other nations, too. As William Becker of the Presidential Climate Action Project puts it, "One of the most self-defeating irrationalities of our time is that nations have talked all these years about the need to reduce carbon emissions while continuing to spend trillions of dollars subsidizing them... It is like trying to put out a fire by throwing gasoline on it."[237]

Top 10 Energy Subsidies

Climate change has been called the biggest market failure in history. The failure has been caused in part by government policies that distort energy prices. Here are the 10 most distortionary policies, according to subsidy expert Doug Koplow of Earth Track Inc.:

1. The absence of charges on greenhouse gas emissions.
2. The failure of oil prices to reflect the cost of protecting supplies.
3. Liability caps for power companies on accidents at nuclear plants.
4. Mandates and tax incentives for the production of ethanol and biodiesel fuels.
5. Cross subsidies in electricity markets; the practice of charging some customers more to allow low prices for other customers.
6. Domestic subsidies for energy consumption.
7. Government assumption of risks associated with storing high-level nuclear waste.
8. Tax exemptions for petroleum used in air and water transportation.
9. Free cooling water for thermal power plants.
10. Feed-in tariffs and purchase mandates for renewable energy.

Note that in the context of reducing carbon emissions, some of these are constructive while others are perverse.

There have been some reports of progress. Global fossil energy subsidies declined in 2014, with nearly 30 countries instituting some kind of reform.[238] But among the G-20 nations – the nations with the world's leading economies – fossil fuel subsidies remained at the equivalent of $1,000 annually for every citizen, even though the G-20 voted in 2009 to eliminate them. The IMF says that in the United States, which proposed the G-20 agreement, fossil fuels are subsidized at $700 billion annually, which is the equivalent of $2,180 for every man, woman, and child.[239]

Lord Nicholas Stern, the British economist who called inaccurate price signals for fossil fuels the greatest market failure in history, reacted to the new data with consternation. "The figures reveal the true extent to which individual countries are subsidizing pollution from fossil fuels," he told the *Guardian*.[240] In the same interview he said, "The failure to reflect the real costs of fossil fuels in prices and policies means that the lives and livelihoods of billions of people around the world are being threatened by climate change and local air pollution... In particular, these figures reveal that the G-20 countries are wasting trillions of dollars each year on subsidies for fossil fuel pollution."

"Today, the most important roadblock for renewable energy implementation is the world's fossil fuel subsidies," adds Fatih Birol, chief economist at the International Energy Agency (IEA).[241] Indeed, if nations shifted their fossil energy subsidies to energy efficiency and low-carbon resources, we would make substantial progress in transforming the world's energy economy.

The IMF is one of several international agencies and private organizations that attempts to estimate the size of global energy subsidies and the potential benefits of reducing them. The result is a dizzying array of differing projections because no international framework exists for monitoring fossil-fuel subsidies.[242] With that caveat in mind, here are some of the numbers:

- Nations are investing $1.6 trillion annually to increase their energy supplies and $130 billion annually on energy efficiency. To meet the word's energy needs, by 2035, these investments must grow by $8.2 billion annually ($4 billion for energy supplies and $4.2 billion for energy efficiency).[243]

- Nations spent $550 billion in 2013 to help consumers buy fossil energy,[244] four times more than their investments in renewable energy.[245] They spent another $100 billion to subsidize fossil energy production.[246]

- The IMF calculates that the indirect costs of fossil energy consumption – mostly its social and environmental impacts – were expected to total $5.3 trillion globally in 2015.[247] The IMF also estimates that eliminating fossil energy subsidies could raise government revenues by nearly $3 trillion in 2015, while cutting greenhouse gas emissions 20 percent and deaths from air pollution by more than half.[248] The net effect after subtracting higher energy costs for consumers would be to free $1.8 trillion for other purposes.[249]

- To hold global warming to 2°C, the world would have to invest $53 trillion in energy between 2014 and 2035, including $40 trillion in energy supply and $14 trillion in energy efficiency, according to the IEA.[250] By 2035, the annual investment in energy supply would have to be almost $900 billion along with $1 trillion in spending on energy efficiency, the IEA calculates. If the IMF's estimates are correct, the net savings in government revenues from eliminating fossil energy subsidies could fund these investments.

- Carbon pricing applied nationally or as a result of an international agreement would produce additional revenues for the energy revolution as well as additional cobenefits such as lower costs for health care and environmental remediation.[251]

The international community would do well to nail down these data with greater precision, but it is clear that by redirecting fossil energy subsidies, switching energy investments from fossil fuels to clean energy,[252] pricing carbon, and developing the policy certainty that attracts private investment, the world could make the transition to clean energy well before mid-century.

Why We Should Care

Because every nation's greenhouse gas emissions have worldwide impacts, all nations have an interest in global reforms of energy subsidies.

The United States is second only to China in the amount of money spent on direct and indirect energy subsidies, according to the IMF. In 2009, President Barack Obama proposed and won approval from G-20 nations to phase out inefficient fossil energy subsidies "in the mid-term." Little progress has been reported. In each of his annual budget proposals to Congress, Obama has called for cutting taxpayer subsidies for the largest oil, gas, and coal companies by $40 billion over 10 years. Congress has rejected the President's requests.

Subsidy reforms have been accomplished or attempted in Brazil, France, Ghana, North Sudan, Malaysia, India, Indonesia, Iran, Poland, and Senegal, according to the Global Subsidies Initiative at the International Institute for Sustainable Development.

In several countries, consumers have responded with protests. However, energy subsidies have proven to be inefficient. The IEA estimates that the bottom 20 percent of the world population in regard to income receives only 8 percent of the value of fuel subsidies. There are better ways to remedy the regressive nature of energy costs, including carefully targeted direct cash payments to low-income consumers.

Sources: IMF at http://www.imf.org/external/pubs/ft/survey/so/2015/ new070215a.htm; *The Guardian* at http://www.theguardian.com/environment/ 2015/may/12/us-taxpayers-subsidising-worlds-biggest-fossil-fuel-companies; Global Subsidies Initiative at https://www.iisd.org/GSI/fossil-fuel-subsidies/case-studies-lessons-learned-attempts-reform-fossil-fuel-subsidies

12 | The Need for Speed

There is such a thing as being too late when it comes to climate change.

– President Barack Obama,
announcing his Clean Power Plan

Once again, the change we must make in national and global energy use must be a rapid transformation rather than a series of incremental transactions. It must be evolution by revolution. It must upend an entire era of fueling the economy by taking carbon from under the ground and dumping it into the atmosphere. The revolution must ultimately replace carbon fuels with resources that are ubiquitous, clean, and sustainable. Those resources are free for the taking and capable of powering the economy without endangering our health, security, or ecosystems.

We need speed because the planetary boundaries[253] that we are in danger of crossing are not subject to negotiation. They are matters of physical law.

We have pushed past physical boundaries before, most notably in defying gravity to "slip the surly bonds of Earth."[254] But manipulating the environmental systems that make the planet hospitable is a far different matter. We do not fully understand many of them, including the complicated forces that influence climate. As they say, it is not nice to fool with Mother Nature, especially when we do not know what we are doing and what the consequences will be.

Back to Fundamentals

To fully appreciate the need for speed, we must go back to the fundamentals of climate change. I noted in Chapter 4 that human emissions of greenhouse gases make their way to the troposphere and linger there to trap the sun's heat near the Earth's surface. Depending on the type of gas, the emissions can remain in the troposphere for hundreds and even thousands of years.[255] Because the emissions are persistent, they are additive. So, today's emissions join those from previous generations to increase the greenhouse effect.

In addition, climate change involves "thermal inertia." This means that the full effects of the emissions are not immediately evident. One estimate is that the results of today's greenhouse emissions will not manifest for another 25–50 years.[256] This means that the impacts of climate change we are experiencing today are the result of greenhouse gas emissions in the 1970s, before anyone under the age of 45 was born. Today's emissions will not be felt fully until around the middle of this century.

The result is a delayed feedback loop. In other words, we do not immediately experience the consequences of our actions. That makes

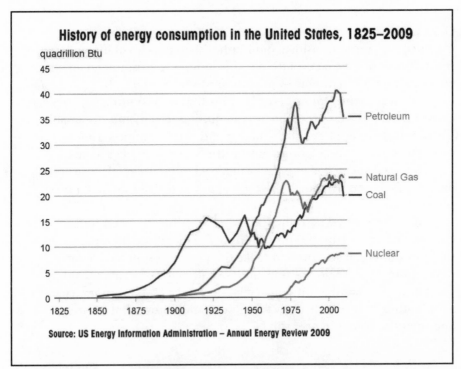

History of energy consumption in the United States, 1825–2009

Source: US Energy Information Administration – Annual Energy Review 2009

Figure 12.1 | The United States has gone through several major energy transitions, most of them taking place over decades or even centuries. (Source: US Energy Information Administration [EIA])

climate change a test of our intelligence as a species – of our ability to foresee what is ahead and to change course.

Because many of us will not be alive to fully experience the results of today's carbon emissions, our motivation to reduce them is less about self-preservation than it is about our ethical obligation to future generations. If we do not act now, we are – as the bumper sticker says – spending our children's inheritance.

Lessons from History

During most of our nation's history, making major changes in energy supplies has taken a half century or more. During the last century, however, we rapidly diversified our energy mix with the advent of nuclear power and the expansion of petroleum, natural gas, and coal production (Figure 12.1).

On the *Scientific American* blog, writer David Wogan explains that past energy transitions have been characterized by three features: They have occurred out of necessity because an energy resource has grown scarce or because we seek advantage from a better fuel, they have increasingly diversified our fuel mix, and they have tended to decarbonize the mix.[257]

All three are characteristics of the energy transition underway today. What is different and what makes this energy shift more difficult, Wogan writes, is that past transitions were motivated by observable developments such as the depletion of forests. Until recently, our awareness of climate change has been "based mostly on indirect observations or anticipated outcomes."[258]

This is changing. The physical, financial, and security impacts of climate change are occurring more rapidly than scientists predicted and they are becoming impossible to ignore. *Rolling Stone* offered a "snapshot" of these changes in August 2015:

> *In just the past few months, record-setting heat waves in Pakistan and India each killed more than 1,000 people. In Washington State's Olympic National Park, the rainforest caught fire for the first time in living memory. London reached 98 degrees Fahrenheit during the hottest July day ever recorded in the U.K.; the* Guardian *briefly had to pause its live blog of the heat wave because its computer servers overheated. In California, suffering from its worst drought in a millennium, a 50-acre brush fire swelled seventyfold in a matter of hours, jumping across the I-15 freeway during rush-hour traffic. Then, a few days later, the region was pounded by intense, virtually unheard-of summer rains. Puerto Rico is under its strictest water rationing in history as a monster El Niño forms in the tropical Pacific Ocean, shifting weather patterns worldwide.*[259]

Dr. Sylvia Earle, the distinguished ocean scientist who has led more than 100 undersea expeditions, reports on another set of consequences that go largely unseen: The oceans have changed dramatically since she began exploring them in the 1960s:

In that time, on the order of 90 percent of many of the big fish have been extracted from the sea. Changes brought on by global warming, overfishing, and pollution have taken their toll on the undersea environment. Coral reefs and kelp forests have been reduced by half, compromising the diets and habitats of the creatures who live there. The decline is heartbreaking.[260]

Climate skeptics accuse climate activists of using scare tactics when they warn that there are more severe impacts to come. But as we say around the Center for the New Energy Economy offices, there is a difference between Chicken Little and Paul Revere.

On the flip side of the climate crisis, there is an enormous economic opportunity in the imperative to cut greenhouse gas emissions. Tens of trillions of dollars must be invested to transform the energy economies of developed nations and to ensure that developing countries grow their economies with clean resources.

Bloomberg Energy Finance projects that there will be major growth in electric capacity worldwide from 2013 to 2030, 54 percent of which will come from non-hydro renewable technologies, while less than 30 percent will come from fossil fuels. Hydropower and nuclear generation will provide the rest. Renewable energy's share could be more than two-thirds of $7.7 trillion in expected electric power development during the period, Pew says.[261] If we in the United States want to capture these emerging markets, or even just compete well in them, speed is key. So far, however, other nations have been more proactive. Although Americans developed the world's first solar photovoltaic cells more than 60 years ago,[262] six of the top 10 solar manufacturers in the world today are Chinese.[263] And although an American invented the first power-generating wind turbine more than a century ago, only one US company (General Electric) was among the world's top 10 wind turbine suppliers in 2014.[264]

As we have seen time and time again, the market diffusion of new technologies can happen very quickly. The world's first commercial call on a mobile phone was placed on April 3, 1973, in New York City. By 2012, there were more cell phones than toilets. By 2014, there were nearly as many cell phone subscriptions (6.8 billion) as people. Most of the growth took place in the space of 20 years. This rapid technology dispersion often is cited as an example of how developing nations can leapfrog over fossil fuels and directly to carbon-free fuels.[265]

America's entry into World War II is our best-known example of an almost inconceivable turnaround in the nation's industries. When climate-action advocates say we need a comparable effort now, they are

Denmark, China, and Germany are the world's top wind turbine suppliers today but the technology was invented in the United States. In 1888, Charles Brush, an Ohio engineer, built this 80,000-pound wind machine. It had 144 blades on a 60-foot tower and it generated 12 kilowatt hours of electricity. The turbine provided Brush's home with power for 20 years. (Source: Google Public Domain Images)

referring to two things. The first is the "Pearl Harbor moment" (and more recently the 9/11 moment) when the nation was awakened to an imminent threat and came together to meet it. The second is the resolve, or political will, to meet a threat with action. It is the resolve with which President Franklin Delano Roosevelt called on the nation to become the "arsenal for democracy," less than a month after the Pearl Harbor moment. Industry responded. Automakers, shipyards, and aluminum, brass, and copper industries transformed their operations almost overnight to produce materials for the war. While US automakers produced three million cars in 1941, they made only 139 during the entire war because they retooled their assembly lines to manufacture fuselages, airplane engines, guns, trucks, tanks, and long-range bombers. The United States ended up making nearly two-thirds of all the equipment used by the Allies, including 297,000 aircraft, 193,000 artillery pieces, 86,000 tanks, and 2 million trucks. American industrial production doubled in size within four years.[266]

What is missing in regard to climate change is that decisive turning point in which a critical mass of Americans recognizes the urgency for action. It would be reassuring to know that we still are able to summon the resolve to defeat an existential threat. Climate change is this century's test. We have yet to show we can pass it.

No Time for Incrementalism

If we had allowed denial and obstructionism to further delay our participation in World War II, the Axis powers would likely have won and the world would be far different today. If the communications industry had settled for incremental growth, the people in developing nations would still have no way to connect with the rest of the world. And if we do not respond forcefully to climate change today, our future will be far less secure, stable, safe, prosperous, and just. A response equal to the threat requires much more than tweaking a price signal here or a building code there. It requires revolutionary changes at the grass roots *and* treetops of public policy. We need courageous, game-changing, forward-looking investments in the tens of trillions of dollars. We need clear and consistent signals from policy makers that the market for clean energy is solid so that capital moves off the sidelines.

As paradigm shifts go, few in history will be judged to be as important, challenging, and historic as moving from an era of digging, blasting, sucking, and burning the ancient remains of plants and animals to an era of harvesting the clean energy all around us in infinite and readily available supply. In the new era, there will be no black lungs and mine disasters, no groundwater poisoned by energy production, no childhood asthma caused by power plant pollution, no ozone days that make it dangerous to breathe, no fish too contaminated to eat, and no vital ecosystems carelessly destroyed. No marine life will be suffocated by oil spills. As one clean energy group puts it, "When there is a huge solar spill, it's called a nice day."[267]

This is a world well within our reach. The technologies we need already exist. The imperative to use them is more evident every year as sea levels rise, weather extremes grow worse, species go extinct, and the extraordinary costs of climate change become more apparent and inevitable.

If some of us have trouble looking ahead to what the world would be like in the grip of global warming, then perhaps we can look back to the future that was entrusted to us. As historian Harvey J. Kaye has written:

> We need to remember who we are. We need to remember that we are the children and grandchildren of the men and women who rescued the United States from economic destruction in the Great Depression and defended it against fascism and imperialism in World War II. We need to remember that we are the children and grandchildren of the men and women who not only saved the nation from economic ruin and political oblivion, but also turned it into the strongest and most prosperous country on earth.
>
> And most of all we need to remember that we are the children and grandchildren of the men and women who accomplished all of that – in the face of powerful conservative, reactionary, and corporate opposition and despite their own faults and failings – by making America freer, more equal, and more democratic than ever before.[268]

13 | Thirsty Energy

*Thousands have lived without love, not one
without water.*

– W. H. Auden

A colleague tells this story: On a hot day in Washington, DC, he took
refuge on a park bench in some shade near the Lincoln Memorial. A
Middle Eastern woman and her young son sat on a bench nearby. When
the boy asked for a drink, his mother handed him a bottle of water. He
took a sip, and then began pouring the rest of it on the ground, apparently
for his amusement. The woman grabbed the bottle and scolded him:
"Never waste water! Water is precious!"

Those who have lived in water-stressed regions understand how
precious water is. Others are learning the hard way. As I write this, four
years of drought have resulted in a historic water crisis in California.
Analysts at the University of California, Davis, estimate that in 2015 alone,
the drought would cost the state's agriculture industry nearly $3 billion
and 18,600 jobs.[269] Having exhausted surface water supplies, farmers are
drilling deep into the ground to withdraw water that fell to the Earth
20,000 years ago. It is a costly process both monetarily and ecologically.
In some areas of the state, the withdrawals are causing land to subside
as much as a foot each year, damaging roads and wells and causing
permanent damage to the water table (Figure 13.1).[270] The National
Aeronautics and Space Administration (NASA) reports that subsidence is
taking place more rapidly than anticipated, including a drop of 13 inches
in ground over an eight-month period in a 60-mile-long section of the
Central Valley.

Texans who underwent a five-year drought also discovered how
precious water is in this era of climate change. The liquid that comes out
of the taps in thousands of Texan households is no longer virgin water.
It is recycled urine. Some 27,000 citizens of West Texas are adjusting to
that unsettling fact as a result of the drought.[271] Other people around the
United States may soon find that they also have to accept "toilet to tap"
water programs.

Welcome to a thirsty world, where water is finally recognized for something that has always been true: It is more valuable than oil, coal, natural gas, and even gold.[272] We can live without those commodities, but we cannot live without water. That fact is becoming a key driver in the energy revolution.

The Energy-Water Nexus

Policy makers worldwide are paying close attention to what they call the "energy-water nexus," the fact that it takes water to make energy and it takes energy to supply water.

One estimate is that the energy we use to obtain, move, and treat the public water supply accounted for nearly 13 percent of

Figure 13.1

An official of the US Geological Survey showed in 1977 where a farmer in the San Joaquin Valley of California would have stood in 1925 and 1955. Land in the Valley sank nearly 30 feet during that period. (Source: USGS)

America's primary energy consumption in 2010, equivalent to the annual energy use of 40 million Americans.[273] In California, water-related electricity use accounts for nearly 20 percent of California's total power consumption. Water-related energy consumption accounted for 5 percent of the United States' CO_2 emissions in 2005, equivalent to the annual greenhouse gas pollution from 53 million passenger vehicles.[274]

To more fully appreciate why the energy-water nexus is so important, we have to drill down into some elementary facts. Water is a finite resource of about 333 million cubic feet planet-wide. It is always in motion on, above, and below the Earth's surface,[275] changing from liquid to vapor and ice in a hydrological cycle that can take a couple of days or a million years.

More than 70 percent of the Earth's surface is covered with water, but only 1 percent of it is available and suitable for human consumption (Figure 13.2). The rest is salt water in oceans, or freshwater stored in underground aquifers, soils, ice caps, and glaciers. The available 1 percent is not evenly distributed. Some 780 million people in the world today are water-poor, meaning they do not have access to potable water.[276]

We humans influence the hydrological cycle and the availability of freshwater in several ways. As I will explain, some activities waste it while others contaminate it. Our most significant influence on the natural hydrological cycle, however, is climate change. As we have seen in many parts of the United States and many other locations around the world, global warming is altering precipitation patterns so that some places get too much rain, others get too little, and still others receive the same amount but in deluges rather than in smaller storms. The results include blizzards, floods, and drought. Intelligence experts expect that by 2030, nearly half the world's population will live in places experiencing high levels of water stress. We already see incidents of water conflicts and even "water terrorism."[277] We can expect more.

The Nexus in the United States

We benefit in the United States from one of the world's most extensive systems for making water widely, if not universally, available. We have nearly 170,000 public drinking water systems, including 54,000 community water systems serving more than 264 million people.[278] More than 1 million miles of water mains deliver potable water to consumers.

Nevertheless, a growing number of Americans can testify that we are not immune from water stresses. In varying degrees of severity, most of the United States has been affected by drought in recent years. During the summer of 2012, moderate to extreme drought affected 61 percent of

Figure 13.2

the lower 48 states, according to the National Oceanic and Atmospheric Administration (NOAA).

As of April 2015, 37 percent of the contiguous United States was still experiencing at least moderate drought.[279] By the end of May 2015, moderate to severe drought affected a large part of the western United States. The *New York Times* notes, "Over the past decade, droughts in some regions have rivaled the epic dry spells of the 1930s and 1950s."[280]

Water conflicts, traditionally associated with the American West, are occurring in other regions of the United States. In what has been called the Tri-State Water Wars[281] for example, Alabama, Georgia, and Florida have been fighting for nearly two decades over water allocations. Georgia wants enough water to serve its growing urban population. Alabama wants to sustain its fisheries. Florida wants to maintain its shellfish industry.

In a 2013 survey, water managers in 40 states said they expected that parts of their states would experience water shortages in the next 10 years.[282] A study in 2010 by Tetra Tech for the Natural Resources Defense Council (NRDC) concluded that one third of the counties in the lower 48 states – more than 1,100 in all – are likely to have water shortages by mid-century. The risk of shortages is extremely high in 400 of them.[283] (Figures 13.3–4)

While climate change is a critical threat to adequate clean water supplies, several other threats are the results of public policies. First, water has been cheap. Public water systems in the United States deliver 100 gallons of water per person every day at the low cost of .002 cents per gallon.[284] That encourages waste. The Environmental Protection Agency (EPA) says that

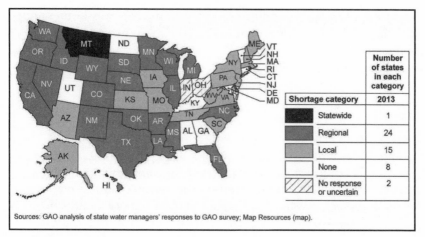

Shortage category		Number of states in each category
		2013
■	Statewide	1
■	Regional	24
■	Local	15
□	None	8
▨	No response or uncertain	2

Sources: GAO analysis of state water managers' responses to GAO survey; Map Resources (map).

Figure 13.3

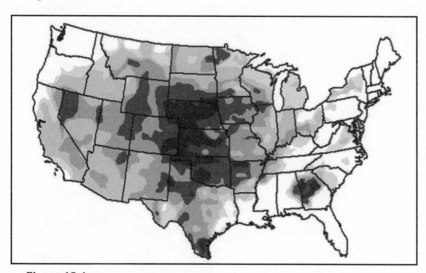

Figure 13.4

A survey by the Government Accountability Office in 2013 found that 40 of the 50 states expect water shortages in the next decade, even with average water conditions. Yet some of the states said they did not expect water problems. Among them – Utah, Kentucky, Alabama, and Georgia – already have suffered abnormal to extreme drought in recent years. Figure 13.4 shows drought conditions in 2012. The darker the shading, the more severe the drought was. Climate scientists say that in the years ahead, we will see more conditions like those in 2012. (Sources: Figure 13.3 – GAO; Figure 13.4 – US Drought Monitor, USDA et al.)

we Americans waste a trillion gallons of water annually in our homes and on residential landscapes, equivalent to the yearly water consumption of more than 11 million households.[285] In farm country, many irrigation systems and conventional tillage methods waste water, too. So do farm policies that subsidize the use of water-intensive crops.

A second incentive for waste is found in water allocation rules. Along the vital Colorado River in the West, some states have use-or-lose policies. If ranchers or farmers find ways to conserve water, they can lose their valuable water allocations. In other cases, communities do not understand that surface and subsurface waters are part of the same systems. When consumers draw water from underground near the Colorado River, the river refills the aquifer, flowing through porous underground soils. ProPublica reporter Abrahm Lustgarten cites the example of Needles,

Water level near capacity (1998)

Water level 2014 record

Water level 2015 record

When this photo was taken in July 2014, Lake Mead was 147 feet below its capacity due to drought. The lake, created by the Hoover Dam, stores Colorado River water for use by farms, cities, and homes in Nevada, Arizona, southern California, and northern Mexico. Most of its water originates from melted snow in Colorado, Utah, New Mexico, and Wyoming. (Source: Ken Dewey via NOAA)

California. "A funny thing happens when Needles pumps its water from underground," Lustgarten writes. "No matter how much the city uses, the water level in the local groundwater wells never drops. Instead, water is sucked out of the Colorado River bed, underground, toward the wells, filling any subterranean void."[286]

Third, water is leaking from our aging infrastructure. Some of the water mains in the United States go back to the Civil War.[287] According to the American Society of Civil Engineers (ASCE), 240,000 water main breaks occur each year.[288] The EPA estimates that 14 percent of the water that flows through the average municipal water system is lost because of leaks; some systems have reported losing 60 percent or more.[289] Repairing our water pipes would cost as much as $1 trillion over 10 years, according to the American Water Works Association.[290]

A fourth cause of water problems is the degradation or destruction of natural systems in the hydrological cycle. Between 2004 and 2009, we lost more than 360,000 acres of water-purifying coastal and inland wetlands to extreme storms, sea level rise, and human development.[291] Healthy soils and vegetation absorb half of the planet's rainfall and help to recharge aquifers. But in our cities, those impermeable surfaces reduce rainfall absorption to only 15 percent.[292]

Pollution is a fifth factor. Storm water runoff in urban areas carries lawn fertilizers, chemicals, trash, and pollutants from roads into freshwater supplies. The Environmental Working Group (EWG) has found more than 140 unregulated chemicals in tap water in 42 US states. The EPA and the United States Geological Survey (USGS) have reported finding that one-third of the water systems in the United States contain traces of at least 18 unregulated and potentially hazardous contaminants.[293]

Thirsty Energy

The protection and conservation of water supplies is becoming increasingly important worldwide, but an equally important factor is wise use. We all know that farm crops are thirsty, but many energy resources are thirsty, too. All forms of the energy we produce consume water at some stage of their lives, whether in mineral extraction and refining, the manufacturing of equipment, the cooling of thermoelectric power plants, or all of the above. Even the most miserly energy technologies such as solar and wind use some water at some stages in their life cycles. Nevertheless, some energy resources are much thirstier than others, and that is likely to become an increasingly important factor in our energy choices.

Competition will become more intense between thirsty energy, thirsty agriculture, thirsty industries, and thirsty people. Energy resources that require significant amounts of freshwater for extraction, processing, and consumption are likely to score lower in sound benefit-cost analyses than resources that use less. Knowing this, here are some of the factors we must weigh as we build a twenty-first century energy economy:

Thermoelectric power plants: Nuclear, coal, and natural gas-fired power plants produce about 90 percent of the nation's electricity. In the process and in aggregate, they draw more freshwater than any other activity in the United States including agriculture.[294] About 40 percent of the nation's freshwater use goes to energy generation, according to the USGS.[295] Every day, power plants withdraw 140 times the daily water used by New York City.[296] The water they extract from rivers, lakes, streams, and aquifers could irrigate the farmland of 17 Nebraskas, according to researchers for the US House of Representatives Natural Resources Committee.[297] Water is used to both generate steam that drives turbines, and also to cool the thermal facilities. While air-cooling is an option for some thermal plants, it is relatively expensive and seldom used.[298]

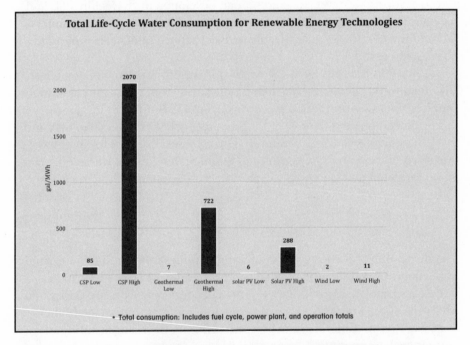

Total Life-Cycle Water Consumption for Renewable Energy Technologies

* Total consumption: Includes fuel cycle, power plant, and operation totals

Different energy resources require significantly different amounts of water during their life cycles. These charts are based on a life-cycle water consumption analysis that includes three stages – the fuel cycle, which pertains only to coal, natural gas, and nuclear generation technologies; power plant, which represents the life cycle of the physical power plant equipment; and operations, which includes

Water stresses already are affecting energy production. Lake Mead supplies hydropower to California, Nevada, and Arizona, but in the summer of 2014, the reservoir dropped to 1,031 feet – a level not seen since the dam was filled in the 1930s. Electric generation was curtailed by 23 percent that year due to water scarcity. At 950 feet, the dam would stop producing power entirely.[299]

Since 2004, problems with water supplies have caused at least a dozen other power plants to either shut down or to reduce their power output.[300] To the extent that climate change is contributing to water shortages, these problems are self-inflicted. The electric sector has been the largest source of US greenhouse gas emissions, responsible for more than one-third of our emissions in 2013. Coal alone is responsible for 77 percent of the sector's carbon pollution.[301]

Oil and gas production: Hydraulic fracturing is a technique that oil and gas producers use to tap into reserves that could not be extracted with older drilling methods. It involves the injection of fluids into rock

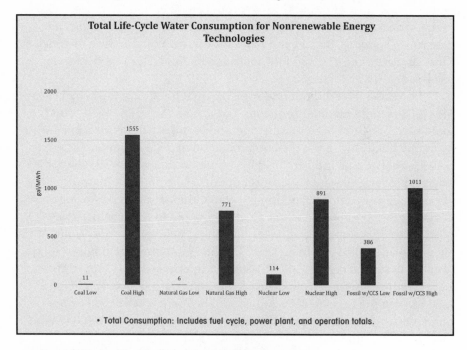

cooling for thermal technologies and all other plant operation and maintenance functions. Water consumption means water that is withdrawn and not returned to the immediate water environment. The charts show the lowest and highest consumption totals possible, without regard for technological compatibility. (Source: J. Meldrum, S. Nettles-Anderson, G. Heath, and J. Macknick [2013])

formations to fracture them and release trapped oil and gas. The fluids are a combination of chemicals, sand, and water. The EPA reports that water makes up 90 percent or more of the volume of the fluids, and each well requires thousands to millions of gallons of water. As many as 30,000 new oil and gas wells used hydraulic fracturing each year between 2011 and 2014. The agency estimates that hydraulic fracturing used an average of 44 billion gallons of water annually in 2011 and 2012.[302]

While hydraulic fracturing uses less water than some other extraction methods and constitutes only a fraction of annual water use in the United States, it has raised concerns about the possibility that fracturing agents will contaminate freshwater supplies in many parts of the United States. In a draft study issued in June 2015, the EPA reported that between 2000 and 2013, some 9.4 million Americans lived within one mile of hydraulically fractured wells. Some 6,800 sources of public drinking water, serving more than 8.6 million people, were located within those areas.[303]

In addition, conventional and hydraulically fractured oil and gas wells both produce "flowback" (aka "produced water"), that comes back to the surface, often containing high levels of salt as well as organic and inorganic chemicals, metals, and naturally occurring radioactive materials.[304] This wastewater must be carefully managed to avoid polluting freshwater resources.

The EPA said it did not find evidence that fracturing fluids had caused widespread contamination problems, but it acknowledged that it found some specific cases where routine operations and accidents associated with hydraulic fracturing led to the contamination of drinking water wells.[305]

Coal: The coal industry uses freshwater and produces wastewater when it processes the fuel after it is mined. Coal companies have disposed of wastewater by dumping it into old mine shafts or storing it in aboveground impoundments. Coal companies in Appalachia have been sued for contaminating water tables and well water by disposing of chemical-laden slurry in mine shafts.[306] Slurry impoundment failures have resulted in several high-profile disasters.[307] In one such incident in 2014, a coal company's storage tank leaked thousands of gallons of a chemical used to wash the fuel after it is mined and before it is burned. The leak, which occurred upstream from a water treatment plant, left 300,000 West Virginians without water.[308]

Another important issue in Central Appalachia is the destruction of surface waters when mining companies dispose of the rock and spoils they remove from mountaintops. The Central Appalachian Coal Basin consists of 12 million acres; as many as 1.7 million acres have undergone mountaintop removal. Since 2009, the practice of dumping mining wastes (called "overburden" by coal companies) into valleys has destroyed nearly 1,200 miles of streams, according to the EPA.[309] Streams below these "valley fill" sites and mountain deforestation have been linked to fish kills, contaminated fish and wildlife, accelerated sediment and nutrient transport, and increased algal production as well as possible human health impacts, the EPA says.[310]

Another water issue on the horizon is the coal industry's plan to use Carbon Capture and Sequestration (CCS) to reduce or prevent carbon emissions. Current estimates are that if CCS achieves commercial application, it can increase the water consumption of power plants by as much as 90 percent per megawatt of electrical output.[311] I explain more about CCS and the future of fossil fuels in Chapter 14.

Nuclear Power: Although nuclear power plants do not produce greenhouse gases when they generate electricity,[312] they are the thirstiest type of thermoelectric power generation. However, much of the water they use is returned to the sources from which it is drawn. A more important concern is the depletion of the sources from which nuclear power plants draw their water. An Associated Press analysis in 2008 found that 24 of the 104 nuclear power plants were located in areas that were suffering the most severe levels of drought.[313] In addition, uranium mining reportedly has contaminated surface and groundwater supplies in 14 states.[314]

Hydroelectric Generation: Hydropower provides only 6 percent of the nation's electricity,[315] but virtually every part of the country receives electric power from federal dams and reservoirs. Hydropower generates as much as 70 percent of the electricity that serves the Pacific Northwest.

Among conventional electric generation operations, hydropower faces the most direct risk from climate change. The Department of Energy (DOE) has advised Congress that, "Future changes to precipitation and runoff could potentially impact hydropower generation, water quality and supply, critical species habitat, and other important water uses that indirectly affect hydropower generation."[316] Extreme water years in the future, both wet and dry, are likely to "pose significantly greater challenges" to hydropower, the DOE says. The prediction already is coming true. The Energy Information Administration (EIA) estimated that hydropower production would drop by nearly 2 percent in 2015 alone because of the California drought.[317]

Other Renewable Resources: Non-hydro renewable resources, including biomass, geothermal, solar, and wind, produced 7 percent of the nation's electricity in 2014.[318] Because solar photovoltaic (PV) cells and wind turbines do not require water to produce electricity, they are the power technologies of choice for conserving water resources. The EIA estimates that power capacity from utility-scale solar plants will increase dramatically in the United States, growing 86 percent in 2015 and 2016 alone.[319]

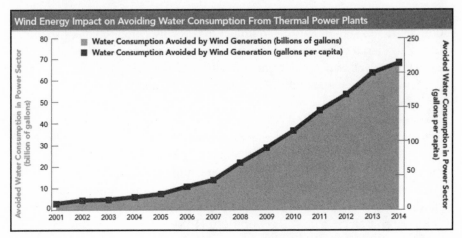

Figure 13.5

In 2014, wind energy saved 68 billion gallons of water in the United States, the equivalent of about 215 gallons per person, or 517 billion bottles of water. In California alone, with a historic drought under way, wind power saved 2.5 billion gallons of freshwater in 2014. (Source: *AWEA US Wind Industry Annual Market Report,* Year Ending 2014)

California is proving the value of wind and solar power generation in areas where water is not abundant. The American Wind Energy Association (AWEA) calculates that wind power saved 2.5 billion gallons of water in 2014 during California's drought – the equivalent of 200 gallons annually per household.[320] Nationwide, wind power saved 68 billion gallons of water in 2014 (Figure 13.5).

Not all renewable energy resources are water-conserving, however. Concentrating solar power plants, now primarily located in the southwestern United States, need water for cooling. Their water requirements can exceed those of coal- and gas-fired power plants.[321] Biofuels are among the most water-intensive fuels in part because of the irrigation water needed to grow feedstocks. One estimate is that producing a gallon of corn ethanol requires an average of 1,000 gallons of water, much more than is needed to produce other liquid fuels such as gasoline.[322]

Geothermal electric plants take advantage of heat below the Earth's crust. The amount of heat 33,000 feet below the Earth's surface contains 50,000 times more energy than all of the oil and natural gas resources in the world.[323] To produce electricity, geothermal plants draw water that has seeped into the Earth and been heated by the subsurface temperatures. In some cases, geothermal plants inject water underground to heat it. Apart from that and some evaporation from steam, most water is returned to the geothermal springs from which it comes.[324]

On our present course, the energy-water nexus will become not only more important but also more contentious in the years ahead. The energy sector is the fastest growing water consumer in the nation today, in part because of existing government policies. Much of the growth of the sector's water demands will take place in regions that already are experiencing intense competition among water users, according to the Congressional Research Service (CRS).[325]

Major trends are causing the energy sector to become even more water intensive. For example, climate change causes heat waves that place higher demands on power production during summer months when water use is highest in many regions.

In the longer term, we can expect some black swans to appear. For example, research published in the *Proceedings of the National Academy of Sciences* predicts that as many as 7 million people may attempt to immigrate across our southern border to the United States over the next 70 years, largely due to declining food crop yields because of drought.[326]

It is clear that smart energy choices can help avert, or at least reduce, the severity of water crises (Figure 13.6). Other strategies include increasing the efficiency of water- and energy-consuming equipment in households and in industry and agriculture; strong enforcement of the Clean Water Act; setting energy and water prices that reflect their true value to society; repairing and upgrading water infrastructure; setting more intelligent government policies; and restoring the natural systems that help store, move, purify, and manage water for free.

As always, the best solutions will be found with the systems thinking described in Chapter 9. For example, desalination is one possible response to freshwater shortages. Desalination plants are being planned on the West Coast, including one that reportedly will soon provide 7 percent of San Diego County's water.[327] But desalination is energy intensive and expensive today, and its energy must be low- or no-carbon so that it won't contribute to climate change.

Saving Water

When the Obama administration issued a rule in 2015 to protect smaller water resources such as streams, wetlands, and tributaries, Democrats as well as Republicans in Congress objected, characterizing the rule as a power grab.[328] A federal judge blocked the EPA from enforcing the

Water Consumption vs. Energy Trends

Energy Trend	Impacts on Water Use
Shift from foreign oil to biofuels	Increases energy's water consumption if domestic agricultural irrigation water (and other inputs) is needed for fuel production.
Shift to shale gas	Natural gas development using hydraulic fracturing may raise water quantity/quality concerns if well development is geographically concentrated in areas with water constraints. However, natural gas from fracturing consumes less US freshwater than domestic ethanol or onshore oil.
Growth in domestic electricity demand	More water used for electricity generation; how much more depends on how the electricity is produced (e.g., smaller quantities needed if electricity demands are met with wind and photovoltaic solar; larger quantities if met with fossil fuels or certain renewable sources).
Shift to renewable electricity	Concentrating solar power technologies can use more water to produce electricity than coal or natural gas; these solar facilities are likely to be concentrated in water-constrained areas. Technologies are available to reduce this water use. Other renewable technologies, such as photovoltaic solar and wind, use little water.
Use of carbon mitigation measures	Carbon capture and sequestration may double water consumption for fossil fuel electric generation.

Source: Congressional Resource Service (CRS)

Figure 13.6

rule one day before it was to take effect. The controversy was one more example of how sensitive the control of water resources is.

Regardless of the outcome of the rule, there are many improvements consumers, communities, and agencies can make in water management with or without federal regulation. For example, they can:

- Make water consumption, water quality impacts, and the prevention of water conflicts fundamental elements of the benefit-cost analyses that states, localities, and significant private water consumers use to prioritize their energy choices.

- Give higher priority to capturing the dual benefits of carbon sequestration and water conservation. Conservation tillage of agricultural lands is one example.

- Eliminate any "use or lose" provisions in laws governing water rights so that the holders of rights are not punished for conservation. They can create ways for the owners of water rights to sell or trade their unused allocations each year.

- Price water to accurately reflect the actual costs of obtaining, moving, and treating it. The actual cost should include the energy required to manage and protect water resources. As a result of local political pressure, many municipalities have kept water rates so low that there are insufficient funds for repairing and upgrading water infrastructure. One recent survey of utility managers in the United States found they would have to double their water rates over the next seven years to cover their costs.[329]

- Prioritize aquifer recharge at the local level. Communities can save both energy and water by creating more permeable surfaces, restoring wetlands, engaging in urban forestry, developing more parks and green spaces, encouraging community gardens and green roofs, recycling wastewater for landscape irrigation, establishing reasonable requirements for wastewater reuse by homeowners and businesses, using natural drainage swales to manage storm water, and encouraging the use of drought-tolerant native species in landscaping.

- In rural areas, require or encourage low-tillage agriculture, drip irrigation, and other water-saving technologies.

- Expand government community development and technical assistance programs to include water conservation and management training. As an example, they could expand the DOE's Industrial Assessment Center program to provide water management and conservation assessments to low- and medium-sized manufacturing plants.

- Improve the energy and water efficiency of electric generation and transmission. This would involve reflecting the costs in energy prices and requiring electric power plants to pay for the water they consume.

- Factor water conservation and protection into plans to upgrade or expand the nation's infrastructure for transportation, energy, and water. They could consider embedded energy and water in choosing materials for infrastructure work, as well as the impacts that infrastructure could have on water quality.

- Provide information and technical assistance to communities on energy-efficient water treatment processes.

- Increase federal support of research on next-generation biofuels that require less water consumption to grow and process feedstocks.

- Incorporate energy-water nexus opportunities into the twenty-first century business models of energy utilities.

- Encourage federal agencies to share their water conservation lessons with local governments and water management agencies. (President Obama has ordered government agencies to reduce water consumption by 36 percent, to cut landscaping and agricultural water consumption by 2 percent annually, and to install "green infrastructure" on federally owned property to help with storm water and wastewater management.)[330]

American poet Wallace Stevens once said, "Human nature is like water. It takes the shape of its container." The same will be true of water and energy policies. Both will be shaped by the physical realities that prescribe what is economically and environmentally plausible as well as socially and morally responsible. Every year, public utility commissions throughout our country are making decisions that will determine how electricity generation will impact water resources for decades to come, yet many commissions do not take the energy-water nexus into consideration. We will reach a point at which thirsty people will no longer tolerate thirsty energy, and the world's water poor will not tolerate water waste. Or, we can start treating water now like the precious resource it is.

14 | The Future of Fossil Fuels

It is time, as a matter of pride, as well as a matter of national security, for the United States to lead the world in the energy revolution.

– Secretary of State John Kerry

In April 2015, Bloomberg New Energy Finance published an article that immediately grabbed the attention of the energy and environmental communities. It began with the headline, "Fossil fuels just lost the race against renewables. This is the beginning of the end." [331]

The turning point came in 2013, Bloomberg said. This was the year in which the world began adding more power generation from renewable resources than from new coal, natural gas, and oil combined. The trend has continued. "The question is no longer if the world will transition to cleaner energy, but how long it will take," Bloomberg concluded.

This begs some important questions for energy policy. If fossil fuels are losing the race, should we continue investing public resources in coal, oil, and natural gas? And given the extraordinary risks that greenhouse gas emissions pose to the fossil energy sector and its investors, will some fossil fuels be forced to drop out of the race? And what about nuclear power? Although it was not covered in the Bloomberg analysis, renewable resources outpaced the growth of nuclear generation, too.

The Big Shift

Energy forecasters have imperfect crystal balls. Energy markets have surprised us so often that we should no longer be surprised by surprises. In 2012, for example, the United States imported more oil than any other country; [332] three years later, the United States was the world's top oil producer.

What does seem clear is that a historic shift is under way in favor of renewable energy resources in the United States and globally (Figure 14.1). Although the United States has not yet put a price on carbon and the world community has yet to reach a sufficient agreement on reducing greenhouse gas emissions, renewables have emerged as the fastest growing source of electric power in the country, and have driven much of the growth in the global energy sector since the year 2000, according to the International Energy Agency (IEA).[333]

In view of uncertainties and market changes such as these, the challenge for policy makers worldwide is to improve the present without ruining the future. Billions of people are trying to rise from abject poverty to a decent standard of living. The definition of "decent" in much of the global South is the quality of life in the global North. With aspirations so high and the need to alleviate poverty so great, and with the environment already stressed from past economic development, the only way to improve

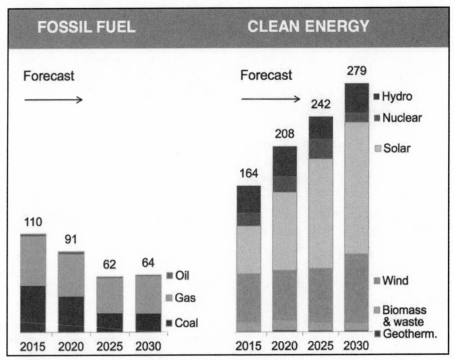

Figure 14.1

Bloomberg New Energy Finance projects that renewable resources will continue outpacing fossil fuels for electric power generation. Bloomberg calls this "the beginning of the end" for the dominance of fossil fuels in providing the nation with electricity. (Source: Bloomberg New Energy Finance)

the present and the future is to transition from finite and polluting energy resources to clean and limitless energy resources.

Given this reality, what are the prospects for our various energy resources in the years ahead? The answer depends in part on how much risk we are willing to accept. The risk of irreversible climate change increases the longer that we and other nations put greenhouse gases into the atmosphere. Much of the world is still waiting for the United States to lead. Entrenched energy interests are fighting to remain entrenched. How willing are we to bet our quality of life in the years ahead, and our children's inheritance, by continuing to burn carbon fuels?

The Carbon Off-Ramp

The most important factor in weighing climate risks seems to be in flux. It is the world's political will to make the clean energy transition. When nations met in Copenhagen to work on a climate treaty in 2009, they failed to produce an agreement but they did reach a consensus that global warming should be held to no more than 2°Celsius (3.6° Fahrenheit) above preindustrial levels. In 2015, during the Conference of Parties in Paris, the international community agreed to attempt to hold warming to no more than 1.5°C.[334]

Since then, a number of experts, including a team led by former NASA scientist James Hansen, have concluded that the risks at 2°C of warming actually are approaching the "highly dangerous" level,[335] and there may be little hope of holding warming to even that level. Less than a year after the Copenhagen climate conference in 2009, the Royal Society – a group of scientists who advise the British government – published the conclusion that "despite high-level statements to the contrary, there is now little to no chance of maintaining the global mean surface temperature at or below 2°C. Moreover, the impacts associated with 2°C have been revised upwards, sufficiently so that 2°C now more appropriately represents the threshold between 'dangerous' and 'extremely dangerous' climate change."[336] (Figure 14.2)

If we continue pumping greenhouse gases into the atmosphere at the rate we do today, we would reach 2°C of warming by 2036 and "cross a threshold into environmental ruin," according to Dr. Michael E. Mann, the highly respected director of the Earth System Science Center at Penn State University and one of the lead authors in the work of the Intergovernmental Panel on Climate Change (IPCC).[337]

These are the reasons the carbon off-ramp must be as steep as possible. Generally speaking, we have three options aside from no action at all: We can switch rapidly to low- and no-carbon energy resources, we can

- As much as $106 billion worth of coastal property will be underwater by 2050.

- States in the Southeast, Great Plains, and Midwest will risk losses of up to 70 percent in average annual yields of corn, soy, cotton, and wheat.

- The average American will see as many as 50 days each year over 95°F, more than three times as many as we experienced over the past 30 years.

- Extreme temperatures caused by climate change will require the construction of 95 gigawatts of new power generation, the equivalent of 200 average coal-fired power plants.

- Residential and commercial ratepayers will see their bills increase as much as $12 billion per year.

Source: *Risky Business* at http://riskybusiness.org/reports/national-report/executive-summary

Figure 14.2

develop ways to keep energy-related CO_2 from entering the atmosphere when we burn fossil fuels – or we can do both.

The Competitors

In assessing the competitors in the race to a clean energy economy, electric generation is a good place to begin. The IEA expects that electric power will be the "largest final energy carrier" in the world by mid-century.[338] We know that coal and gas used in power generation emit the most carbon (Figure 14.3).[339] The renewable resources emitting the most greenhouse gases during their life cycles are, from highest to lowest, solar photovoltaic technologies, geothermal energy, concentrated solar power, and wind.

Even if it were possible to hold global warming to 2°C or less, the carbon intensity of energy production – the amount of carbon necessary to make one unit of energy – would have to decline by 60 percent, according to the IEA.[340] Assuming there are no big surprises, here are some of the scenarios that different analysts predict for the role of fossil fuels in a carbon-constrained economy:

Coal: Over the past 200 years, coal has been vital to the nation's progress, prosperity, and quality of life. No workers have labored harder for their families and for the American people. Few have worked at greater personal risk. Now, it appears that we are witnessing the death of this great American industry. We can no longer afford the environmental and social problems of coal production and consumption, even without counting its indirect costs.

Environmental regulations and market forces are limiting coal's future. Since its boom in production, natural gas rather than coal has dominated the power market. China appeared to be a major export market for US coal producers, but it has issued an energy strategy that would cap its coal consumption in 2020.[341] The World Bank, among others, has decided it will not finance new coal-fired power plants around the world except in "rare circumstances."[342] And wind and solar are competing head-to-head with coal in some areas of the country. The Energy Information Administration (EIA) predicts that more than one-third of new generation capacity between now and 2040 will be from renewable fuels.[343]

These realities have severely diminished coal's performance in financial markets. The Dow Jones Coal Index dropped 87 percent between 2011 and 2015 (Figure 14.4). As 2015 began, both Moody's Investors Service and Standard & Poor's rated the industry's publicly traded debt as junk bonds.[344] According to CNBC, "Investors should not be fooled into thinking it is just regulation that has crimped coal demand and all it would take is a pushback against the EPA (Environmental Protection Agency) and Obama administration to change the equation."[345]

"We have the absolute destruction of the coal industry," says Bob Murray, the CEO of Murray Energy, the largest underground coal mining company in the United States. "If you think it's coming back, you don't understand the business... because it's not going to come back."[346]

Capturing Carbon

There is a chance, however, that coal can extend its life in the new energy economy. That chance is carbon capture and sequestration (CCS), a technology that would trap carbon at the power plant so it can be buried underground.[347]

The coal industry and the Department of Energy (DOE) have invested billions of dollars to develop CCS. Although the technology is expensive and more resource intensive than conventional coal power, EPA Administrator Gina McCarthy has testified that she regards CCS as technically and economically feasible.[348] Technical experts and scientists with whom I have discussed CCS feel strongly that its use is vital to reduce emissions from the expansion of coal-fired generation in rapidly developing countries such as China and India. But as the DOE has noted,

Life Cycle GHG Emissions

Life-cycle greenhouse gas emissions (expressed in CO_2 equivalents) from various commercially available and precommercial electric technologies

Technology	CO_2eq/kWh*
Currently commercially available technologies	
Coal-PC	820
Biomass-cofiring with coal	740
Gas-combined cycle	490
Biomass-dedicated	230
Solar PV-utility scale	48
Solar PV-rooftop	41
Geothermal	38
Concentrated solar power	27
Hydropower	24
Wind offshore	12
Nuclear	12
Wind onshore	11
Precommercial technologies	
CCS-Coal-PC	220
CCS-Coal-IGCC	200
CCS-Gas-Combined cycle	170
CCS-Coal-oxyfuel	160
Ocean (tidal and wave)	17

* grams of CO_2 equivalent per kilowatt hour of generation

(Source: Intergovernmental Panel on Climate Change via *Wikipedia*)

Figure 14.3

CCS would increase the cost of electricity and the energy and intensity of power production,[349] and it would not solve the significant environmental and social impacts of coal mining, cleaning, and transportation.[350]

Petroleum: There is mixed news for the future of oil. On one hand, the United States is now the world's top petroleum producer. On the other, we have achieved this goal just as the world must dramatically reduce its use of carbon fuels and at a time that domestic gasoline consumption appeared to be flattening.[351] In addition, the oil and gas industry must contend with several unknowns, including emerging policies to reduce carbon emissions, changing demographic trends and preferences, competition from nonpetroleum fuels, and the growing fuel efficiency of the nation's vehicles.

Some of these deserve more explanation. Demographic influences on oil consumption include the movement of millennials and baby boomers to city centers, where services are closer and automobile ownership is less critical. The *Washington Post* explains:

> *There's a lot of evidence that Millennials don't drive as much – or care as much for cars in general – as previous generations their own age did. They're less likely to get driver's licenses. They tend to take fewer car trips, and when they do, those trips are shorter. They're also more likely than older generations to get around by alternative means: by foot, by bike, or by transit...*
>
> *These nascent millennial indicators would have major implications not just for car dealers and gas stations, but for how the United States invests in transportation.*[352]

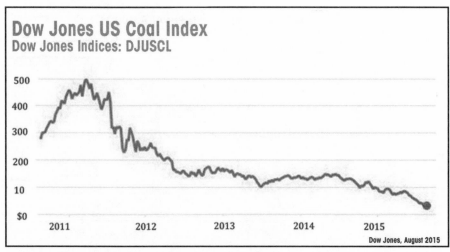

Dow Jones US Coal Index
Dow Jones Indices: DJUSCL

Dow Jones, August 2015

Figure 14.4

The Down Jones US Coal Index has shown steady decline over the last five years, perhaps an indication that coal's role in the nation's energy mix is reaching its end. (Source: Dow Jones US Coal Index is proprietary to and is calculated, distributed, and marketed by S&P Opco, LLC [a subsidiary of S&P Dow Jones Indices LLC], its affiliates and/or its licensors and has been licensed for use. S&P® is a registered trademark of Standard & Poor's Financial Services LLC, and Dow Jones® is a registered trademark of Dow Jones Trademark Holdings LLC. ©2015 S&P Dow Jones Indices LLC, its affiliates, and/or its licensors. All rights reserved.)

These changing choices contributed to a drop of 7 percent in vehicle mile traveled (VMT) over the last decade (Figure 14.5). In May 2014, the Federal Highway Administration predicted this trend would continue with a "significant slowdown" in vehicle miles traveled compared to the last 30 years.[353]

In addition, vehicles of all sizes are improving their fuel efficiency because of historic increases in federal fuel economy standards instituted by the Obama administration. By model year 2025, cars and light trucks will be required to get nearly 50 miles per gallon compared to 27.5 miles per gallon when President Obama took office. The EIA projects that households will spend $550 less on gasoline in 2015 because of the standards[354] and that fuel efficiency would contribute to a decline in gasoline consumption at least through 2040.[355]

It is also important to factor in the world oil market's control of petroleum prices. Although consumers celebrated when gasoline prices

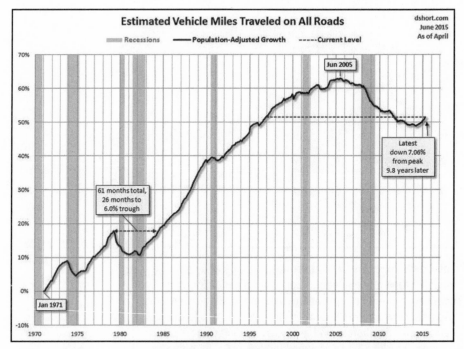

Figure 14.5

Against a 1971 baseline, and adjusted for population, vehicle miles traveled (VMT) on American roads peaked in June 2005, and declined for much of the following decade. This graph illustrates VMT for all drivers over the age of 16, including millennials. (Data: US Department of Transportation).

dropped in 2014–2015, the rapid change was fresh evidence of volatility in oil markets. Michael Levi at the Council on Foreign Relations warns that this volatility poses an immediate risk to the global economy.[356]

"Volatility also scares investors and consumers, deterring them from investing in oil infrastructure and from buying more efficient cars and trucks," Levi says. "Policymakers should therefore not view falling prices only as a sign of relief, but also as an indicator of trouble."[357]

The biggest uncertainty for oil and other fossil fuels, however, is the calculation by scientists that the world cannot keep climate change in check unless most of the world's proved fossil energy reserves remain unburned (see the section below on the world's "Carbon Budget"). If enforced, that constraint threatens the financial future of the fossil energy sector.[358]

Four Carbon Factors

Four carbon-related factors will help determine the future of fossil fuels. They are carbon pricing, the carbon budget, the carbon bubble, and carbon sequestration.

Carbon Pricing: Momentum appears to be slowly growing in the United States and internationally for assigning a price to carbon – in other words, adding a surcharge to fossil energy prices to better reflect their true costs to the environment and society. As British economist Lord Nicholas Stern notes:

The science tells us that (greenhouse gas) emissions are an externality; in other words our emissions affect the lives of others. When people do not pay for the consequences of their actions, we have market failure… This externality is different in four key ways that shape the whole policy story of a rational response. It is global; long term; involves risks and uncertainties; and potentially involves major and irreversible change.[359]

The most prominent options for pricing carbon are a carbon tax or carbon trading – a system that allows polluters to buy and sell emission permits, creating a carbon market that proponents say would encourage technical innovation and emission reductions. Congress rejected the idea of a national cap-and-trade regime in 2009, but northeastern states have implemented trading systems. Several prominent Republican leaders in the United States have since come out in favor of a national carbon tax.[360] Boulder, Colorado, established a local carbon tax in 2007; the Bay Area in California established one in 2008.[361]

In the rule the EPA issued in August 2015 to regulate carbon emissions from existing power plants, the Obama administration created the structure to facilitate multistate carbon emissions trading with "Emission Reduction Credits." The EPA observed, "The availability of trading reduces overall costs to the industry by focusing the controls on the particular sources that have the least cost to implement controls."

At the international level, Finland, Norway, Sweden, Denmark, British Columbia, and the United Kingdom have established carbon taxes.[362] In June 2015, the CEOs of six of the world's largest energy companies called on governments to create "clear, stable, long-term, ambitious policy frameworks" on carbon reductions, including a carbon tax.[363] Such a tax would accelerate the market penetration of several low-carbon and carbon-free renewable energy technologies by immediately making their prices more competitive with fossil fuels.[364]

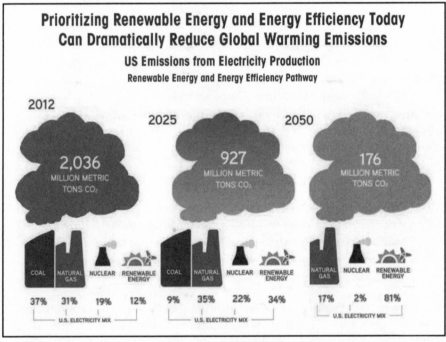

Prioritizing Renewable Energy and Energy Efficiency Today Can Dramatically Reduce Global Warming Emissions
US Emissions from Electricity Production
Renewable Energy and Energy Efficiency Pathway

2012 — 2,036 MILLION METRIC TONS CO₂
2025 — 927 MILLION METRIC TONS CO₂
2050 — 176 MILLION METRIC TONS CO₂

	COAL	NATURAL GAS	NUCLEAR	RENEWABLE ENERGY
2012	37%	31%	19%	12%
2025	9%	35%	22%	34%
2050	—	17%	2%	81%

U.S. ELECTRICITY MIX

Figure 14.6 — The carbon budget requires a dramatic global decline in the use of fossil fuels to generate electricity. Nevertheless, there is a wide disparity between different projections of what the nation's energy mix will be decades from now. These two charts show the disparity between the projections of the Union of Concerned Scientists (UCS) (Figure 14.6) and the EIA (Figure 14.7). The UCS projects that coal must disappear from America's power industry by mid-century and the use of natural gas must decline to 17 percent. Renewable

The Carbon Budget: The carbon budget is the estimated amount of greenhouse gases we can put into the atmosphere before crossing the line into climate catastrophe. One calculation is that the carbon budget is 900 billion metric tons of CO_2 in the atmosphere. We have put 592 billion metric tons into the atmosphere since 1780. To stay within the budget, somewhere between 60 percent and 80 percent of the world's proved reserves of oil, gas, and coal must remain unburned between now and mid-century.[365] While this calculation was done some years ago, it has only recently come to wider public attention.

Calculating the carbon budget is relatively simple. The harder task will be to decide how to allocate it among nations. Disagreements on the responsibilities of developed versus developing nations have been one of

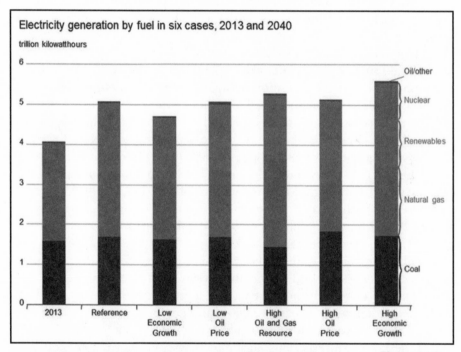

Figure 14.7

resources would produce the overwhelming majority of power (81 percent). This scenario agrees with analysis by the DOE's National Renewable Energy Laboratory that, with sufficient investment, renewable resources could provide 80 percent of the nation's electricity by 2050. On the other hand, EIA projects that coal and natural gas will still be significant sources of electric power by 2040. EIA's "reference case" assumes no changes in current policies. (Source: Union of Concerned Scientists and US Energy Information Administration)

the most stubborn barriers to finalizing a global climate agreement over the last two decades. When a global agreement is finally achieved, it will likely allocate most of the remaining carbon budget to developing rather than developed economies like the United States'.

The Carbon Bubble: The world's underground reserves account for trillions of dollars of the value of fossil energy companies today. Henry Paulson, among others, points out that when fossil energy companies continue valuing themselves as though they can use potentially unusable assets, the result is a "carbon bubble" similar to, but much larger and more dangerous than, the credit bubble that brought down the economy in 2008. "We're staring down a climate bubble that poses enormous risks to both our environment and economy," Paulson says. "The warning signs are clear and growing more urgent as the risks go unchecked."[366]

The Carbon Balance: The most fundamental purpose of climate action is not to reduce our use of fossil fuels. The most basic objective is to restore the Earth's carbon balance.

In general, carbon emissions are produced in two ways. There are natural sources such as animal and plant respiration, volcanic eruptions, and the decomposition of organic matter. Then there are "anthropogenic," or human-caused, emissions from burning fossil fuels; industrial processes; and activities such as intensive livestock farming. The world has experienced climate change before due to natural forces. Climate change today is mostly the result of burning fossil fuels.

The problem today is that the carbon cycle is badly out of balance because we are emitting enormous amounts of carbon while human activities have destroyed or degraded many of the biosphere's storage systems. When they are healthy, vegetation, soils, wetlands, and oceans absorb CO_2 and serve as "carbon sinks."

The performance of natural carbon sinks is expected to decline unless more is done to restore and protect them (Figure 14.8). For example, *Scientific American* reports there are more than 3 trillion trees in the world today. Before agriculture began 12,000 years ago, there were twice that many. Today, the world is losing 10 million trees each year. Worldwide, 231 million hectares of forests, equal in size to Texas and Alaska combined, were lost between 2001 and 2013, according to Global Forest Watch. More than 1.7 million hectares of tree cover were lost in the United States.[367]

"Fossil carbon combustion amounts to just five percent of the 200 billion tons per year of total carbon circulation, but the resulting imbalance adds enough CO_2 to the air to destabilize the climate," explains John DeCicco at the University of Michigan Energy Institute.[368]

When healthy, the biological sequestration by vegetation, soils, wetlands, and oceans absorbs CO_2 and serves as a "carbon sink." The

EPA reports that in 2013, soils and forests offset about 13 percent of the nation's total greenhouse gas emissions.[369] Given the urgency of preventing higher atmospheric concentrations of greenhouse gases, it makes sense to immediately begin maximizing biological sequestration. There are proven and relatively low-tech, low-cost carbon sinks with priceless cobenefits from ecosystem services. Improvements in biological sequestration should be part of every international, national, local, and corporate climate plan. That is not what is happening today.

Instead of CCS – or as an interim step while CCS is developed, or even as a backstop in case CCS proves to be unworkable – it would be sensible to immediately begin maximizing biological sequestration. There are proven and relatively low-tech ecosystem services that act as low-cost carbon sinks with priceless cobenefits.

It does not require much imagination to envision – and it should not take much political debate to create – a world in which corporations and philanthropies contribute more to groups that conserve grasslands and forests, or in which AmeriCorps engages young Americans in replanting forests decimated by insects, fire, and drought.[370]

If Congress and state legislatures want a relatively low-cost, high-return way to mitigate emissions, they should ensure that government programs for ecosystem restoration are adequately funded, including the US Forest Service's program to reforest damaged woodlands[371] and the Department of the Interior's[372] efforts to reclaim and replant the thousands upon thousands of abandoned mine sites around the United States.[373]

Shareholders Are Restless

Some of the world's biggest energy companies have been slow to acknowledge their climate risks, and their shareholders are growing restless. In 2008, 15 members of the Rockefeller family mounted a small rebellion against ExxonMobil. The family members were descendants of John D. Rockefeller, who founded Exxon's predecessor, Standard Oil.[374] They wanted Exxon to take global warming more seriously, to reduce its greenhouse gases, and to begin investing more in renewable energy. As one family member put it, "ExxonMobil needs to reconnect with the forward-looking and entrepreneurial vision of my great-grandfather."

The Rockefellers introduced shareholder resolutions to improve management of the company. None prevailed, but their rebellion was highly symbolic, and it was one of the first widely publicized signs of investor concerns about whether fossil energy companies fully understand or accept the forces that are shaping their future.

Natural Carbon Sinks

The US Geological Survey (USGS) is one of several federal agencies concerned about biological carbon sequestration. USGS says that forests, wetlands, and farms in the eastern United States alone sequester approximately 300 million tons of carbon each year, comparable to the annual greenhouse gas emissions of all the nation's cars. In coming years, USGS predicts that:

- America's ecosystems will continue absorbing CO_2 through 2050, but the overall rate of carbon storage could drop as much as 25 percent because of increases in urbanization and agriculture as well as growing demand for forest products.

- Wildfires in the western United States are expected to increase in number, scope, and intensity. When forests burn, they release the CO_2 stored in trees and other vegetation. Emissions from western wildfires could increase as much as 56 percent by mid-century.

- The eastern United States stores more carbon than all of the rest of the lower 48 states combined, even though the region has less than 40 percent of America's land base. Forests cover about half of the land in the East and account for nearly 13 percent of its annual carbon storage.

- The rate of sequestration in eastern states is projected to slow by up to 20 percent by 2050, mostly because of declines in forest cover.

Figure 14.8

Even though it was not successful in 2008, the Rockefeller rebellion has grown into two movements among energy company shareholders. One movement is encouraging institutions to divest their holdings in fossil energy companies and to move their money to clean energy. In the other movement, shareholders are retaining their stock so they can introduce resolutions that require companies to engage in a variety of environmental practices. The nonprofit group Ceres tracks these resolutions. It found that between 2011 and 2015, more than 600 resolutions urged corporations to strengthen their commitments to cutting greenhouse gas emissions, improving energy efficiency, using water more efficiently, and preventing deforestation.[375] The environmental news organization E&E Publishing notes:

> *Such resolutions have become a perennial event, and relatively few of the climate change resolutions garner overwhelming, or even majority, support from shareholders. But backers of the resolutions maintain that they do have an effect, and shareholder support for such measures has*

grown – in some cases from the single and low double digits to upwards of 40 percent when companies' environmental risks and liabilities are well understood.[376]

In 2014, ExxonMobil again became a poster child for investor unrest by dismissing the existential threat that it and other oil and gas companies face because of climate change.[377] Shareholders urged it to assess and publish its climate-related risks, including the possibility that its proved reserves would become stranded assets. Exxon responded that it is "confident that none of our hydrocarbon reserves are now or will become 'stranded'" because the people of the world striving to escape poverty and reach the middle class would not stand for it.[378] That confidence is based on the faulty assumption that only fossil fuels can lift people out of poverty.

As shareholder movements pick up momentum, some business leaders have pushed back, arguing that corporate executives should focus on profits and good shareholder returns rather than on environmental concerns. But there is ample evidence that good environmental performance and good economic performance are good business. In a 2013 study, for example, the World Wildlife Fund and the British nonprofit CDP concluded that if US businesses acted now to reduce emissions by an average of 3 percent annually, they could save up to $190 billion in 2020 alone and $780 billion over 10 years.[379]

It is becoming increasingly difficult for corporations to justify to their shareholders – and for elected leaders to explain to voters – why the United States should not capture the enormous emerging global market for clean energy technologies, why clean energy is not a higher priority for creating new businesses and jobs, why we are not proactively managing the risks of climate change, and why we should not be leading the global energy revolution.

Many of the United States' largest and most lucrative businesses – those that produce the energy resources that drove America's industrialization – are fighting to sustain an energy mix that is unsustainable in the twenty-first century. Their actions put themselves, their investors, and the United States itself at considerable risk.

15 | The Future of Natural Gas

Nobody disputes that cheap natural gas would be a good thing for the economy. The question is, is this sustainable new development that can be counted on for decades to come, or simply a "bubble" brought on by a land grab and drilling frenzy?

– Jeff Goodell, author

The Vermejo Park Ranch is a sprawling outdoor paradise that stretches from the Great Plains to the Sangre de Cristo Mountains on the Colorado–New Mexico border. With 584,000 acres, it is three-fourths the size of the state of Rhode Island. It is home to elk, deer, bison, cougars, black bears, and bighorn sheep; 180 species of birds; and brown, rainbow, and cutthroat trout. The black-footed ferret, an endangered species, thrives there thanks to collaboration between the ranch and the US Fish and Wildlife Service.

The range is also home to a 300-year reserve of coal, natural gas, and oil. Coal mining began there in 1880, at one time providing jobs for nearly 3,400 workers.

The land eventually came under the ownership of EP Energy Corporation (EPE), an oil and gas company that produced coal-bed methane. When the company put the ranch up for sale in 1996, it caught the eye of media mogul and philanthropist Ted Turner.

Turner wanted to add to his substantial land holdings in the United States. EPE wanted to retain the subsurface mineral rights – in other words, the right to continue producing coal-bed methane. Turner told the company he had no interest in owning land that would be blighted by gas production. So, Turner's attorneys and the company worked out a deal. EPE would collaborate closely with Turner's people on if, when, and how gas would be produced.

Under the agreement, 30 percent of the property has been designated as "areas of special sensitivity," where no gas extraction is allowed. There is a limit on the number of wells that can operate at one time. There can be no more than one well for every 160 acres. Wells must be placed to minimize interference with the ranch's spectacular views. Well sites must be reclaimed when they are retired, power lines must be buried, and production is not allowed during elk breeding season.

In addition, the oil company must disclose full information about the composition and quantity of chemicals used in extraction, and it must collaborate with Turner's company in monitoring the impact of gas production on ground and surface waters. Today, visitors to Vermejo Park are unlikely to notice gas production there.

Very few landowners have Ted Turner's lawyers or financial clout, of course, but his agreement with EPE has become a model used by the Western Landowners Alliance to help others negotiate agreements that "balance the responsible development and delivery of all forms of energy with the protection of important environmental and human values."[380] Agreements such as this may be an answer to Jeff Goodell's question at the start of this chapter: It *is* possible for natural gas to be produced responsibly, preserving ecosystems, water quality, and natural beauty in the "spirit of cooperation," to paraphrase the Vermejo contract.

By mid-2015, nearly 480 communities in the United States had approved bans or restrictions on hydraulic fracturing, according to the group Food & Water Watch.[381] New York's governor and Maryland's legislature banned the practice. Bans have been imposed or considered in Canada, Argentina, the Czech Republic, Germany, South Africa, Romania, Bulgaria, France, Spain, Germany, and the United Kingdom.[382] In Colorado, several communities approved bans on hydraulic fracturing, which were later struck down in court. When hydraulic fracturing opponents said they would resort to a statewide vote, Governor John Hickenlooper appointed a commission to study how the interests of communities and the industry could both be protected.

Citizens in these places worry – legitimately – that the chemicals in the fracturing fluids will find their way into groundwater supplies. They worry that flowback water might contaminate drinking water with methane gas, hydrogen sulfide, oil, water, salt, sand, heavy metals, barium, and radium, as well as the chemicals in the fracturing fluids.[383] Objections to gas production extend to air pollution and noise from generators and other equipment, land disturbances such as access roads, the safety of wells that have been retired, and even earthquakes that in some places appear to be caused by the practice of injecting wastewater deep underground.[384]

These represent local and regional environmental impacts. An even larger issue, which has national and global implications, is gas leaks from wells, storage tanks, aging pipelines, and other parts of the natural gas infrastructure. Natural gas is composed mainly of methane, which is a potent greenhouse gas. Recent studies have shown that in some parts of the gas industry's value chain – for example, at gas gathering and processing facilities – leaks are a larger problem than the government or industry thought.[385] Credible research shows that if leaks become excessive, they can negate any climate benefit and even make gas as detrimental to climate stability as coal.[386] According to the Environmental Defense Fund (EDF), which is working with the gas industry to study the leak issue:

While it is true natural gas burns cleaner than other fossil fuels, methane leaking during the production, delivery, and use of natural gas has the potential to undo much of the greenhouse gas benefits we think we're getting when natural gas is substituted for other fuels.[387]

Nevertheless, the value of natural gas is evident across the nation. It is replacing coal in power plants, providing an alternative fuel for vehicles, powering industry, and providing many other services. Nationwide, 6.2 million homes are heated with fuel oil, with 87 percent of the consumption in the Northeast.[388] Replacing #6 fuel oil with #2 fuel oil reduces pollutants, but the impact is even more dramatic when replacing #6 oil with natural gas as a heating fuel, as it reduces CO_2 emissions 30 percent.[389]

In its fact sheet on natural gas, the Natural Resources Defense Council (NRDC) asks, "Can natural gas help curb climate change?" Its answer:

Yes, but we can only ensure this result with stricter standards… We do not need to wait for better data on current emissions before putting stronger safeguards in place to protect against the full array of harmful impacts from inadequately regulated natural gas production… There are proven, cost-effective technologies and practices that improve the operational efficiency of natural gas production and reduce methane emissions at the same time. Less methane leakage translates into not only less heat-trapping pollution, but also more natural gas to sell, meaning that tightening up the production process can actually be profitable. Fortunately, some companies are already adopting these practices. The rest of the industry should be required to follow suit.[390]

Michael Levi agrees:

Shale gas is no panacea, but with the right policies to protect communities where gas is produced and to harness the fuel as part of a broader climate strategy, it can play a critical role in confronting global

How Long Is the Natural Gas Bridge?

Recent research shows how complicated it can be to define the role of natural gas in cutting US carbon emissions. It also shows that while the EPA's Clean Power Plan will significantly help cut carbon pollution, it is only the next step in a longer series of actions the United States must take.

David Biello reports in *Scientific American* that scientists used a technique known as "structural decomposition analysis" to study US carbon emissions between 1997 and 2013. They found that carbon emissions continued growing prior to 2007 largely because of an expanding economy. After 2007, carbon emissions dropped, with about 80 percent of the decrease due to the recession combined with a shift away from heavy industry. A warm winter in 2012 also played a role.

The new analysis shows that the energy sector's shift to natural gas in recent years has compensated for new emissions due to population growth. The nation's new natural gas abundance has kept 160 new coal-fired power plants from being built. Together with renewable resources such as wind and solar, natural gas has taken up the slack in electric power caused by the reduced use of coal. The coal/gas tradeoff is significant from a climate standpoint: Replacing one coal plant with a natural gas plant can save 1 billion metric tons of CO_2 pollution, in addition to cutting other pollutants.

However, natural gas also is replacing some nuclear power plants, which produce no greenhouse gases when they generate electricity. And, without policies that require the use of renewable energy, low-priced natural gas could also prevent wind, solar, and geothermal power facilities from being built.

The question, Biello says, is whether the world can reach the international community's goals of an 80 percent reduction in carbon emissions by 2050 and a carbon-free economy by the end of this century. Biello concludes, "Natural gas makes for a weak bridge to a zero-pollution future and truly clean power – one that cannot span more than a few decades. Still, a bridge made of gas is better than none at all."

Source: David Biello, "Fact or Fiction? Natural Gas Will Reduce Global Warming Pollution," *Scientific American*, August 3, 2015, http://www.scientificamerican.com/article/fact-or-fiction-natural-gas-will-reduce-global-warming-pollution. Biello is an associate editor of *Scientific American* and the host of *60-Second Earth*, a *Scientific American* podcast covering environmental news.

warming. Without shale gas, US greenhouse gas emissions would be higher, our climate policies would be weaker, and the odds of slashing future carbon dioxide emissions and meeting US climate goals would be greatly reduced.[391]

According to the Massachusetts Institute of Technology's Energy Initiative, natural gas is a carbon-based resource that will "need to make way for other low- or zero-carbon sources of energy in the future."[392] In the meantime, the environmental impacts of shale development are "challenging but manageable" and domestic supplies are "likely to grow considerably and contribute to significant reductions in greenhouse gas emissions for decades to come."[393]

For many climate scientists, the long-range goal is to become a carbon-neutral world by the end of this century. The United States is believed to have sufficient gas reserves to last many years into the carbon down ramp implied by that scenario. Ultimately, however, natural gas's long-term future in the nation's energy mix will be determined by increasingly competitive renewable energy options, by carbon pricing, and by limits on the carbon we can put into the atmosphere. The role of natural gas on the carbon down ramp relative to other fossil fuels has been indicated by scientists at the University College London's Institute for Sustainable Resources.[394] They estimate that the US contribution to greenhouse gas reduction requires that we leave 92 percent of our coal reserves unburned, along with 6 percent of oil reserves, and 4 percent of natural gas reserves. The researchers conclude that as the cleanest burning fossil fuel, natural gas could indeed serve as a "bridging fuel or a transition fuel to a low carbon energy future," if most of the world's coal reserves remain unburned.[395]

There is one more factor that will influence how long natural gas remains a significant bridge fuel. That factor is the support of the American people.

A Contract with America

The question is whether the oil and gas industry is willing to enter into a Vermejo-like "contract" with the American people – a social contract in which the industry commits to responsible production.

From 2011 to 2015, the Center for the New Energy Economy (CNEE) and Colorado State University's (CSU) Energy Institute hosted five symposia to discuss the future of the fuel. Oil and gas executives, academic experts, policy makers, environmental leaders, and regulators were among the participants. Industry leaders have emphasized that they want to maintain a "social license to operate" and that they welcome reasonable regulations and government oversight, especially to prevent some companies from seeking unfair advantage by ignoring environmental stewardship.

In March 2015, the federal government issued its definition of responsible production in the form of a new regulation from the Bureau of Land Management (BLM) regarding oil and gas production on public lands. The BLM allowed an unusually long period for public input before finalizing the rule. It received and considered more than 1.5 million comments.[396]

Nevertheless, several industry groups and oil- and gas-producing states sued the BLM shortly after the rule was finalized and a federal judge ordered that its implementation be delayed.[397] The judge reportedly kept the door open to issuing an injunction that could delay the rule for years as the lawsuit made its way through the courts.

Whether or not the rule deserved intervention by the courts, the industry would have done more good for its social license by complying voluntarily with the BLM's production requirements on both public and private lands. It might have helped dispel the perception that the natural gas boom is "a land grab and drilling frenzy." [398]

There are other ways the industry can strengthen its social license to operate. Better communication and collaboration with affected landowners and communities is one. More willingness to be transparent would help, such as by fully disclosing the chemical components of fracturing agents. Another boost for the industry's social license would be to identify the market failures that inhibit responsible production practices and back legislation to fix them. "The question isn't where the next regulation should be, it's always where has the market failed," says Dan Grossman of the EDF. "Where has an externality not been internalized? How can new public policy address that market failure?" [399]

Yet another way to build public confidence is being demonstrated at CSU in a project called Colorado Water Watch.[400] CSU has placed monitors at oil and gas sites in northeastern Colorado's Denver-Julesburg Basin. Real-time data is transmitted to researchers who watch for indications of groundwater contamination. The monitoring allows a quick response if contamination occurs. The public can also access the data in the form of charts and graphs on the Internet.

Competing with Renewables

Renewable energy advocates are concerned that the boom in natural gas production will retard the growth of wind, solar, and other renewable resources. Some of the market forces I have mentioned – carbon pricing, the additional costs of more environmental safeguards, the competitiveness of wind and solar power, and state renewable energy requirements – should ease those concerns. But there also are opportunities for solar and gas industries to collaborate with mutual benefits. The NRDC notes:

> As the nation continues to build up renewable energy sources, natural gas can play a supportive role by providing a backup for renewable energy generation. Natural gas is an important source of operational flexibility on the grid, meaning that natural gas plants can quickly respond to signals in the market to smooth out load and help meet demand, given that the output from renewable energy sources can vary. Natural gas plants are one of a number of ways to help integrate scaled up renewable energy sources into our electricity system, helping us to get a larger fraction of our electricity from renewable energy like wind and solar. Additionally, natural gas and renewable energy investment profiles are complementary, which assists in their co-investment... Both technologies can potentially benefit from policies that seek to reduce carbon emissions.[401]

There remains a wide variety of opinion on how long natural gas should remain in America's energy mix – or whether it should remain there at all. In my view, natural gas will be an important part of the world's as well as America's energy mix for decades to come. Whether that turns out to be the case, however, depends in no small part on the industry's willingness to enter into a social contract with the communities that are worried about modern oil and gas production.

16 | Harvesting Energy: The Future of Renewables

I'd put my money on the sun and solar energy. What a source of power! I hope we don't have to wait until oil and coal run out before we tackle that.

– Thomas Edison, 1847–1931

This quote from Thomas Edison is cited often in renewable energy circles, but it usually doesn't include Edison's next seven words: "I wish I had more years left." Unfortunately, he would have had to live another full lifetime to witness the dawn of the solar era.

But dawn has come. We did not have to run out of oil or coal to get here; instead, we had to run out of nature's ability to accommodate their detritus. And there are those who are still trying to shove the sun back down below the horizon.

Edison's appreciation of solar energy was a no-brainer. The energy comes from a power plant 93 million miles away (no worries about living next door) yet it delivers energy to all parts of the world in only eight minutes. We have a 5 billion year supply, give or take a billion years. New solar energy, as opposed to the ancient solar energy stored in carbon fuels, emits no pollution. We can use it directly for electric power and heat, or indirectly in one of its many manifestations – winds, waves, rivers, and plants.[402] It provides all this for free. Edison would be astounded that it has taken us so long to "tackle" it.

The role of renewable energy in the United States economy has been a story of fits and starts going back at least to the oil crises of the 1970s. Society's interest has waxed when there have been shortages in, interruptions of, or price spikes for conventional energy. It has waned again when oil, gas, and coal were stable.

Some renewable resources have always been used in the background, eclipsed by the incredible energy intensity of coal, oil, and natural gas. Wind has turned pumps on farms and milled wheat; wood was eclipsed by coal in the 1800s as the nation's principal energy resource, but it still is the second largest source of renewable energy in America today. Passive solar heating has always been available for those smart enough to point their windows in the right direction and to add a little thermal mass.[403]

But it is only recently that solar and wind energy are able to compete head-to-head with the price of fossil fuels. They are now the fastest growing sources of new electric power in the United States and in the world, and their growth will continue. The Energy Information Administration (EIA) predicts they will remain the fastest-growing power technologies at least through 2040, which, at the time of this writing, is as far into the future as EIA has looked.[404]

And this estimate might be conservative; EIA's critics point out that it has consistently underestimated the future contribution of these two technologies.[405]

The Renewables Boom

The benefits of renewable energy are no secret. Many are clean, inexhaustible, and homegrown. Most states, as described in Chapter 18, have put policies in place to promote them. Another big driver is the growing popularity of "distributed" solar and wind systems that produce electricity close to its point of use – including neighborhood-scale wind turbines and building-scale photovoltaic solar technology found not only on rooftops but also incorporated into walls, windows, and roofs. Federal regulations against greenhouse gas emissions and other harmful pollutants from power plants and industries will also drive the markets for the lowest-carbon renewables in the years ahead.

The renewable energy boom is enabled, too, by innovative new ways to help people purchase or lease the technologies. In several states (Figure 16.1), commercial building owners can get loans from their municipalities for energy efficiency and renewable energy improvements. Known as Property Assessed Clean Energy (PACE) financing, the loans are repaid with installments on annual property tax bills. In August 2015, the Obama administration announced that PACE financing will also be available for residential renewable energy systems that meet certain conditions.[406] In addition, some utilities offer "on-bill" financing for renewable energy and energy efficiency improvements, allowing building owners to repay the loans on their monthly utility bills. For its part, the federal government allows borrowers to get an extra few thousand dollars for renewable energy and energy efficiency improvements to their homes with Energy Efficient Mortgages (EEMs) offered by the US Housing and Urban Development (HUD) and the Veterans Administration.[407]

But the biggest financial innovation to boost the solar market has been third-party financing, where a solar company does all the work and pays all the initial costs, then sells the generated electricity to the building owner. It has opened the market to people who cannot afford the initial costs of purchasing and installing solar equipment.

Partly as a result of these financing options, more solar panels were installed on America's rooftops in the first three months of 2015 than in any previous quarter, according to the Solar Energy Industries Association (SEIA).[408] In fact, 51 percent of the new electric generation capacity that came online in the United States during those three months was solar. Although most of the United States' rapidly growing solar capacity has taken place in large-scale solar arrays built by utilities, the solar movement is turning more toward systems for individual

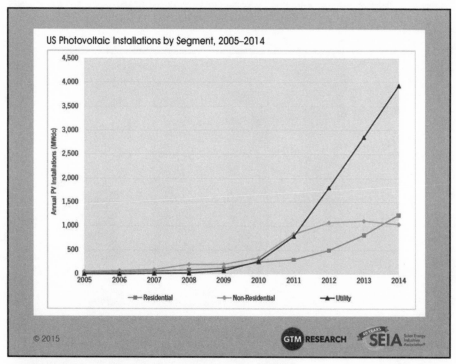

Figure 16.1

Solar photovoltaic (PV) installations have grown rapidly in recent years, particularly those installed by utilities, but increasingly as a result of residential applications. (Source: Solar Energy Industry Association [SEIA])

consumers.[409] SEIA predicts that 3 million new rooftop solar systems will be installed over the next five years.[410]

Wind turbines are located in 39 states today, generating nearly 5 percent of America's electricity.[411] In the summer of 2015 alone, wind projects were under way in 24 states, most of which are "red" states such as Texas, Oklahoma, Kansas, and North Dakota. While federal tax benefits have helped fund the development of both solar and wind technologies, their prices are becoming so competitive that even some solar companies now feel that the tax credits can be phased out. One CEO willing to say that publicly is Camilo Patrignani at Greenwood Energy, an engineering, procurement, and construction company in the clean energy field. He wrote in the *New York Times* that the principal tax benefit for solar development – the Investment Tax Credit (ITC) – should be reduced in 2017 and phased out altogether in 2018. "It may seem odd for a solar CEO

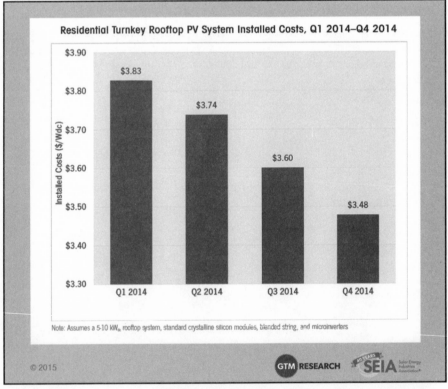

Figure 16.2

The installed cost of rooftop solar systems has declined rapidly in recent years, including a 3.3 percent decline quarter-by-quarter in 2014. (Source: Solar Energy Industries Association [SEIA])

to call for such a move, but we won't need the ITC if we're given a smooth glide path to prepare as an industry," he says.[412] He notes that despite California's decision to end its incentive for rooftop solar panels, "the state's solar industry is growing faster than ever."[413] The glide path that Patrignani referred to was created by Congress in December 2015, when it extended federal tax credits for wind and solar energy.

At the end of 2014, the investment firm Lazard reported that the price of unsubsidized solar energy was about $.072 a kilowatt hour (kWh), while the price for wind was $.037/kWh. That compared to $.061/kWh for natural gas and $.066/kWh for coal. But wind and solar are even less expensive in long-term power purchase agreements. SEIA reports that the price of solar-generated electricity has dropped 70 percent since 2008 under long-term contracts in large-scale projects (Figure 16.2). Austin Energy recently signed a 20-year agreement for solar energy at less than $.05/kWh.[414] NV Energy, a utility owned by Berkshire Hathaway (whose CEO is Warren Buffet), negotiated the lowest price ever for solar energy – $.038/kWh in a 25-year purchase agreement with SunPower. With this deal, NV Energy beat its own record low price of $.046/kWh cents for a similar project in Boulder City, Nevada.[415] In August 2015, the Department of Energy's (DOE) Lawrence Berkeley National Laboratory reported that the national median price of an installed residential solar system dropped 9 percent over the previous year, while the price for nonresidential systems dropped between 10 and 21 percent, depending on the system's size.[416]

"The cost of providing electricity from wind and solar power plants has plummeted over the last five years, so much so that in some markets renewable generation is now cheaper than coal or natural gas," the *New York Times* reports.[417] The leading solar industry analyst at Deutsche Bank predicts rooftop solar panels will reach grid parity in all 50 states by 2016.[418]

Building on the momentum, President Obama went on a multistate tour in August 2015 to announce several new executive actions to "create a clean energy economy for all Americans." The initiatives included $1 billion in federal loan guarantees for distributed energy projects; a new tool to help homeowners increase their borrowing ability by calculating the lower operating costs of their energy-efficient homes; and $24 million for 11 projects in seven states to double the amount of energy each solar panel can produce.[419]

Bullish Expectations

Some clean energy experts and organization are predicting surprisingly rapid growth in renewable energy in the United States, far above the rate forecast by number crunchers at the EIA. The National Renewable Energy

Laboratory (NREL) is one. In an analysis that involved more than 110 contributors from 35 organizations including other national laboratories, NREL concluded that renewable energy could supply 80 percent of America's electricity needs in 2050 if the right investments are made in electric infrastructure.[420]

At Stanford University, author and lecturer Tony Seba lays out in detail how solar energy, electric vehicles, and self-driving cars will make fossil fuels obsolete by 2030. The reason is what he calls "extraction economics" – the rising costs of extracting fossil fuels as conventional reserves are depleted, while solar energy experiences exponential growth. Other experts disagree that the energy transition can occur that rapidly. Seba replies that solar energy is a very disruptive technology and that "when disruption happens it happens swiftly, within two decades or even two years."[421]

In the meantime, the DOE predicts that new technical developments will spur the rapid expansion of wind power in the years ahead. It says, for example, that taller turbines will expand the land area available for wind development by 54 percent. By 2030, the benefits of catching more wind will include $125 billion in avoided greenhouse gas emissions, $42 billion in other air pollution reductions, 173 billion gallons per year in water savings, 375,000 jobs, and $1.8 billion in leasing and tax revenues.[422]

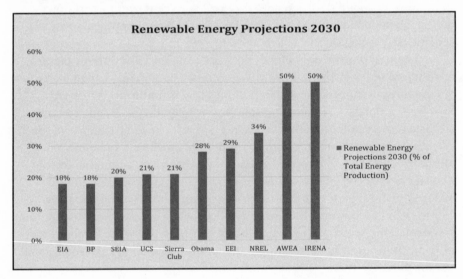

Solar-Brewed Tea in Georgia

Until recently, it was against the law in Georgia for anyone but an electric utility to produce and sell electricity. The law secured the status of electric utilities as monopolies there – power companies with no competitors.

America's Energy Pioneers

Leading the Nation

In 2012, California established the nation's most ambitious requirement for how much power production must come from renewable resources. It now is closing in on its goal of getting 33 percent of its electricity from renewables by 2020 while creating 163,000 green jobs. So during his fourth inaugural address in January 2015, California governor Jerry Brown upped the ante. He announced that in 15 years, the state expects to generate fully half of its electric energy from renewable resources. The new goal moves California ahead of Hawaii, which plans to achieve the goal of 40 percent of its energy from renewables by 2030. Governor Brown did not stop there. He also set two other new goals. California will work to cut automotive oil consumption in half and to double the energy efficiency of its buildings, also by 2030.

Going All the Way

Texas is famous for several things: oil production, conservative politics, and the nation's highest rate of greenhouse gas emissions. But Texas produces more wind energy than any other state. So, perhaps it should not have been a surprise when one of its cities decided to get 100 percent of its electricity from wind and solar power. That decision by Georgetown, Texas, had more to do with economics than with climate change. Georgetown is a city of about 50,000 residents, 25 miles from Austin. When the staff of its municipal utility studied its energy supply options, they found that renewable energy was cheaper than fossil energy in a long-term power purchase agreement. So, the city signed a 25-year contract with SunEdison, which will provide more than 9,500 gigawatt-hours of clean energy to Georgetown through 2041.

Rhode Island's Development of Offshore Wind Resources

Some of America's best wind resources are offshore. The Global Wind Energy Council estimates that offshore wind turbines could meet the nation's energy needs four times over. However, offshore wind has been stalled for years over concerns such as whether the technology installations will damage ocean views. Now a Rhode Island-based company, Deepwater Wind, plans to build five turbines 12 miles from the state's shore. The project will cost $225 million and generate 30 megawatts of electricity. Deepwater Wind reportedly is considering a 250-turbine offshore project covering 260 square miles of ocean off the coast of Rhode Island in federal waters.

Figure 16.3

The law did not sit well with at least two groups. One was the Sierra Club. The other was the Atlanta Tea Party Patriots, the state's Tea Party affiliate. The Sierra Club did not want anything to stand in the way of alternatives to coal-fired power plants. The Tea Party believed that people should have a choice of where they get their electricity. Although their motivations were different, solar became their common cause. The Sierra Club and the Atlanta Tea Party joined forces to get the law changed. They also persuaded utility regulators to require the Georgia Power Company to offer net metering to its customers.

Debbie Dooley, who founded the Atlanta Tea Party chapter, has taken some flack from her colleagues. Some called the partnership "laughable." Others asked her if a certain well-known liberal billionaire was funding her. Writing on the left-leaning *Grist* blog, she responded:

> *It's time for a new party. I'm calling it the Green Tea Coalition. The premise is simple: Those who believe in the free market need to reexamine the way our country produces energy. Giant utility monopolies deserve at least some competition, and consumers should have a choice. It's just that simple, and it's consistent with the free-market principles that have been a core value of the Tea Party since we began in 2009.* [423]

The coalition now has taken its solar energy campaign to Florida, Louisiana, Idaho, Indiana, Nevada, Minnesota, Wisconsin, Michigan, Colorado, and South Carolina – all of which are red or purple states, except Minnesota.

"As I travel the country advocating for solar using a free-market message, I am seeing an awakening among conservatives in this area," Dooley writes. "There are many areas that conservatives and progressives strongly disagree on, but both are united in a desire to pass on a legacy of true energy independence to future generations of Americans. The right to solar energy is an American issue – not a partisan one." [424]

Breakthrough stories are emerging all around the United States (Figure 16.3). Awakened to the vulnerability of conventional power by Hurricane Sandy, New York offered $40 million in incentives for communities to build microgrids – small-scale electric systems that can be detached from the power grid when necessary. [425] Where states allow it, communities are creating neighborhood-scale shared solar systems – a gratifying development because in 2010, I signed the nation's first community solar law to enable customers to bypass the limitations of buildings not suitable for rooftop systems. [426]

These are the power systems the American people want. [427] They are producing jobs as well as energy. The latest survey by the Solar Foundation [428] found that the solar industry alone has created more than

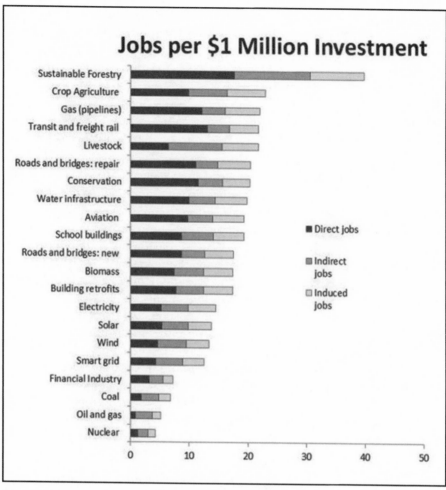

Jobs per $1 Million Investment

Sustainable Forestry
Crop Agriculture
Gas (pipelines)
Transit and freight rail
Livestock
Roads and bridges: repair
Conservation
Water infrastructure
Aviation
School buildings
Roads and bridges: new
Biomass
Building retrofits
Electricity
Solar
Wind
Smart grid
Financial Industry
Coal
Oil and gas
Nuclear

■ Direct jobs

▨ Indirect jobs

☐ Induced jobs

0   10   20   30   40   50

Researchers at the University of Massachusetts Political Economy and Research Institute calculated the number of jobs created by investments in different parts of the economy. The lowest numbers of jobs for each $1 million of investment were in nuclear energy, oil and natural gas, and coal. Elements of the clean energy economy showed higher job returns, including investments in smart grid, wind, solar, building retrofits, and sustainable forestry (for carbon sequestration). (Source: From "The Reality of Coal Mining Jobs," by Eric de Place, Copyright 2012, Sightline Institute, based on data from "How Infrastructure Investments Support the US Economy: Employment, Productivity, and Growth," Political Economy Research Institute, January 2009; used with permission.)

Figure 16.4

705,000 jobs in companies that build, install, service, and support solar energy equipment. Over five years, solar-related employment has increased by a remarkable 86 percent, the census found (Figure 16.4).

Future Shock for Utilities

With all this success, we might think that the barriers to renewable energy have all been overcome. We would be wrong. Several developments need to occur before wind and solar power have made a serious dent in greenhouse gas emissions. The electric grid and rate structures must be updated in ways that accommodate distributed power generation. To deal with the intermittent nature of sunlight and wind, we need more advances in energy storage and better interconnections between the nation's three major grids so that wind and solar power can be transmitted to locations where the wind is not blowing and the sun is not shining. And we need to overcome the resistance of traditional energy interests.

The toughest barrier, however, involves the nation's electric utilities. The growing interest among utility customers to become power producers is challenging the twentieth century utility business model of big central power plants and hundreds of thousands of miles of transmission lines. Utility executives tell me they are handicapped by regulatory lag; they say the clean energy revolution is 10 years ahead of power companies and power companies are 10 years ahead of regulators.

In a dialogue that the Center for the New Energy Economy (CNEE) facilitated with utility executives, senior officers of several of the nation's largest electric utilities and transmission and distribution companies offered this situation analysis:

> The nation's energy technologies and needs are advancing faster than rules, rate regimes, and federal administrative processes. It is not only the utility and energy sectors that must be reinvented for the twenty-first century; it is the entire system of government regulation and private financing. Electric and gas utilities rely on private markets and private incentives to deliver reliable energy to the American people. The rules of investment and financing must be aligned with advances in technology to expedite the transition to modern business models and energy resources.

But some of the "lag" is coming from utilities themselves, including efforts to slow down solar installations. Here is how the *Washington Post* described it in March 2015:

> Three years ago, the nation's top utility executives gathered at a Colorado resort to hear warnings about a grave new threat to operators of

Out of the Spotlight

Many other renewable resources do not get as much attention as wind and solar. Some are cleaner and more sustainable than others – a fact that full-cost accounting reveals. Here are examples:

Wood: The United States is a major exporter of wood pellets today, mostly to Europe. Wood was still our second-largest source of domestic renewable energy in 2014. It is not an optimal, climate-friendly fuel because it emits greenhouse gases when it is burned. Trees absorb carbon dioxide when they are alive, but most of them have long growing cycles that delay their carbon offset.

Biofuels: Most common biofuels are made from plants that contain sugar and starches, including wood products, farm crops, and crop residues. The biofuels in widest use today – corn ethanol, for example – use carbon fuels, fertilizers, and water when they are cultivated, processed, and transported. Efforts are under way to commercialize more advanced biofuels made from plant materials that do not need cultivation. Used in transportation, the more advanced fuels can reduce life-cycle greenhouse gas emissions by at least 50 percent compared to conventional biofuels and 85 percent compared to some gasolines.

Algae: Algae can be made into "green crude" – similar to petroleum – without using potable water or agricultural land. It grows from sunlight, its wastes can be recycled, and it can be used as a drop-in fuel, meaning that vehicles do not need special equipment to use it. DOE's Argonne National Laboratory says that algae fuels have a greenhouse gas footprint at least 50 percent smaller than conventional diesel fuels.

Bio-Methane: This fuel can be obtained from landfills, food wastes, animal wastes, and other biological materials as they decompose. It can be used in transportation, electric generation, and heating. At last count, there were more than 600 operating landfill-to-energy projects in the United States, but fewer than 40 produce renewable natural gas (RNG). There were 58,000 milk cow operations, but the EPA reported that fewer than 200 were producing RNG by mid-2013.

Hydrogen: The only thing that comes out of a hydrogen vehicle's tailpipe is water. Hydrogen stores energy from other resources, which ideally are low-carbon fuels such as sunlight and wind. Hydrogen fueling stations and vehicles are in use today mostly for demonstration purposes. Barriers include the lack of distribution infrastructure and the relatively high costs of the larger vehicle fuel tanks, because hydrogen has lower fuel density than gasoline or natural gas.

Wave and Tidal Power: Tides are more predictable than wind and solar power. Underwater turbines are powered by tides or currents. The DOE has concluded that wind and tidal power could provide 15 percent of the nation's electricity by 2030, with the highest potential on the West Coast and the coasts of Alaska and Hawaii.

America's electric grid: not superstorms or cyberattacks, but rooftop solar panels. If demand for residential solar continued to soar, traditional utilities could soon face serious problems, from "declining retail sales" and a "loss of customers" to "potential obsolescence," according to a presentation prepared for the group. "Industry must prepare an action plan to address the challenges," it said. The warning, delivered to a private meeting of the utility industry's main trade association, became a call to arms for electricity providers in nearly every corner of the nation. Three years later, the industry and its fossil-fuel supporters are waging a determined campaign to stop a home-solar insurgency that is rattling the boardrooms of the country's government-regulated electric monopolies.[429]

In some states, utilities and fossil energy supporters are attempting to roll back net metering policies and renewable energy standards. Other utilities are attempting to levy monthly surcharges for solar systems, making them harder for some customers to afford. Some utilities as well as customers complain that solar customers who use the conventional power grid for backup are not paying their fair share of costs to maintain the grid.

Other utilities are seeking to enter the marketplace. Perhaps in a nod to its founder, Thomas Edison, New York's ConEd is starting an unregulated subsidiary to finance third-party rooftop solar systems,[430] competing with companies such as SolarCity and Sunrun. Arizona's largest utility, Arizona Public Service (APS), is installing free solar panels on the rooftops of 1,500 customers and paying them $30 each month for 20 years. The power is fed directly into the grid.[431] Elon Musk has partnered with SolarCity to install his new Tesla wall-mounted energy storage systems in residences.[432] SolarCity, meanwhile, has partnered with Google to create a $750 million fund to help homeowners pay the upfront costs of rooftop solar systems in 14 states and the District of Columbia.[433] Homeowners will pay SolarCity for the power the panels produce, or monthly rent if they wish to lease the panels.

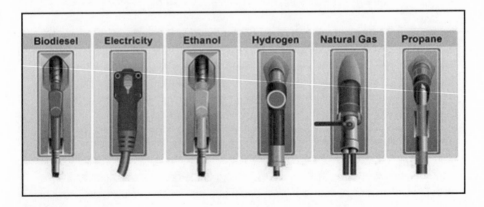

While I have focused on renewable electricity in this chapter, I would be remiss not to mention the forward momentum of alternative fuels in transportation, a sector that accounts for nearly a third of US energy consumption. In addition to the nation's historic progress in vehicle fuel efficiency, DOE's most recent data show there were 1.2 million vehicles on American roads powered by alternative fuels of all types, including electricity, liquefied petroleum gas, compressed natural gas, liquefied natural gas, methanol, ethanol, and hydrogen.[434]

During his State of the Union Address in 2011, President Obama set the ambitious goal of getting 1 million electric vehicles (EVs) on US highways by 2015. Unfortunately, that has not happened. Analysts cite several reasons, including worries about the relatively short range of EVs, lower gasoline prices, and the lower operating costs of more efficient conventional vehicles.[435] Nevertheless, the United States led the world in EV deployments in 2014, according to Germany's Centre for Solar Energy and Hydrogen Research,[436] which said, "What that means practically speaking is that roughly one in every three or so EVs in the world is on US roads."[437]

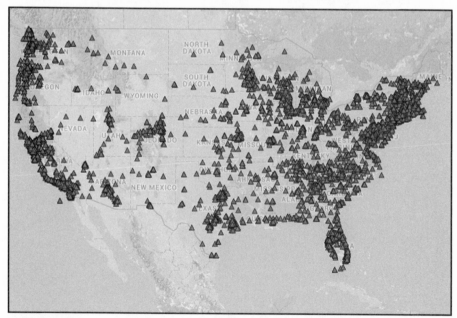

Figure 16.5

By 2015 there were more than 10,000 electric vehicle charging stations (Figure 16.5) around the United States and more than 20 models of plug-in electric vehicles available in the marketplace from BMW,

Chevrolet, Cadillac, Fiat, Ford, Honda, Kia, Mercedes, Mitsubishi, Nissan, Porsche, Tesla, Toyota, Audi, Hyundai, Volkswagen, and McLaren.[438] The market research firm Frost & Sullivan reports that while there are still improvements to be made in electric vehicles, more luxury carmakers are beginning to produce them, building on the success of Tesla Motors, BMW, and the Daimler Group.[439] Some forward-looking analysts predict that fully charged electric vehicles parked at charging stations could provide utilities with power during peak consumption periods.[440]

Whether electric vehicles qualify as contributors to a clean energy economy depends on the type of energy used to generate their power. As our electric generation becomes cleaner, electric vehicles will continue to reduce emissions in the transportation sector.

In other words, the energy revolution is classically disruptive, introducing innovative financing arrangements and new technologies to the marketplace. The old business models of the old energy economy no longer work well. The old power structure – including regulators, utilities, and investors – will need to adapt or will face ongoing friction with customers, increasing pressure from air regulators, and problems integrating new energy technologies into their twentieth-century systems. Few of us claim the disruptions will be easy, but there is no question that they are necessary.

17 | Responsible Capitalism

Whatever is fragile, like the environment, is defenseless before the interests of a deified market.

– Pope Francis

Since assuming the papacy, Pope Francis has severely criticized capitalism, and he has been severely criticized for it. A common response from his critics is that a pope's job is to address moral issues, not politics.

I am a practicing Catholic, a former governor, and the leader of an organization deeply involved in the energy revolution. I straddle the worlds of faith and public policy every day. Separation of church and state notwithstanding, I have rarely encountered an issue of public policy that does not have a moral dimension.

In regard to climate change, the interaction between moral principle and politics should be clear. The need to do something about global warming is without question a moral issue. The specific goals we must achieve are matters of science. What we do about climate change is a political issue. None of these should have become a partisan issue.

The pope's critics have reacted as if Francis has attacked the essence of America itself. Capitalism, they have responded, has done more to lift people out of poverty than any other force in history. There is some debate about whether government policies or unfettered capitalism deserve the most credit for reducing poverty, but there should be little question that capitalism at its best has driven incredible economic progress and done enormous good.

The question today is what "enormous good" means when 7 billion people (double the number of 45 years ago[441] and on the way to 15 billion by the end of this century[442]) are consuming resources, when we already need another half a planet to restore the carbon balance,[443] and when we are in danger of crossing several other planetary boundaries.[444] The reality is that the United States cannot do its part to reduce global carbon emissions without the active participation of the business and industrial sectors, and without major investments of private capital – about $150 billion annually, according to estimates from the University of Massachusetts Political Economy Research Institute (PERI) and the Center for American Progress.[445]

An obvious exercise of responsible capitalism is for corporations to engage actively in America's transition to clean energy. Doing so is not necessarily altruistic. When asked to identify their most significant long-term risks, nearly 900 participants in the World Economic Forum listed these four issues: international conflict, the rapid spread of infectious diseases, weapons of mass destruction, and the failure to adapt to climate change, in that order.[446] All but weapons of mass destruction are among the impacts scientists say will be exacerbated by global warming.

The Bigger Picture

While the pope's criticisms of capitalism have freshened the debate about the morality of economic systems, various groups have been thinking for a long time about how we might reform the architecture of capitalism to produce more just and beneficial outcomes for the "triple bottom line" – economy, environment, and social well-being. Among these ideas are sustainable development, natural capitalism, regenerative capitalism, and the "natural step."

Sustainability: The term *sustainable development* emerged in 1987 from the work of the World Commission on Environment and Development, more commonly known as the Brundtland Commission after its chairwoman, Gro Harlem Brundtland, a former prime minister of Norway. The commission's report defined sustainable development as meeting the needs of the present generation without compromising the ability of future generations to meet their own needs.[447] Since then, sustainable development has also been defined as the practice of simultaneously addressing the needs of the economy, the environment, and society. One of the industrial pioneers of the practice was the late Ray Anderson, chairman and founder of Interface, Inc., who set out to make his carpet company a zero-carbon enterprise. Figure 17.1 contains thoughts about the sustainability challenge from Mr. Anderson and two of his colleagues along with the classic 2004 table from the Worldwatch Institute on spending in developed nations compared to the needs of developing economies.

Since the issuance of the Brundtland report, many organizations have been founded to promote sustainable business practices, among them the World Business Council for Sustainable Development (WBCSD) – an organization of CEOs striving to "take shared action" on sustainability.[448]

The Twenty-first Century Business

While a few visionary companies have been founded on the principles of sustainability, most businesses will require radical change. In coming decades, business models and mindsets must be fundamentally transformed to sustain companies' value to their customers, shareholders, and other stakeholders.

At the societal, business, and personal levels, the understanding and adoption of sustainability practices is limited less by technical innovation than by people's inability to challenge outdated mindsets and change cultural norms. Paraphrasing Edwin Land, physicist Amory Lovins has observed, "Invention is the sudden cessation of stupidity...[that is,] that people who seem to have had a new idea often have just stopped having an old idea."

To achieve this degree of change, leaders must put forth bold visions, and they must engage their organizations in different, deeper conversations about the purpose and responsibility of business to provide true value to both customers and society. – **Ray Anderson, Mona Amodeo, and Jim Harztfeld**

Spending in developed countries		Needs of developing countries	
Makeup	$18 billion	Reproductive health care for all women	$12 billion
Pet Food (US and Europe)	$17 billion	Elimination of hunger and malnutrition	$19 billion
Perfumes	$15 billion	Universal literacy	$5 billion
Ocean cruises	$14 billion	Clean drinking water for all	$10 billion
Ice Cream (Europe)	$11 billion	Immunization for every child	$1.3 billion

Sources: "Changing Business Cultures from Within," 2010 State of the World, Worldwatch Institute, January 2010, pp. 96–102, http://blogs.worldwatch.org/transformingcultures/wp-content/uploads/2009/11/SOW2010-PreviewVersion.pdf; and "Annual Expenditures on Luxury Items Compared with Funding Needed to Meet Selected Basic Needs, Worldwatch Institute, 2004, http://www.worldwatch.org/state-world-2004-consumption-numbers. The late Ray Anderson was the founder and chairman of Interface, Inc., a carpet manufacturing company that pioneered sustainability practices.

Figure 17.1

The United Nations continues to be the world's principal advocate and leader on sustainable development. Secretary General Ban Ki-moon has called for a clean industrial revolution. "The clear and present danger of climate change means we cannot burn our way to prosperity," he says. "We need to find a new sustainable path to the future we want."

Natural Capitalism: Three prominent experts in energy, environment, and business – Hunter Lovins, Amory Lovins, and entrepreneur Paul Hawkins – published this concept in 1999. Their book, *Natural Capitalism: Creating the Next Industrial Revolution,* advocated three steps toward greater sustainability:[449]

1. Buy time by using resources much more productively. The result would be less resource depletion, less pollution, more jobs, lower costs for business and society, an end to degradation of the biosphere, and greater social cohesion.

2. Redesign industrial processes and the delivery of products and services to do business as nature does, using approaches such as biomimicry and cradle-to-cradle analysis.

3. Manage all institutions to regenerate natural and human capital.

Hunter Lovins, who later founded the organization Natural Capitalism Solutions,[450] argues that international climate negotiators must change their conversation from sacrifice to opportunity – from who will make economic sacrifices to limit carbon pollution, to who will be first to capture the enormous economic advantages offered by clean energy. "The reality is that acting to protect the climate does not impose a financial penalty," she says. "Being one of the first countries drastically reducing its emissions is not a disadvantage. Both developed and developing nations are moving rapidly to renewable energy sources, not because it is morally the right thing to do, but because it's the route to prosperity. The numbers show that there is a strong first mover advantage."

The investment advisory company CDP has substantiated that argument. In late 2014, it compared the performance of S&P 500 industry leaders that have climate management strategies and those that do not. The companies managing climate had 18 percent higher returns on investment than those that did not. They also experienced 50 percent lower volatility in their earnings and provided 21 percent greater dividends to shareholders.[451]

"We hope to shine a light on the link between strong climate change management and measures of financial performance," CDP explained, "and at the very least, to put to rest the common misconception that taking action on climate change exacts a cost to profitability. Our data shows the opposite."[452]

Regenerative Capitalism: Regenerative Capitalism is advocated by the Capital Institute, an organization based in Greenwich, Connecticut. It has created a group of distinguished advisors as a brain trust to "explore and effect the economic transition to a more just, regenerative, and thus sustainable way of living on this earth through the transformation of finance."[453] Its goal is to "create a self-organizing, naturally self-maintaining, highly adaptive, regenerative form of capitalism that produces lasting social and economic vitality for global civilization as a whole."

"Instead of viewing moral issues as irrelevant to 'rational' economic decision-making, in Regenerative Capitalism, human and moral concerns become central to decision-making, and policymakers view those concerns as critical to the maintenance of a healthy whole," the institute says.

The Natural Step: The Natural Step was initially developed in the late 1980s by Swedish cancer scientist Karl-Henrik Robert.[454] His work led him to the idea that human society, like the human cell, might be healthier if it conformed to "system conditions" fundamental to life. He drafted a document in which he described these conditions and circulated it to doctors, scientists, physicists, chemists, and ecologists for peer review. The document went through 21 drafts before the reviewers reached consensus. With help from the king of Sweden, Robert circulated the document to every school and household in that country.

Since then, members of the Natural Step movement say they have worked with thousands of corporations, communities, academic institutions, and nonprofit groups to educate them on four science-based system conditions for sustainability. They call it the Framework for Strategic Sustainable Development (FSSD). In plain language, the four conditions are:

1. We cannot remove stuff from the Earth at a rate faster than it naturally returns and replenishes.

2. We cannot make chemicals at a rate faster than it takes nature to break them down.

3. We cannot cause destruction to the planet at a rate faster than it takes to regrow.

4. We cannot do things that cause others to not be able to fulfill their basic needs.

These deceptively simple statements are rooted in science and in the idea that natural systems can show human society how to better organize itself. "The FSSD has taken people beyond the arguments of what is and is not possible; beyond politics of left or right wing perspectives," the organization says. "Instead, the Framework builds on a basic understanding of what makes life possible, how our biosphere functions, and how we are part of the earth's natural systems."

These organizations and their approaches to capitalism have at least two things in common. First, they advocate a systems approach to economics – a "mindset capable of seeing connections, patterns, and systems structure, as well as a sightline far beyond the quarterly balance sheet or the next election," according to environmental educator and author David Orr.

Second, they have been benchwarmers in our usual conversations about economics in the United States. If we want a more moral, more just, and more sustainable economy, perhaps it is time to bring them into the game.

Corporate Pledges

The dark side of the corporate response to climate change has been the alleged funding by oil companies of think tanks and political candidates who try to discredit climate science and deny that anthropogenic global warming is occurring. On Capitol Hill, incumbent industries use their wealth to "rent seek," which is the practice of using the prospect of campaign contributions to obtain special favors from lawmakers, often in the form of tax breaks.

But a brighter side is emerging. At this writing, the CEOs of 200 companies representing $7 trillion in revenues are members of the WBCSD.[455] The American Sustainable Business Council says it reaches out to business associations representing more than 200,000 companies and 325,000 business executives, owners, and investors.[456] *Business News Daily* reports that 66 percent of midsize companies in the United States say they are working to establish or improve their corporate social responsibility efforts.[457] In July 2015, 13 of the nation's biggest corporations[458] committed to invest more than $140 billion in energy efficiency, emissions reductions, and renewable energy. They also promised to support a strong international climate agreement. Their pledges are part of a White House initiative called American Business Act on Climate Pledge.[459]

Prior to this, the White House announced commitments of $4 billion by foundations and institutional investors to fund climate change solutions.[460] That merely scratches the surface of the potential of the philanthropic community. Only 2 percent of all philanthropic dollars are being spent today on climate action.[461] To improve this situation, organizations such as the Climate and Energy Funders Group and Confluence Philanthropy are focusing on "impact investments" in groups and projects that are combatting global warming.

Investments in clean energy should not be a hard sell for the business community. The cost-savings potential of energy efficiency needs no explanation, except to point out again that lower energy bills mean higher net revenues that can be reinvested in capital expansion, employee benefits, or new jobs. Distributed energy systems ranging from building integrated solar cells to combined heat and power systems – especially when backed up by storage – can help companies avoid the substantial financial losses caused by outages in the conventional grid.

In the bigger picture, companies can do their part minimizing climate impacts by decarbonizing their operations and supply chains – a goal the world's largest corporation, Walmart, has been working on for several years. In its eighth annual *Global Responsibility Report,*[462] the company says it now obtains 26 percent of its electricity from renewable sources, on the way to the goal of 100 percent. As 2015 began, Walmart had more than 380 renewable energy projects in place or in development in 17 states and five countries. By 2020, it plans to double the number of stores with renewable energy systems, compared to 2013. By the end of 2015, it intends to eliminate 20 million metric tons of greenhouse gas emissions from its supply chain.

Mindy Lubber, who leads Ceres and tirelessly champions sustainable business practices, tells a story on the small end of the size spectrum. Tom Benson, owner of the "World's Largest Laundromat" in Berwyn, Illinois,[463] operates 153 clothes washers and 148 clothes dryers. The washers use thousands of gallons of hot water every day, costing Benson 25 percent of his monthly revenues. Benson installed a solar water heating system on his roof. It heats 2,400 gallons of water every day and saves $25,000 a year.

"Tom Benson is tired of listening to conservative industry groups' bluster that climate change is bad for business," Lubber says. "That's because clean energy saved his."[464]

Finding a Green Niche

Although it is apparent that America's incumbent carbon sector has a regressive influence on energy policy, the ideal outcome of the energy revolution is not to shut down the world's coal, oil, and gas companies. The ideal outcome would be to enlist them in the revolution, to help them transform their business models for a transition into the green economy, and to put their extraordinary resources and talents to work on the development and deployment of clean energy technologies. Instead, the largest oil and gas companies have spent billions of dollars in recent years exploring for new reserves that climate scientists say we cannot use if we are serious about avoiding a future we will not like.[465]

Several of the world's largest oil and gas companies have ventured into renewable energy in the past, but most have pulled back. British Petroleum (BP), whose slogan was "Beyond Petroleum," once invested in wind and solar energy. It pulled out of solar energy in 2011 and wind energy in 2013. Chevron had a renewable energy subsidiary, but sold it in 2014. Several of the major oil companies are active in biofuels. But as energy analyst Matthew Morton reports:

Over the last two decades, the large Western international oil and gas companies, or IOCs – BP, Chevron, ConocoPhillips, ExxonMobil, Shell, and Total – have largely followed a common path with regard to renewable energy sources... Initial moves into a wide range of technologies have been followed by a general withdrawal from many renewable positions. As of early 2015, the IOCs' activities in renewables are mainly limited to biofuels. This pattern of engagement and then partial disengagement has been driven by a number of different factors, most of which are, unsurprisingly, rooted more in these companies' core oil and gas activities than in external developments in renewables.[466]

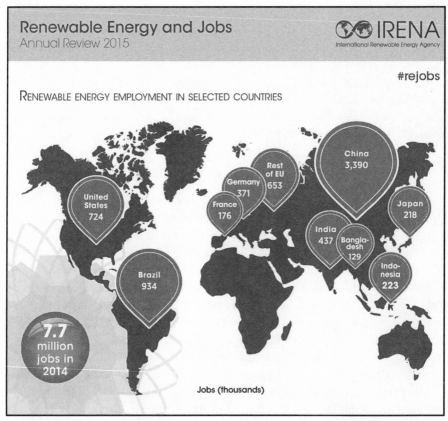

Figure 17.2

The International Renewable Energy Agency (IRENA) reports that 7.7 million people worldwide were employed in the renewable energy sector during 2015, up 18 percent from the year before. (Source: IRENA)

Morton notes that pressure from environmental campaigns was a factor that pushed some oil companies into renewable energy ventures in the past. That pressure continues today and could push the companies back into the green space "as a form of redress for the impact of their core operations on the environment," he writes.[467] But while their public image and the integrity of their brands are important to companies, so are profits. Sustainability has proved to be a profitable objective for companies, and clean energy has proved to be an engine for job growth (Figure 17.2).

What is certain is that the fossil energy sector can expect continuing seismic shifts ranging from carbon pricing to international commitments for near-term reductions in greenhouse gas emissions and increasing incidents of extreme weather that change the politics of climate change and clean energy. History has been on the side of carbon fuels, but the future is not.

Pope Francis is not the first moral leader to criticize the destruction of the world's natural systems. In 1971, Pope Paul VI wrote, "Due to an ill-considered exploitation of nature, humanity runs the risk of destroying it and becoming in turn a victim of this degradation."[468]

Forty-four years later, people worldwide are using 60 billion tons of raw materials each year, the weight of 41,000 Empire State Buildings, according to Friends of the Earth Europe.[469] In developed countries, we use up to 10 times more natural resources than people in developing economies do.[470]

Like Pope Paul VI, Francis writes that he is deeply concerned about the "delicate equilibria" between humankind and nature. But he also recognizes there is some progress. "Following a period of irrational confidence in progress and human abilities, some sectors of society are now adopting a more critical approach," he wrote in his landmark encyclical on the environment. "We see increasing sensitivity to the environment and the need to protect nature, along with a growing concern, both genuine and distressing, for what is happening to our planet."[471]

That trend must grow dramatically and rapidly. Responsible capitalism is an imperative in the transition to a new energy economy. The corporate sector should make it an imperative for the sake of its future as well as ours. At the same time, our environmental watchdogs have a responsibility to monitor progress and to prevent greenwashing, while consumers have an obligation to reward sustainable companies and products with the power of the purse.

18 | States: Where the Action Is

No matter what our illustrious Congress desires or attempts, and regardless what our current president intends, at the end of every American day, the sun sets on 50 states and a handful of territories that are free and independent governments... It is still at the state level that the majority of business gets done... And lo and behold, the states have decided that renewable energy is good.

– Renewable energy attorney
Lee Peterson[472]

National media as well as many thought leaders regard Washington, DC as the Big Dance, the Superbowl of American politics and public policy. In many cases, however, the real leadership in the energy revolution is taking place in the 50 states and nearly 90,000 local governments outside the Beltway. When President Obama points out that the United States has reduced its carbon emissions more than any other country in recent years, much of the credit belongs to progress at the state and local levels.[473] On the front lines of the revolution, states and localities also are the arenas where most of the skirmishes take place over energy policies.

There is a reason that state and local governments are filling the void left by an inactive Congress. States, and to a lesser extent localities, have most of the legal authority to reduce greenhouse gas emissions and other energy-related pollution and to introduce renewable energy technologies into the economy. The three largest sources of greenhouse gas emissions in the United States are buildings, transportation systems, and power plants. State and local governments regulate or otherwise influence each of them. The Department of Energy (DOE) periodically issues a model of national energy building codes, but it is legislatures that turn these into laws, and it is up to local governments to enforce them.[474] State public utility commissions regulate the rates and activities of investor-owned gas and electric utilities, while local governments manage municipal utilities. As one utility CEO told me, 90 percent of the policies that allow utilities to recover their costs come from state public utilities commissions; the remaining 10 percent comes from regulators at the federal level. States and localities decide how federal transportation funds are invested. Local zoning and land use planning determine the density and location of urban development, with major impacts on the energy consumption and air emissions attributed to mobility and traffic congestion. In general, states regulate and oversee oil and gas production. While the Environmental Protection Agency (EPA) administers the national laws designed to keep our air clean, states are in charge of developing and implementing the plans to comply with the EPA's requirements for limiting greenhouse gas emissions and other air pollutants.

According to the DOE's data, 37 US states and territories have voluntary or mandatory standards that determine the amount of wind, solar, and other sustainable energy resources in their energy mixes.[475] Some 230 million Americans live in states with mandatory renewable energy portfolio standards (RPS), every state but one has net metering standards that allow solar customers to sell electrons back to utilities, more than half offer tax incentives for renewable energy, and 46 guarantee citizen access to solar energy. An estimated 240 million Americans live in states with formal plans to reduce greenhouse gas emissions. In aggregate, the population of these states would be the fifth largest country in the world.

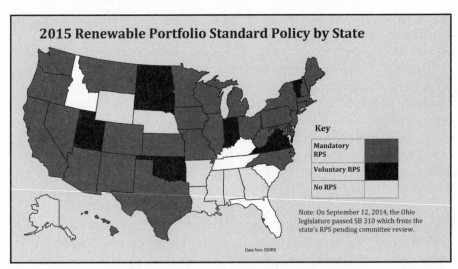

2015 Renewable Portfolio Standard Policy by State

Key

Mandatory RPS

Voluntary RPS

No RPS

Note: On September 12, 2014, the Ohio legislature passed SB 310 which froze the state's RPS pending committee review.

Data from DSIRE

Some 260 million Americans live in states that have either mandatory or voluntary goals for using renewable energy. (Source: Database of State Incentives for Renewables and Efficiency)

Trading Carbon

In cap-and-trade programs, states establish firm limits on greenhouse gas emissions, lower the limits each year, and hold regular auctions to sell emission allowances to polluters.

Polluters also are allowed to sell emission credits to each other. The requirement for polluters to purchase emission allowances and the opportunity to sell credits if emissions are reduced encourages companies to adopt technical innovations, clean energy, and greater energy efficiency.

In the meantime, states earn auction revenues that can be spent on clean energy programs. California's quarterly auctions of emission allowances are earning approximately $4 billion annually.

States participating in the Regional Greenhouse Gas Initiative (RGGI) report they have used $700 million in auction proceeds to fund a variety of energy efficiency and clean energy initiatives that are expected to result in more than $2 billion in energy cost savings for residents of the nine participating states.

Sources: July 30, 2015, email communication with Patrick Cummins; *Regional Investment of RGGI CO$_2$ Allowance Proceeds*, 2012 (Regional Greenhouse Gas Emission, February 2014), http://www.rggi.org/docs/Documents/2012-Investment-Report.pdf.

Figure 18.1

Twenty-four states have established mandatory or voluntary Energy Efficiency Resource Standards (EERS) that require electricity savings.[476] These states account for more than 60 percent of the electricity sold in the United States, according to the American Council for an Energy Efficient Economy (ACEEE). If they sustain their targeted energy efficiency levels out to 2020, they will save the equivalent of the combined power consumption of Maryland, Washington, Minnesota, Vermont, and Rhode Island.[477] As a result of EERS, energy efficiency programs offered by electric utilities tripled from $2 billion in 2008 to $6 billion in 2012, ACEEE reports.[478]

The widespread adoption of EERSs and RPSs demonstrates unequivocally that energy productivity and clean energy technologies are not partisan issues. Democrat and Republican governors, mayors, and legislators have all been among the leaders. New Jersey governor Chris Christie signed legislation in 2011 requiring solar purchases by the state's utilities. Michigan governor Rick Snyder has made a public commitment to reduce the state's use of coal and replace it with renewable resources and energy efficiency; he has called on the legislature to increase Michigan's RPS by 2015.[479]

In Georgia, as I mentioned earlier, the all-Republican Public Utility Commission voted in 2013 to require the nation's largest public utility, Georgia Power, to buy 25 megawatts of solar power by 2016.[480] In North Carolina, the state's largest utility – Duke Energy – has supported continuation of the RPS there, while conservatives turned back an attempt to repeal the state's RPS.

In 2012, California launched a cap-and-trade program, part of an initiative by Republican governor Arnold Schwarzenegger and the legislature to cut the state's emissions to 1990 levels by 2020 (Figure 18.1).[481]

In 2013, under Democratic governor Jerry Brown, California and Quebec partnered in a carbon-trading program among industries. In 2015, they expanded it to become the only economy-wide cap-and-trade program in the world, according to Patrick Cummins, the executive director of the Western Climate Initiative. In 2009, the governors of 30 US states and territories formed the bipartisan Governor's Energy and Climate Coalition in support of a federal cap on carbon emissions. In 2008, nine Northeastern states began implementing a regional cap-and-trade program known as the Regional Greenhouse Gas Initiative (RGGI).

There will be more to come.

State Experiences

Hawaii is one among many examples where we see the challenges of the clean energy transition under way in the utility sector. The state has relied on expensive oil to generate electricity; as a result, Hawaiians pay the highest electric rates in the nation. Policy makers there set the goal of obtaining 40 percent of the state's electricity from renewable resources by 2030; in 2015, the state legislature established the goal of universal renewable energy – 100 percent – by 2045.[482] To encourage progress, the state offers a 35 percent tax credit for solar installations.

Nearly 10 percent of the customers served by the state's largest utility – the Hawaii Electric Company (HECO) – have rooftop solar systems. By 2013, so much solar power was surging through its grid that HECO worried these clean electrons would overwhelm its circuits and cause power disruptions. HECO decided it would stop connecting solar systems to its grid until it conducted a study of each new rooftop array to determine whether it would force the utility to upgrade its equipment. If so, the upgrade would be done at the customer's expense.

In response, Hawaii's Public Utility Commission (PUC) came down squarely on the side of solar-energy-producing customers. It declared, "The best path to lower electricity costs includes an aggressive pursuit of new clean energy resources."[483] In 2013, the PUC ordered HECO to develop a new business model to accommodate rooftop solar systems. A year later, the PUC rejected the business plans submitted not only by HECO but also by two other utilities, the Hawaii Electric Light Company and the Maui Electric Company. The PUC ruled they had not demonstrated an acceptable "course correction" to accommodate clean distributed energy. The commissioners declared that Hawaii had "entered a new paradigm" in which "the best path to lower electricity costs includes an aggressive pursuit of new clean energy resources."[484]

The PUC finally issued its own roadmap to Hawaii's future power system, recommending that HECO integrate the "maximum level of cost-effective renewable resources while maintaining adequate reliability of the electric grid," and that it consider investing in energy storage and the modernization of its grid to handle renewables while retiring older, inefficient power plants. HECO now is planning to build a facility to store solar electricity – one of the largest of its kind in the United States. "Hawaii is definitely a postcard from the future," said the PUC's former chair, Hermina Morita.[485]

Here are a few of the many other states and cities that are leading the energy revolution:

California:

Most analysts agree that the principal pioneer among states has been California, whose economy is so large that if the state were a nation it would rank eighth in the world, comparable to Italy, Canada, and the Russian Federation.[486] California responded to global warming by passing AB 32, the Global Warming Solutions Act of 2006.[487] The law requires the state to cut its greenhouse gas emissions to 1990 levels by 2020 and to obtain one-third of its energy from renewable resources by 2020 – the most ambitious requirement of its kind in the nation.[488]

In 2015, the state legislature went even farther by increasing the state's RPS to 50 percent by 2030, and by increasing the efficiency of buildings by 50 percent. In addition, California has created two programs to finance "green" energy; the programs have issued more than $13 billion in tax-exempt bonds to offer low-interest loans for energy efficiency improvements and tax incentives for manufacturers of clean energy technologies. With Proposition 38, the California Clean Energy Jobs Act,[489] the state allocated corporate income tax revenues to a clean energy job creation fund. An estimated $550 million annually, over five years, may be spent on projects to expand the use of energy efficiency and clean power technologies in schools.[490]

According to a ranking system developed by the research firm Clean Edge, California is America's leader in clean technologies and has been for several years.[491] Over the past several decades, the state's energy consumers have saved an estimated $65 billion because of appliance efficiency rules going back to the administration of Governor Ronald Reagan. Household electric bills are 25 percent lower than the national average, a savings attributed only partly to the state's relatively moderate climate.

In addition, California, with its 3 million apartment units, has partnered with the federal government to reduce the administrative hurdles to commercial Property Assessed Clean Energy (PACE) financing for multifamily housing. The partnership is part of the Obama administration's goal to install 100 megawatts of solar energy in federally subsidized multifamily housing by 2020.

Connecticut:

This state created a solar lease program in 2008 to help homeowners install solar energy systems without upfront costs. The program provides rebates for nearly half the installed costs of rooftop solar electric systems; for the rest of the cost, a public-private program called Connecticut Solar Leasing offers zero-down leases for 15 years. After that, the homeowner can extend the lease, buy the system, or have it removed.[492]

In 2012, Connecticut formed the nation's first "green bank" – a quasi-government entity that uses attractive interest rates, loan loss reserves, and other incentives to attract private capital for clean energy development. Other states have followed. New York created a green bank late in 2013 to finance projects that help the state meet its clean energy goals that cannot otherwise be met using only private investment. Hawaii plans to establish a $150 million green bank.[493]

Nevada:

Nevada is among the states with the greatest solar energy potential. Its RPS requires that 25 percent of its power come from renewable resources by 2025. Of that amount, 6 percent must come from solar energy. In addition, a law passed by the legislature in 2013[494] directs state utilities to begin phasing out coal-fired power generation in favor of alternative forms of energy. Among other results, NV Energy has announced it will completely end its reliance on coal by 2019, switching to natural gas and solar energy to produce electricity. Nevada reportedly attracted $5.5 billion in new investment to bring renewable energy projects online between 2010 and 2014. As of January 2015, it had nearly 22,000 jobs related to renewable power, energy efficiency, and other conservation industries.[495]

Minnesota:

The state's public utilities commission has adopted a method to calculate the value of solar energy produced and put back into the grid by homeowners and businesses. The environmental and social benefits of solar energy are part of the calculation, called the Value of Solar Tariff (VOST).[496] In several states with net metering policies, utilities have objected that people with rooftop photovoltaic systems are not paying for their use of the grid. The VOST separates compensation going to solar customers from the electric rates paid by all customers. That helps nonsolar customers understand the value they receive from the power generated by their neighbors, while ensuring that solar customers are compensated for that value. Minnesota's plan will require all customers to pay the same rates for their electricity, but will provide a VOST credit on the bills of solar customers.[497] The state now gives utilities the choice of keeping their net metering policies or switching to VOST as an alternative.

Elsewhere:

Around the nation, 11 states generate more than ten percent of their power from non-hydro renewable resources. The US Energy Information Administration (EIA) reports that electric power from solar, wind, and other non-hydro renewable resources is routinely surpassing hydroelectric generation – a significant milestone.[498] Iowa, the first state to implement a renewable energy standard, now obtains 40 percent of its electricity from renewables, in part from 3,000 wind turbines that have created 4,000 jobs.[499] It is ahead of schedule to achieve its goal of installing 10,000 megawatts of wind power capacity by 2017. Kansas is getting more than 20 percent of its electricity from renewable resources, and has created 12,000 jobs in the clean energy sector. As I mentioned elsewhere, the city of Bloomberg, Texas, has negotiated agreements with wind and solar power producers to provide 100 percent of its energy at costs that are competitive with carbon fuels. Iowa, Kansas, Nevada, and Texas all are led by Republican governors – further evidence that clean energy is not a partisan issue.

The Predictable Pushback

The birth of the clean energy economy is not without complications and opposition. Red and blue states are attempting to become so green that opponents of climate action and clean energy have turned their guns to the states. As a result, several states are not only laboratories of energy innovation; they have also become battlegrounds where a few organizations are attempting to roll back progress. The most frequent skirmishes are over efforts to weaken or repeal existing RPSs. Chambers of commerce and several conservative think tanks are lobbying states with RPSs to freeze, suspend, or reduce them.

Conflicting conclusions about the costs and benefits of RPS policies have contributed to the debate. In 2012, Robert Bryce of the Manhattan Institute for Policy Research reported it had found evidence that the costs of RPSs may be too high and "may not only outweigh any environmental benefits but may also be detrimental to the economy, costing jobs rather than adding them."[500] In 2014, however, Lawrence Berkeley National Laboratory (LBNL) came to a different conclusion. Its study found that the cost of complying with RPSs would be no more than 10 percent of retail electric rates, and in several states would be less than 5 percent.[501] Based on the average monthly residential electric bill in the United States ($107.28 according to EIA), the highest increases would be about $10 per month. When it surveyed states that count the benefits of avoided emissions due to their RPSs, LBNL found the benefits ranged from $25 to $92 per month, far exceeding additional charges on customer bills.[502]

Avoided emissions are only one of several RPS benefits. Pike Research reports that in 2011, businesses providing the products and services for a clean energy economy were adding nearly $14 billion to federal tax revenues and nearly $7 billion in tax revenues for states and localities.[503]

One of the most prominent organizations promoting the rollback of RPSs is the American Legislative Exchange Council, a group funded principally by corporations and corporate foundations.[504] Its published mission is to "advance limited government, free markets, and federalism at the state level through a nonpartisan public-private partnership of America's state legislators, members of the private sector, and the general public."[505]

In 2012, the American Legislative Exchange Council (ALEC) produced a model bill called the "Electricity Freedom Act," designed to dismantle or weaken state RPSs. ALEC's director told Bloomberg, "We're opposed to these (clean energy) mandates, and 2013 will be the most active year ever in terms of efforts to repeal them."[506] Data maintained by the Center for the New Energy Economy (CNEE) in our Advanced Energy Legislation Tracker shows the score at the end of the 2013 legislative season. By mid-June, 26 bills had been introduced that would in some way roll back a state's RPS by extending compliance deadlines, reducing renewable energy goals, allowing nonrenewable resources, or repealing the standards altogether.[507]

In April 2013, Bloomberg carried an article with the headline, "US States Turn Against Renewable Energy as Gas Plunges."[508] It read in part:

> *More than half the US states with laws requiring utilities to buy renewable energy are considering ways to pare back those mandates after a plunge in natural gas prices brought on by technology that boosted supply. Sixteen of the 29 states with renewable portfolio standards are considering legislation that would reduce the need for wind and solar power.*[509]

But when the 2013 legislative season ended, none of the rollback bills had become law. In fact, the net effect of RPS legislation in 2013 was

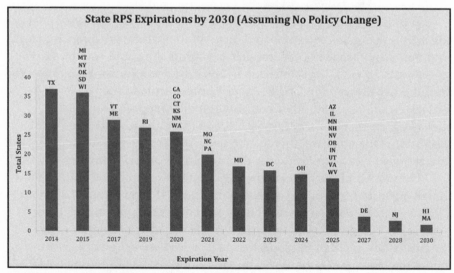

By 2025, most of the RPSs created by states will expire or have met their targets. States will face the question of whether to extend the standards, let them expire, or replace them with one or more other policies that promote the growth of clean energy. (Source: Center for the New Energy Economy)

Figure 18.2

to increase the size of the RPS market.[510] Colorado and Nevada expanded their RPS policies that year. ALEC continued its effort in 2014, predicting that it would be more successful. It had some success, although limited. In April, the Kansas House defeated a bill to roll back the state's RPS after the state senate approved the legislation. In May 2014, Ohio's effort to weaken its RPS by reducing the amount of energy required from renewable resources was changed to a temporary "freeze" while a legislative committee studied the issue.[511] Elsewhere, Governor Chris Christie withdrew New Jersey from the Regional Greenhouse Gas Initiative,[512] and although the Midwestern Regional Greenhouse Gas Reduction Accord remains on the books, the states that signed the accord are not pursuing it, reportedly because of changes in leadership.[513]

Challenges on the Horizon

The states that successfully defend their renewable energy standards will soon face another challenge: What to do when their RPS sunsets. The majority will expire before 2025 (Figure 18.2). In the best scenario, RPSs will have transformed America's energy markets and made renewable energy technologies cost-competitive with fossil energy so that government mandates and incentives will not be necessary.

It is more likely, however, that the many benefits of renewable energy will encourage states to extend and increase their RPSs, or to replace them with more sophisticated policies such as binding emissions standards.

In a 2013 workshop convened by the Advanced Energy Economy Institute (AEEI) and the CNEE, experts brainstormed other policies that states, utilities, and other companies might adopt to continue their progress on clean energy – a "beyond the EERS and RPS" policy discussion. One common theme emerged: Allow greater customer choice and access to clean energy rather than relying on utility mandates.

Opponents of clean energy policies are fighting on other fronts, too, in well-organized, ground-level assaults. In mid-2015 after the EPA issued its Clean Power Plan – the rule to limit carbon emissions from power plants,[514] a group of conservative states prepared to sue the administration to block the rule.[515] Several Republican leaders in Congress were urging states to ignore the regulation until the lawsuits were resolved. CNEE's Advanced Energy Legislation (AEL) Tracker found that as of spring 2014, 19 bills or resolutions had been proposed in 17 states to resist the EPA's regulation.[516] The rule's proponents point out that compliance need not be onerous. The rule gives states unusual flexibility on how they may comply, including energy efficiency and renewable energy initiatives in other sectors beyond pollution control measures at power plants.

In short, the cutting edge of the energy revolution and the front lines of resistance both are located in states and communities. There are many things the federal government can and should do to accelerate America's energy transition, but among the most important is to empower more state and local leadership and, in some cases, to simply get out of the way.

19 | A Just Transition

You load sixteen tons, what do you get?
Another day older and deeper in debt.
St. Peter don't you call me 'cause I can't go.
I owe my soul to the company store.

– From the song "Sixteen Tons"

Revolutions are disruptive by definition. They overthrow established orders. The clean energy revolution is no exception. The established order that is being overthrown is the energy economy of the carbon era. The disruption already is under way in the United States and in other industrialized economies that grew up with fossil fuels.

This is not America's first revolution, of course. We know that we cannot have progress without change, and we cannot have change without disruption. As Frederick Douglass put it, "If there is no struggle, there is no progress." In fact, American history is the story of struggle writ large, from the American Revolution to the Civil War to civil rights and women's rights and all of the smaller achievements in between.

I have described several of the challenges inherent in the clean energy revolution. There are others, to be sure. A common denominator for all of them is the need to make sure that the transformation to clean energy is fair and just. There are many tools already available to help most of us adjust to the disruption and to seize the opportunities inherent in the energy revolution. We need to pick up and use those tools with the same spirit of common cause and patriotism we saw during World War II, when families grew victory gardens, bought war bonds, and conserved resources to support the war effort "for the duration."

Like the war, the energy revolution is not a spectator event. It is not something that should be imposed by government on a passive and compliant citizenry. It is change we can believe in and must all participate in. Many revolutionaries already are at work, including states that have set clean energy goals, the rapidly rising number of renewable energy enterprises and their employees, homeowners with solar roofs, and communities that have entered into long-term agreements to purchase solar and wind energy. Some of America's largest corporations are greening their stores and supply chains. Our most creative entrepreneurs are working on next-generation batteries, alternative fuels, and electric vehicles that can travel much farther between charges. We will soon have cars and trucks that sip fuel more efficiently than we could have imagined just a few years ago. We have mind-boggling technology that allows cars to drive themselves, their computers serving as our chauffeurs. We already are constructing buildings that produce more energy than they use.

In the process, the revolution is upsetting the business models of electric utilities, oil and gas companies, and many of the industries that support them. It is forcing evolution in the automotive and construction industries. It will change the flow of capital into the very industries that have enlisted in the revolt. It will change investment strategies as the carbon budget constrains the production and consumption of coal, oil, and eventually natural gas. As the United Nations Industrial Development Organization (UNIDO) foresees, "Over the next generation and further into the future, all owners of fossil fuel assets, including public sector entities as well as private oil, coal, and natural gas corporations, will, by necessity, experience a major decline in the value of these fossil fuel holdings."[517]

Of all these forces, the most influential will be energy markets after we fix the broken price signals for oil, gas, and coal to reflect their actual costs to society and the environment. Like other energy consumers in other parts of the world, we have been buying energy at a deep discount, disconnected from real costs that have been externalized and subsidized to separate consumers from the consequences of their choices. Like diners who do not want to think about where the meat on their plates came from, we have ignored the unpleasant parts of how our energy is made or where its wastes go. We have bought these fuels without having to pay for childhood asthma or wars in the Middle East. Someone is paying of course, but not those of us who use the fuels.

When these costs finally are incorporated into energy prices, this fundamental flaw in energy markets will be repaired. Markets will take over much of the work that has been delegated by default to government agencies and regulators, leading to complaints about big government, its costs, and its interference in our lives.

It is not only industries and markets that are affected by the energy shift, however. The shift is disrupting the lives of American workers, families, and communities whose livelihoods are derived from fossil fuels.

The old energy economy has many faces. Some are covered in coal dust or smeared with oil. Some are the faces of fourth-generation soft-rock miners or young men learning to be third-generation wildcatters. Others are teenagers who dropped out of high school to earn $70,000 a year driving coal trucks, and young men and women working dangerous jobs on drilling rigs for more than $100,000 a year.

These are the heavy lifters whose work played central roles in making America the most prosperous country on the planet. The idea that coal and oil are somehow bad for America is an insult as well as a threat to their security. Their natural response is to defend their vocations.

It is understandable that the coal industry feels the federal government has declared a "war on coal," even though the actual war is against climate change and other collateral damages from energy production. While scientists and environmentalists talk about parts per million, miners and rig operators worry about barrels per well, tons per day, and dollars per hour. They are focused not on what the weather will be generations from now, but whether they will have jobs tomorrow and pensions when they get old.

These worries are stoked by the most potent weapon in our cultural energy wars: fear. One side raises the real and frightening prospect that climate change will become irreversible and inadaptable; the other side warns that the world is being taken over by socialists and tree huggers who, as Rush Limbaugh has warned, are "coming for your SUV."[518]

It is the people who produce and distribute fossil fuels who are the point of the spear, threatened by new science, regulations, competitors, and technologies, as well as by the dangers inherent in their work.

It is mechanization, not environmentalism, that has caused coal jobs to disappear since the 1920s. Nearly 2 percent of the jobs in the United States were in coal mining then; today only 0.12 percent of the labor force works in the entire coal industry, including mining, transportation, and power plants.[519] It is not only government regulations that are affecting coal markets today; it is also competition from natural gas.[520] The Energy Information Administration (EIA) projects that even without more environmental regulations or carbon constraints, crude oil production in the United States will start to decline after 2020.[521]

We do not have to go far in Colorado to see what disruption looks like, whatever its cause. One example is the town of Craig, population about 9,300. It is located near the Colowyo coal mine, one of the state's largest surface mining operations. The mine employs about 220 people and reportedly generates more than $200 million annually for the region's economy. Colowyo supplies one of Colorado's largest coal-fired power plants – a plant able to generate electricity for nearly 1 million homes.

In 2007, state and federal authorities approved a plan to expand the mine, but an environmental organization filed suit alleging that federal officials had not done an adequate job assessing environmental impacts.[522] A US District Court judge agreed and threatened to close the mine if the environmental impact assessments were not improved. Hundreds of people have rallied in Craig to protest the lawsuit. At this writing, the mine's future remains unresolved.

A different story is part of the history of a town called New Castle on Colorado's Western Slope. A rich coal vein called the Grand Hogback built New Castle's economy during the coal boom of the 1880s.[523] But New Castle suffered two of Colorado's worst mining disasters, including one in 1896 that killed 49 miners and another in 1913 that killed 37. The mine exploded again in 1918, triggering the end of coal production in the community. Nevertheless, New Castle survived. Today it is a "quaint town situated in a narrow valley with views of mountain peaks," several annual festivals, and a prize-winning golf course. Its principal industries are tourism and recreation.[524]

New Castle also is a micro-example of how the market penetration of renewable energy will not always be smooth. A solar developer recently proposed to install 1,600 photovoltaic panels on a four-acre site near a subdivision in the community. The space was owned by the town, which agreed to lease the acreage to the developer. Neighbors protested that the array was an industrial facility that could lower their property values. The town and solar developer agreed to look for another site.[525]

Then there is Somerset, Colorado, which has two coal mines and a third one nearby. At the beginning of 2013, the mines provided jobs for 1,000 people, paying an average salary of $100,000 – more than twice the median income elsewhere in the county. But 142 workers were laid off after an underground fire forced one of the mines to close.[526] The closure put $1 million in annual property tax revenues at risk. Now, oil and gas companies have begun hydraulic fracturing near the community, raising concerns about water contamination and mountain views. "There's bumper stickers on nearly every car," townsman Scott Morley, who worked in the mines for more than 30 years, told a reporter. "The county is probably half environmentalists and half coal miners."[527]

Rifle, Colorado, is also familiar with the liabilities of relying on fossil energy production. As the Rifle Chamber of Commerce recalls:[528]

May 2, 1982 will always be remembered as Black Sunday in Rifle, Colorado. It was the day Exxon locked the gates and more than 2,000 people were suddenly unemployed. People came from all over to work in the oil shale business. Rifle's population doubled nearly overnight, jumping from 2,700 to around 4,500 people. There were thousands of workers in town. On May 2, 1982, the Colony oil shale project came to a sudden and dramatic halt. Workers were locked out of the site when they reported to work on Monday, May 3. Initially, the reaction from the Rifle community was defiant. But the impact was felt community wide. The banks began to have problems, people left town immediately, and local U-Haul businesses instantly became the busiest place in the United States.

Twenty-five years later, a reporter from a local newspaper found that hardly anyone remembered Black Sunday. One resident who did remember blamed the lack of a national energy policy for the shutdown. "We didn't have one in '82, and we don't have one now," he said. The town's merchants reportedly "have gained a renewed respect for diversifying the local economy."[529]

But Rifle has earned bragging rights on the vanguard of the energy revolution, due in large part to leadership by its former mayor, Keith Lambert. Among America's large cities, Honolulu ranks number one in solar energy per person, generating 276 watts per capita at the end of 2014.[530] Rifle, which apparently is too small to be considered in the rankings, generated significantly more solar energy than Honolulu – 325 watts per person. City government in Rifle is now a net-zero energy operation, producing as much power as it draws from the grid. The value of its solar power is estimated at a half-million dollars, money that remains in the community to help its economy. In addition, Rifle is one of eight local governments in Garfield County, Colorado, that are collaborating to help residents, businesses, and local governments improve their energy efficiency and switch to clean energy for a "stronger, more resilient economy."[531]

"Extractive forms of energy have a lifespan," Lambert says. "If we're not working toward the other side of the lifespan, we're fooling ourselves and are going to get caught flat-footed at some point."[532]

Expand these Colorado examples to the coalfields of Appalachia and the Powder River Basin in Montana and Wyoming, and the many states sitting on top of huge gas resources,[533] and we have a better sense of the challenges inherent in fossil fuel production as well as in the transition to cleaner fuels.

What Is a Just Transition?

What exactly is a "just transition"? Although international climate negotiations have been under way for more than two decades, it was

Transition Programs

Robert Pollin points to several examples of how investments can target regions disproportionately affected by new energy policies.

From 1994 to 2004, the US Department of Energy (DOE) administered a Worker and Community Transition program to help diversify the economies of 13 communities that were heavily dependent on the nuclear industry and were having to adjust to nuclear decommissioning. One initiative turned a nuclear test site in Nevada into a solar proving ground.

The federal Trade Adjustment Assistance (TAA) program, launched in 1962, could be a model for a new "Worker Adjustment Assistance Superfund," Pollin says. The TAA provides wage subsidies, health insurance, retraining, counseling, and funding to cover job search expenses for workers who lose their jobs as a result of international trade. The program cost $826 million in 2012, or about $10,000 per worker.

Pollin calculates that even if the cost per worker was four times higher, the Superfund would require $800 million per year, which is a fraction of the federal budget and the subsidies the government provides every year to encourage more production of fossil and nuclear energy.

Robert Pollin et al., "Coal Miners and the Green Agenda," *New Labor Forum* 23 (2013): 88–91, https://www.americanprogress.org/issues/green/report/2014/09/18/96404/green-growth/.

Figure 19.1

not until around 2006 that negotiators began trying to define it. The European Trade Union Confederation (ETUC), composed of 90 national trade union confederations in nine countries, offers this straightforward description:

> A *"Just Transition"* to the green economy is about recognizing and planning fairly and sustainably for the huge changes that climate change policies will have for the whole economy.[534]

Justice and fairness are issues for workers and communities, low- and middle-income consumers, and the carbon industry itself. Per UNIDO:

> Workers tied to the oil, coal, and natural gas industries will inevitably face job losses as a consequence (of the energy transition). Economic policies are therefore needed in all countries to assist these workers, as well as their

families and communities, with transitional support into new areas of economic activity, where decent job opportunities are expanding. In most countries, the energy efficiency and clean renewable energy sectors will be among the most important new areas of expanding job opportunities.[535]

The ETUC lists five principles it says should be followed in transition assistance:

1. Consultations with those who are impacted

2. Investments in "green and decent" jobs

3. Education and training for workers

4. Respect for labor and human rights

5. Social programs that protect those who need them.[536]

Several ideas have been put forward on how such a transition could be done (Figure 19.1). In its *Powering Forward* report to the White House, the Center for the New Energy Economy (CNEE) recommended that the federal government give coal and oil regions a leg up in the competition for existing economic development funds. Along those lines, the Obama administration designated five localities as Promise Zones, including the Kentucky Highlands.[537] In his fiscal year 2016 budget, the president proposed a $55 million program of job training, job creation, and economic diversification in coal country, principally in Appalachia.[538] It will be up to Congress and future administrations whether these types of transition assistance programs are implemented.

Fairness for Low-Income Households

Census data show that 45.3 million Americans lived in poverty in 2013. Forty-four percent of the nation's children live in low-income households, half of them in poverty.[539] While most households in the United States spend four percent of their total annual income on energy, low-income households typically spend 17 percent.[540] Some people find themselves deciding between food, medicine, or paying their utility bills.

There are several options for helping these households cope with the transition to low-carbon energy and especially with carbon pricing. One is to use revenues from a carbon price to increase public assistance programs. California offers an example: It is spending nearly $15 million from its cap-and-trade program to provide free solar installations on homes in disadvantaged neighborhoods.[541] Another option under discussion is direct cash payments to all energy consumers, commonly called the "cap-and-dividend" approach.

Carbon pricing revenues and money redirected from fossil energy subsidies could increase the budget for DOE's Weatherization Assistance Program (WAP) and the Department of Health and Human Service's Low Income Home Energy Assistance Program (LIHEAP). WAP hires local crews to weatherize homes; LIHEAP helps families pay their energy bills in emergency situations. The highest priority of both programs should be home weatherization to prevent rather than simply respond to family energy emergencies.

The Obama administration has implemented several initiatives to help low-income households acquire renewable energy systems. In 2013, President Obama established the goal of installing 100 megawatts of solar and other renewable energy systems in affordable housing by 2020. In July 2015, the administration announced the goal had already been achieved. The president then set a new goal of installing 300 megawatts of renewable energy in affordable housing. That is enough solar power for 50,000 homes. In addition, the administration is offering technical assistance to affordable housing groups so they can install solar systems, and AmeriCorps announced it will train 200 people living in poverty to get jobs with solar companies.[542]

Sometimes, it is little-known adjustments in existing federal regulations that can free capital and opportunities for low-income populations. In 2015, for example, the Comptroller of the Currency issued guidance that awards points under the Community Reinvestment Act to local banks that provide capital for energy efficiency and renewable energy improvements in low-income neighborhoods.[543] The guidance could trigger billions of dollars in low- and no-interest loans and grants for clean energy investments in these communities.

At the state and local levels, many utilities also offer programs to assist low-income customers. So do states that have created public benefit funds with a small charge on electric bills, and that use the money for energy efficiency and renewable energy improvements.[544]

Fairness for the Middle Class

Several tools already are available to help middle-income households participate in the energy revolution and to cope with higher prices for fossil fuels. The most readily available and cost-effective tool is energy efficiency. Significant structural improvements in energy efficiency already are in the nation's economic pipeline. The fuel efficiency of new cars and light trucks will double by 2025 compared to 2011 because of standards set by the Obama administration. The new efficiency levels will reach 54.5 miles per gallon by 2025 and are expected to save consumers $1.7 trillion in fuel costs.[545]

The DOE is required by law to periodically review efficiency standards for appliances and equipment. Its mission is to make sure the equipment and appliance industries take advantage of the latest cost-effective energy efficiency technologies. The DOE already has established efficiency standards for 60 different types of appliances and equipment. As a result, consumers saved nearly $60 billion on their utility bills in 2014. By 2030, the DOE says, cumulative savings in consumer operating costs will reach nearly $1.8 trillion. Society will benefit because the higher standards will prevent 7 billion tons of greenhouse gas emissions.[546]

The DOE also develops model energy codes for homes and commercial buildings. States can use these as models for their own building codes and standards. How well the codes perform depends largely on how well they are adopted and enforced by municipalities. The agency says the codes have the potential to save consumers $330 billion by 2040 and to avoid more than 6 billion metric tons of CO_2 emissions.[547]

There is enormous potential for more savings of energy, emissions, and money. "Many US consumers simply aren't very energy efficient," McKinsey & Company points out. "While they are increasingly aware of the benefits of using less energy and the proliferation of products to help them do so, it's hard to get them to make even modest behavioral changes."[548] Yet those modest changes could reduce household energy use by 20 percent with little to no impact on lifestyles, McKinsey says. Low cost, high-payoff energy efficiency measures, along with voluntary behavioral changes, are available to people at all income levels. In industry, the money-saving, pollution-preventing opportunities include more efficient motor systems and combined heat and power systems in which the heat thrown off by electricity generators is used for space heating and industrial processes.

Renewable energy technologies also help consumers cope with higher fossil energy costs, especially when systems are financed by third parties that do not require up-front payments and share the customer's savings on utility bills.[549] Public interest also is growing in community-sized "solar gardens," in which a single solar installation serves multiple buildings. Solar and wind technologies are immune from carbon pricing and vicissitudes in energy markets because they produce no carbon and their "fuels" are forever free.

Fairness in the Design of Carbon Pricing

Carbon pricing is an idea whose time has come, although perhaps not yet everywhere. Again, it is the practice of adjusting the price of carbon fuels upward to reflect their true costs to society and the environment. The two most common forms of carbon pricing are a tax or surcharge on carbon fuels, or a cap-and-trade system in which a ceiling is put on carbon emissions. Polluters who stay below their emissions cap can sell their unused allowances to polluters whose emissions are too high. Because lowering emissions has economic value, cap-and-trade regimes are supposed to encourage innovation and greater efforts by polluting companies to bring their emissions down as an income proposition.

As of mid-2014, 39 nations and 23 subnational jurisdictions had implemented carbon pricing programs that cover nearly 25 percent of the world's greenhouse gas emissions. The World Bank has valued the global emissions trading market at $30 billion.[550]

In the United States, nine states in the Northeastern and Mid-Atlantic regions have launched a carbon-trading program called the Regional Greenhouse Gas Initiative (RGGI). It generated $1.3 billion in net economic benefits across the region from 2012 through 2014. Electric consumers in households, businesses, and industries saved $341 million, while those using natural gas and heating oil saved $118 million on their energy bills. The trading program was responsible for creating 16,000 job years of employment while reducing the region's CO_2 emissions.[551]

As I mentioned in Chapter 18, California and Quebec launched their own economy-wide cap-and-trade program in 2013. It is producing more than $4 billion annually, dedicated by law to climate change mitigation and adaptation.[552] In the absence of a national policy to price carbon, we are likely to see more multistate carbon trading schemes as states find ways to comply with the Environmental Protection Agency's (EPA) regulation of power plant emissions.

Several prominent Republicans, GOP advisors, and conservative think tanks have spoken in favor of a nationwide tax on carbon, among them Henry Paulson, former Secretary of State George Shultz, and supply-side economist Arthur Laffer. I have mentioned the polling by Stanford University and Resources for the Future, which found that 61 percent of Americans support the creation of a carbon tax and 67 percent would be in favor if the revenues would be used to provide rebates to households.[553]

In effect, a price on carbon would transfer the externalized costs of fossil fuels from taxpayers to consumers who purchase, burn, and create emissions from oil, coal, and gas. The principle is called "polluter pays." Nothing could be more fair.

I believe that carbon pricing will become the norm in the United States, whether it is implemented in multistate, national, or international initiatives. When that happens, it will create a fairness issue not only among workers and consumers, but also in the fossil energy sector. In fairness and in the interest of effective policy, carbon pricing should be applied to all greenhouse gas emissions, not just to carbon dioxide. It should occur upstream at the point where fossil fuels enter the economy – the wellhead, the mine mouth, and the port, for example. As a result, the price correction would be economy-wide rather than affecting some energy-using sectors and not others.

Where Will the Money Go?

Fairness will be an issue, too, in how the revenues of carbon pricing are used. The World Resources Institute (WRI) has calculated that based on the EPA's count of carbon emissions in 2012 and on a very modest carbon price of $15 per ton, government revenues would be above $100 billion annually.[554] The ideas that have surfaced include using the revenues for deficit reduction, investing in measures to combat and adapt to climate change, providing transitional assistance for fossil industry workers, cutting

Preventing the Rebound Effect

An unintended consequence of energy efficiency programs is the "rebound effect," in which consumers use their savings to consume more energy, for example by purchasing a more fuel-efficient car and then driving more.

Michael Shellenberger and Ted Nordhaus of the Breakthrough Institute have written about this. "Over the last several decades there has been a broad consensus that energy efficiency is a cheap and easy way to reduce carbon emissions," they say. "But behind the scenes, a growing group of energy researchers were quietly discovering a more complicated reality. In making driving and lighting more efficient – and thus cheaper – people in many situations drove more and used more lighting. Basic economics suggests that a lower price may increase demand – at least sometimes and in some places."

To prevent rebounding, political and thought leaders should emphasize that net carbon reductions are a civic duty and the national goal, as well as a personal opportunity for more disposable income. Tax deductions and other monetary incentives should be rewarded not simply for making energy-efficient improvements, but also for documented net savings of carbon in each major energy-using category – household utility bills and transportation spending, for example – with each year compared to the previous year.

Source: Michael Shellenberger and Ted Nordhaus, "Why Energy Efficiency Can Increase Energy Consumption in Poor Countries," The Breakthrough, October 9, 2014, http://thebreakthrough.org/index.php/voices/michael-shellenberger-and-ted-nordhaus/why.

Figure 19.2

corporate and/or individual income tax rates, or making direct payments to consumers. The WRI observes, "Using a portion of the revenues to address either the actual or perceived 'losers' from a carbon price may increase the fairness and political viability of the policy." There are many other options, too, of course, including climate-friendly infrastructure improvements or restoring the carbon sinks that have been lost as America's forests have succumbed to insects and fire.

If Congress chooses to reduce the corporate income tax rate, fairness could come up in the context of the wealth gap. The public perception is likely to be that Congress is pandering to economic elites and making the gap bigger. If Congress decides to minimize constituent angst with direct payments – the "tax and dividend" approach – the payments should include measures to minimize the so-called rebound effect that could undermine the climate benefits of carbon pricing (Figure 19.2).

Finally, to avoid contradictions and offsetting effects in federal fiscal policy, carbon pricing should be done as part of comprehensive tax reform. The American people can help by insisting that Congress move beyond talking about tax reform to actually doing it. Broader tax reform should include a revenue-neutral shift of fossil energy subsidies to activities that support the energy revolution. Among them are more clean energy research and development, full US participation in a global carbon-cutting plan, technical and financial assistance to developing countries with the intention of expanding markets for US clean energy products and services, changes in tax policies to trigger more private investment in clean energy, and job-training programs related to emerging clean energy industries.

Intergenerational Fairness

The clean energy revolution must be carried out in ways that are fair and just for future generations. There is merit to the view that allowing greenhouse gas emissions to continue unabated would be an intergenerational crime. The climate disruption we are experiencing today is the result of greenhouse gas emissions a generation ago; the climate our children will experience will be the result of our emissions today.

What does intergenerational justice require? It requires that we build a robust and secure economy, a stable environment with healthy ecosystems, and a world less vulnerable to resource shortages, conflicts, and war. It requires substantial progress on eliminating global poverty in sustainable ways. It requires that the world we leave for our children and their children offers greater prospects for life, liberty, and the pursuit of happiness.

The most frequent pushback from opponents of the energy revolution is that clean energy will have the opposite results, including catastrophic impacts on the economy and on jobs. These warnings have been around for a long time and they have consistently turned out to be unfounded. Markets adjust. Innovators innovate. New technologies achieve economies of scale. Entrepreneurs and industries find ways to make new energy technologies accessible to the American people.

Common sense tells us that the costs of doing nothing about climate change far exceed the costs of acting now. Experience has proved that the benefits of clean energy far exceed their costs. Several studies have found that investments in renewable energy create several times as many jobs as investments in fossil energy, largely because many of the green jobs are more labor intensive and many – such as insulating a building or installing a solar panel on a roof – cannot be exported to other countries. The United Nations, among others, has concluded that investments in green energy "generate more jobs for a given amount of spending than maintaining or expanding each country's existing fossil energy sectors."[555] The American Council for an Energy Efficient Economy (ACEEE) contends that, "The economic benefits of energy efficiency extend far beyond lowering energy bills for consumers." It elaborates:

> An energy efficiency investment creates more jobs than an equivalent investment in either the economy on average or in the utility sector and fossil fuels. As an example, a $1 million investment in a building efficiency improvement will initially support approximately 20 jobs throughout the economy. By comparison, the same $1 million investment in the economy as a whole supports 17 jobs...
>
> Another – and greater – job creation benefit of efficiency results from the consumer savings on energy bills. When a business or household lowers their energy costs, they are then able to spend that money elsewhere in the economy, resulting in additional jobs. On average, this shift in spending supports 17 jobs per $1 million compared to the 10 jobs per $1 million supported through energy generation and distribution.[556]

Jobs in the US solar industry alone grew 20 percent in 2013, 10 times the national average. Solar jobs were expected to grow another 16 percent in 2014.[557] "Renewable energy is a booming business and that's a big opportunity for investors and job seekers alike," according to the financial services company Motley Fool.[558]

Robert Pollin of the Political Economy Research Institute in Amherst, Massachusetts, points out that implementing a clean energy agenda will require large-scale investments in all areas of the country, creating many careers beyond manufacturing, installing, and servicing the hardware for clean energy production.[559] In addition to improving the energy efficiency of America's building stock, industries,

America's Clean Energy Jobs Engine

Here are some of the data being circulated by a variety of organizations that study the jobs impact of clean energy:

- A dollar invested in the green economy creates three times more jobs than a dollar invested in fossil energy.
- Solar employment grew 22 percent in 2014.
- Solar energy added 50 percent more jobs than petroleum and gas extraction in 2014.
- The solar industry created one of every 78 new jobs during 2014.
- Solar companies planned to add another 36,000 employees in 2015.
- There were 3.4 million "green jobs" in the United States by the end of 2011, based on the latest available government data.
- The EPA's regulation of carbon emissions from coal plants is expected to create more than 274,000 jobs and save more than $37 billion on the electric bills of households and businesses.
- Some 1.2 million green job opportunities were posted in the United States between January and March 2015.
- There were 724,000 jobs in renewable energy in the United States and 7.7 million renewable energy jobs worldwide in 2014.
- Robust investment in energy efficiency could save $1.2 trillion by 2020 and create as many as 1.3 million jobs by 2030 and 2 million jobs by mid-century.
- To double the nation's energy productivity by 2030 – a goal set by President Obama – households, businesses, and government agencies would need to invest $166 billion each year. The average household would save more than $1,000 annually in energy costs; American businesses would save nearly as much as the corporate sector paid in federal income taxes in 2011.
- By doubling energy productivity, the United States would cut its CO_2 emissions 22 percent below 2005 levels by 2020 and 33 percent by 2030.

Note: Under political and budget pressures, the Bureau of Labor Statistics stopped publishing reports of jobs in the "green" sector in 2013. Its most current date is from 2011. A variety of nongovernment organizations now are estimating jobs in the clean energy sector.

Sources: Robert Pollin/New Labor Forum, http://www.peri.umass.edu/fileadmin/pdf/other_publication_types/magazine__journal_articles/Pollin--Getting_Real_on_Jobs-Environment---NLF_9-12.pdf; *Fortune,* http://fortune.com/2015/01/16/solar-jobs-report-2014; Natural Resources Defense Council, Environment and Energy Study Institute, http://www.eesi.org/papers/view/fact-sheet-jobs-in-renewable-energy-and-energy-efficiency-2014, International Renewable Energy Agency

and electric system, the shift to a low-carbon economy includes the expansion of public transportation systems and the reinvention of significant parts of the nation's infrastructure.

In 2014, the Center for American Progress (CAP) projected that the United States will need to invest $200 billion a year in clean energy from both public and private sources to cut its energy-related emissions 40 percent over the next 20 years compared to 2005 – a reduction consistent with international targets.[560] The government's share would average $55 billion annually, well within the revenues a national carbon tax or more regional cap-and-trade programs could earn.[561] CAP calculates that the result would be 2.7 million net new jobs.[562]

Finally, communities will find that their investments in clean energy and resilience will improve their business climates. In this era of climate change, the business-climate criteria are changing. Local assets such as an educated workforce and good transportation systems are still on the checklist, but so are reliable and affordable energy supplies, access to freshwater, and the ability to withstand and recover from shocks including extreme weather events and outages in the conventional power grid. Physical resilience is especially important to the small businesses that create most of America's jobs. More than 40 percent of small businesses do not reopen after a weather disaster, according to the Federal Emergency Management Agency (FEMA).[563] John Arensmeyer, the CEO of the nonprofit organization Small Business Majority, writes:

With these (weather) events taking such a toll on small businesses, owners are starting to take note of the factors causing them. Nearly six in 10 small businesses agree climate change and the extreme weather events it creates are a problem that can disrupt the economy and hurt small employers, and they support clean energy policies aimed at lessening the impacts of climate change and that benefit their bottom lines.[564]

Even Environmental Regulations Create Jobs

If we want examples of how past environmental policies have affected jobs, we can find them in longstanding federal laws such as the Clean Water Act and the Endangered Species Act. They have created a "restoration economy" that has resulted in jobs as well as multiple economic and environmental cobenefits. "What has been almost entirely missing from this public debate is a detailed accounting of the economic output and jobs in the United States that are actually created through environmental conservation, restoration, and mitigation actions," say researchers from Yale University and the University of North Carolina at Chapel Hill.[565]

"Despite the commonly held idea that environmental regulations like the Clean Water Act and Endangered Species Act impeded development, there is ample evidence that the public and private investments driven by these regulations have a stimulating effect on economic output and employment."[566]

They estimate that domestic ecological restoration activities directly employ 126,000 workers and generate $9.5 billion in economic output each year, plus 95,000 jobs and $15 billion in economic output from indirect spending.[567] With the mitigation of and adaptation to climate change adding to the restoration economy, the job and economic benefits could be incalculably higher.

All Fairness Is Local

Earlier in this chapter, I cited "consultations with those who are impacted" as one of the criteria for transition assistance. Whatever we identify as the universal features of a transition program, the final definition should be shaped by the residents of communities the energy revolution is disrupting. Some elements of fairness are unique to localities; some are elements that outsiders could not have anticipated.

One example comes from residents of central Appalachia, where persistent poverty and mountaintop removal coal mining are issues. When local people and organizations were asked to identify principles for diversifying the region's economy, they agreed on several, including these:

- If new resources become available, the best resource managers may not be the same government agencies or local leaders whose policies failed to solve poverty in the past. The best managers will be a region's civic organizations, educational institutions, nonprofits, and nongovernment organizations.

- Economic renewal should give people greater control over their lives and communities. That might include incorporating communities, creating locally owned lending and investment institutions, and helping people own the land on which they live and work.

- Economic development should preserve unique local heritage. Steve Berry, best-selling author of *The Columbus Affair*, points out, "A concerted effort to preserve our heritage is a vital link to our cultural, educational, aesthetic, inspirational, and economic legacies – all of the things that quite literally make us who we are."[568] In remaking themselves for the clean energy economy, most communities do not want to become carbon copies of others or the kind of standard strip-mall development that James Howard Kunstler calls the "geography of nowhere." A twenty-first century community that develops sustainably need not lose its sense of place.

- Economic renewal should build upon local talents, customs, and resources. In Appalachia, those resources range from edible forest plants traditionally harvested and bartered to lands around abandoned mines that could be developed for renewable energy production and other uses. The Appalachian Regional Commission calls this "asset-based economic development" that focuses first on "what already exists rather than inventing or building something new."[569]

Government assistance to help communities adapt to the new energy economy should begin with and be guided by broad citizen participation. Communities know best what is fair and just.

It is not the government's job alone to ensure that the energy revolution produces a fair, just, and positive transition. It is a society-wide responsibility that should be supported by public and private organizations including foundations, educational institutions, city councils, economic development boards, civic groups, and so on. Just as climate change requires adaptation, so does the shift to clean energy. Our first job is to make sure that the communities and populations most vulnerable to disruption are among the most resilient.

20 | Conclusion: Why America Should Lead

It is a true privilege to be an American. It was also my great honor to serve as the governor of Colorado, an experience I will treasure for the rest of my days. Every administration has mixed success, but our best work always involved both sides of the aisle working together. Unfortunately, energy policy and politics in the United States have become increasingly divisive, especially in Washington, DC. I suspect there are even some who will read this book suggesting an energy revolution and think that I am not a patriot. They would be wrong. I believe that a global crisis is looming on the horizon and that the United States not only can but must take the lead in addressing it, in large part through a dynamic overhaul in how we produce and consume energy. The well-being of people around the globe depends on us doing just that.

In the spring of 2015, I was invited to Rome to participate as a delegate with a small international group that wrote a document sent to the Vatican prior to the release of the Papal Encyclical, *Laudato Si'*.[570] The delegation included climate experts, economists, diplomats, environmentalists, and journalists from around the world. I was the lone American.

Two things quickly became apparent. First, I had traveled a very long way from the Colorado wheatfield where I posed with wind turbines for my campaign commercial in 2006. Second, among this body of experts, there were many who held an overriding sense of urgency that is not widely shared by most American policy leaders. The common refrain from this group was that we, as a global community, are in grave danger of doing way too little, much too late. It would be fair to say I was more pragmatic than many of my fellow delegates, and at the same time more optimistic about the potential for actually solving the problem of climate change, and solving it in time.

It is true that much of the world has waited for America to take the lead for the better part of the last 20 years. And, because most of the foreign media cover the inaction in Congress, it is certainly understandable why my fellow delegates were cynical about America's willingness and ability to act. Instead of leading the charge against climate change for the past two decades, our Congress has chosen to argue about the science and to collaborate in a denial campaign taken directly from the playbook of the tobacco industry.

But that is not the whole story in America. The rest of the story includes the substantial executive authority of the president to act, the significant role that state and local governments play in an energy revolution, and the desire on the part of the American people to see that transition take place. The revolution will come about far more rapidly if members of Congress pay attention to the wishes of their constituents, and we should all work for that day to arrive soon. If Congress does not act, it is my firm belief that states, local governments, and a bold and willing US president can still oversee an energy revolution in America. The open question is whether the revolution will come in time.

After years of working on these issues as a governor, and, since 2011, working with the White House and with states on energy and environmental issues, my bottom line is this: The United States of America can and should take the lead on transforming energy systems here at home. The United States can and should demonstrate for the rest of the world that reliable energy, affordable energy, and clean energy are not mutually exclusive anywhere in the world.

Why should America lead? First, we have the ability to invest in clean energy in a big way. We are among the richest nations in the world in terms of total GDP, per capita GDP, and natural resource wealth.[571] We are second among nations in renewable energy investment,[572] and we could be first. We have world-class technical expertise. Eight of the top 10 ranked universities in the world are located in the United States, along with seven of the world's best universities in science.[573] Our research assets include production plants and 22 national laboratories at the US Department of Energy (DOE) that have produced 115 Nobel Laureates.[574] One of those facilities – the National Renewable Energy Laboratory (NREL) in Colorado – is arguably the world's premier research facility devoted to energy efficiency and renewable energy research and development.

We are among the world's 10 most innovative nations.[575] We rank first in high-tech companies, with nine of the world's 10 largest.[576] We are the country that invented solar and wind energy technology. Our national laboratories have reduced the cost of wind power by 80 percent, developed power lines that transmit electricity with virtually no

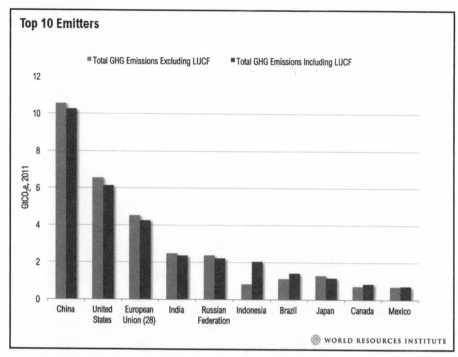

Top 10 Emitters

■ Total GHG Emissions Excluding LUCF   ■ Total GHG Emissions Including LUCF

GtCO₂e, 2011

China, United States, European Union (28), India, Russian Federation, Indonesia, Brazil, Japan, Canada, Mexico

WORLD RESOURCES INSTITUTE

Figure 20.1

China emits more greenhouse gas pollution than any other nation today. The United States is second. This graph shows total greenhouse gas emissions with and without counting land use changes such as deforestation. The United States is also the world's second-largest source of greenhouse gases per capita. Canada ranks first and China seventh on a per capita basis. (Source: World Resources Institute)

energy loss, played a key role in improving batteries, created technology to reduce acid rain, and even demonstrated how 3-D printing can be used to manufacture vehicles.[577]

Importantly, our 50 states are dynamic policy laboratories that are demonstrating the efficacy of a wide variety of public policies and programs related to transforming energy systems, creating economic opportunities, and simultaneously addressing environmental issues. In fact, because of state action, there is light at the end of the tunnel.

The United States is responsible for 27 percent of the greenhouse gases put into the atmosphere between 1850 and 2011. That is more than any other nation in the world. We remain the world's second largest source of carbon pollution (Figure 20.1). As the international community sees it, no other economy has used more of the planet's carbon budget or has a greater obligation to conserve what is left. All developed nations share responsibility for the pollution lingering in the atmosphere today, and all countries must make efforts to slow and adapt to the impacts of global warming, but America's failure to make that commitment in the past has caused other nations to hesitate since climate action without us would be pointless.

We *can* and *should* lead because the American people want us to. The Benenson Strategy Group found that 72 percent of the respondents in one of its recent national polls said they wanted President Obama to sign an international climate agreement in which all countries commit to cut their carbon emissions. Fifty-two percent of the Republicans in the poll agreed.[578] A clear majority of Americans thinks that Congress and the president should do more about global warming and that the United States should reduce its greenhouse gas emissions no matter what other countries do.[579] More than 60 percent of us believe that protecting the Earth and its natural resources are "humankind's responsibility."[580]

We *can* and *should* lead because it is in our national interest to do so. Although we have lost the lead in renewable energy production to other countries, we still have an opportunity to be a first mover in the world's rapidly growing markets for clean energy. The clean energy sector already is a $300 billion "fixture in the world economy," according to Pew Charitable Trusts.[581] Sixty percent of all new electric generation around the world is expected to come from renewable resources by 2030, and renewable energy capacity is projected to increase nearly 600 percent during the 2012–2030 period. The International Energy Agency (IEA) calculates that to keep global warming to no more than 2°C, the world will have to invest $1 trillion each year for many years to come. There are substantial new business opportunities and jobs to be won in this massive emerging market, and the United States should compete for them.

We *can* and *should* lead because we are the United States of America. Our country is still held in high regard in much of the world. In a survey of 39 nations in early 2015, the Pew Research Center found that nearly 70 percent of the world has a favorable opinion of us.[582]

In spite of that, the international community is witnessing that our Congress is paralyzed by partisanship. The world is likely questioning why the American people tolerate that paralysis when it comes time to vote. The world notes that our market economy has created the greatest wealth gap of any well-to-do nation in the world, with 10 percent of households holding nearly 80 percent of the nation's wealth.[583]

Others are curious to see whether the United States of America can find the right answers to several questions. Can a capitalist republic deal effectively with major, even existential, issues such as climate change? Is capitalism capable of protecting the commons? Will the American people use their ultimate power, the vote, to cast out obstructionists from government and overcome partisan gridlock? Can the generations alive today live up to the standard of courage and morality set by the Americans who fought World Wars I and II and who braved death in the fight for civil rights? Can the United States remain the "shining city on the hill whose beacon light guides freedom-loving nations everywhere" – the image that President Ronald Reagan invoked? I believe the answer is yes, but I also believe we have to prove that to the rest of the world, and to ourselves. Throughout this book, I have suggested things we should do to create a future we want. We should define a vision of that future; tear down the stovepipes and echo chambers that reinforce polarization; come to a much deeper appreciation of our interrelationship with and responsibility to the rest of the biosphere; challenge old assumptions that bind us to the past; empower states and communities; learn the difference between good and bad government interventions; engage in capitalism with a conscience; count the hidden costs of our decisions; find better ways to define and measure progress; and make sure that the energy revolution is fair and just.

The Remaining Challenge

There is one more task to discuss because it affects our ability to tackle most of the others. It is the corrupting influence of money on our electoral system and government. As it exists today, campaign finance is threatening to turn our democracy into a plutocracy.

Political leaders of both parties have seen this corrupting influence and some have tried to implement reforms. Those attempts generally have been blocked as unconstitutional by the US Supreme Court. In its most recent rulings, the Court has lifted some important restrictions on political contributions and made corporate money equal in status to constitutionally protected free speech. "Money talks" is now the law of the land. But if money is protected speech, then it follows that wealthy individuals and organizations are freer to speak more often and more loudly than the majority of Americans. It is common knowledge that large contributors expect that they will be repaid once their favored candidates assume office.

The Court has ruled there are no limits to the amount of money certain groups can give in support of political candidates, so long as the contributions are made to organizations not directly associated with the candidate's campaign. It has ruled that donors who channel their campaign money through nonprofit "social welfare" groups can remain anonymous. And it has eliminated limits on the amount of money individuals can give to multiple candidates and political parties during an election cycle.[584]

The law still prohibits contributions made directly to a candidate in exchange for political favors, but the Court has said there is no prohibition against campaign donations that create "the general gratitude a candidate may feel toward those who support him or his allies, or the political access such support may afford." There is a very thin line between buying "general gratitude" from officials and buying favors from them. Writing on the Court's decision to remove the cap from individual campaign contributions, Justice Stephen Breyer acknowledged this. "Who, after all, can seriously contend that a $100,000 donation does not alter the way one thinks about – and quite possibly votes – on an issue," he wrote. "It's only natural and it happens all too often, that a busy senator with 10 minutes to spare will spend those minutes returning the call of a large soft money donor rather than the call of any other constituent."[585]

Even some of the people inside the system admit the political power of wealth. Senator Bernie Sanders of Vermont has said, "I think many people have the mistaken impression that Congress regulates Wall Street. The real truth is that Wall Street regulates the Congress."[586] This is not new. When a congressional committee questioned Charles Keating during the savings-and-loan scandal of the 1980s, one member asked him whether the $1.5 million Keating gave to elected officials could really buy influence. "I certainly hope so," Keating replied.[587]

In 2014, researchers Martin Gilens of Princeton and Benjamin Page of Northwestern University looked at nearly 1,800 policy changes in the United States between 1981 and 2002, focusing on whether the changes most reflected the wishes of middle-income Americans or of high-income Americans and influential special interests.[588] They found that economic elites and business interests have significant impact on public policy while average citizens do not. Their findings, they said, support the theory of Economic Elite Domination rather than Majoritarian Electoral Democracy.

Rigging the Game

The amount of money spent on national elections in the United States was just over $1.6 billion in 1998; by the general election in 2012, it had grown to nearly $6.3 billion.[589] The system gives the appearance that the public policy process is rigged. "Wage stagnation for the vast majority (of American workers) was not created by abstract economic trends. Rather wages were suppressed by policy choices made on behalf of those with the most income, wealth, and power," concludes the Economic Policy Institute, a union-supported think tank.[590] In other words, the current relationship between wealth and political power leads to the conclusion that the rich have been rigging the "equal opportunity" game.

Sometimes influential donors want inaction rather than action. With a touch of hyperbole, perhaps, Columbia University economist Joseph Stiglitz has written, "The top one percent may complain about the kind of government we have in America, but in truth they like it just fine: too gridlocked to re-distribute, too divided to do anything but lower taxes."[591] The two immediate past sessions of Congress – the 112th and 113th – were the least productive in American history in terms of legislation.

If solving the problem of campaign finance were easy, I assume it would have been done already in ways that would withstand legal challenges. Nevertheless, it is important to find a way to draw a line between free speech on one hand and influence buying and peddling on the other. As the Supreme Court has interpreted it, the current system creates lawmakers with purchased ideologies and an electorate with deep distrust in government. As the 2016 presidential campaign began taking shape, only 13 percent of likely voters told pollsters from Rassmussen Reports that they think that Congress does a good job.[592] Nearly 60 percent of voters across the political spectrum believe that most members of Congress are willing to sell their votes for cash or campaign contributions; 56 percent believe their congressperson has done so. Fewer than one in three voters think their representative in Congress agrees with them ideologically, an indication of the perception that members of Congress vote the views of their largest campaign donors rather than the views of their constituents.

The influence of big money is affecting the quality of Congress itself, including the willingness of lawmakers to find common ground so the nation's business can be done. Many of the most moderate and influential members of Congress have left the building for good. In the early months of the 114th Congress, which was seated in January 2015, nine chairs of key committees ranging from the House Ways and Means and Senate Armed Services Committees left or announced their intentions to leave Congress. The exodus included prominent names such as Boxer, Mikulski, Waxman, and Dingell. Although the 273 members of Congress who have left over the course of the last three sessions have done so because of illness, election losses, or retirement as well as frustration, the concern is that the exodus has included many of the "legitimate purveyors of bipartisan legislation," as Dave Wasserman of the Cook Political Report put it.[593] The *New York Times* reported in 2012 that, "Retirements of fed-up lawmakers and campaign spending by special interests is pushing out moderate members of both parties, leaving a shrinking corps of consensus builders."[594]

In addition, Congress has become a "millionaires club," further distancing it from the lives of most Americans. For the first time in American history, more than half the members of Congress were millionaires in 2013 during the 113th Congress.[595] As the Center for Responsive Politics (CRP) explained, it took the combined wealth of more than 18 average American households to equal the median net worth of one member of Congress. "Even the 2010 election, with its promises to 'take our country back,' produced a freshman class of senators with a median net worth of close to $4 million," CBS reported.[596] The CRP's David Levinthal points out, "Most Americans are being represented by people who, any way you cut it, are in the elite of the financial elite."[597]

At times and on very significant issues, the influence of special interests has resulted in the legislative branch taking positions quite different from those the electorate would like it to. That has been the case with energy and climate policy. As I have documented, public opinion research consistently shows that the American people – regardless of political party – favor renewable energy over fossil energy; the majority of voters accept that climate change is real, and most agree that the EPA should limit carbon emissions from power plants. As the 114th Congress began in January 2015, however, 68 percent of Republican leaders in both houses rejected the finding of anthropogenic climate change, including a large majority of the GOP members of the two committees overseeing the topic – the House Science Committee and the Senate Environment and Public Works Committee.[598] The most recent Congresses have focused on stopping the EPA from carrying out its responsibility to limit carbon pollution from power plants under the Clean Air Act. A recent survey by Rassmussen Reports found that only 11 percent of likely voters felt that the average congressperson listens to them. Half of the respondents said their own representative does not care what they think.[599]

The influence of money is a problem for voters regardless of party, but it may be producing unintended consequences for conservatives. Sheldon Richman, the vice president of the conservative Future of Freedom Foundation, contends that the corrupting effect of money on the political process leads to increasing government interventions in the economy, including interventions that conservatives oppose in principle. "Financial intervention on behalf of well-heeled, well-connected groups begets recessions, depressions, and long-term unemployment," Richman writes, "which in turn beget vulnerable working and middle classes who, ignorant of economics, are willing to accept more powerful government, which begets more intervention on behalf of the wealthy, and so on – a vicious circle indeed."[600]

Despite all this, we should not think of wealthy Americans as a monolithic secret society that is trying to subvert democracy. Nor should we assume that the only way to restore the integrity of government is to engineer a massive redistribution of wealth. Even though most Americans are fully aware of the growing gap between rich and poor, believe it will continue, and think the tax system is biased toward the rich,[601] we still admire people "who get rich by working hard."[602] And we should. It is not a redistribution of wealth that we need; it is a redistribution of political power back to voters and the restoration of equal opportunity for all.

At the Crossroads

In the introduction to this book, I made the point that business-as-usual is no longer an option, and that we have to make a choice between designing our future or being its victims. We stand at a crossroads. One road leads to a future in which we have failed our ethical obligation to one another and to generations to come, where we struggle to adapt to chronic disasters and international insecurity, and where we must cope with stresses, shortages, government deficits, instability, and conflict.

On the other road, we not only sustain our shining city on a hill; we make its lights burn brighter and we help make sure they never go out.

I have attempted in these pages to describe some of the things that each of us must know about America's challenges and opportunities right now – challenges that are moral and mundane, physical and psychological, political but patriotic. If doing our part requires that we find common ground, then we must find it. If it requires more knowledge, then we must acquire it. If it requires that we take power back from those who do not have the nation's best interests in mind, then we should take it. And if it requires disruption, which we know it does, then we must help each other through it.

Although he was speaking at a different time about a different place, Robert Kennedy's words seem especially relevant now:

> *The responsibility of our time is nothing less than a revolution – a revolution which will be peaceful if we are wise enough; compassionate if we care enough; successful if we are fortunate enough. But a revolution will come whether we will it or not. We can affect its character; we cannot alter its inevitability.*[603]

It is neither desirable nor possible for us to stand still, so let us choose to power forward.

Notes

1. *Aesop's Fables*, ed. Laura Gibbs (Oxford, UK: Oxford University Press, 2002).

2. For a longer history of this report and President Johnson's actions, see Marianne Lavelle, "A 50th Anniversary Few Remember: LBJ's Warning on Carbon Dioxide," *Daily Climate*, February 2, 2015, http://www.dailyclimate.org/tdc-newsroom/2015/0X2/president-johnson-carbon-climate-warning, and Lyndon B. Johnson, "Statement by the President in Response to Science Advisory Committee Report on Pollution of Air, Soil, and Waters," November 6, 1965. Online by Gerhard Peters and John T. Woolley, The American Presidency Project, http://www.presidency.ucsb.edu/ws/?pid=27355. For the full text of his address to Congress, see *Public Papers of the Presidents of the United States, Lyndon B. Johnson*, 1965 (Washington, DC: Government Printing Office, 1966), vol. I, entry 54, pp. 155–165, http://www.lbjlib.utexas.edu/johnson/archives.hom/speeches.hom/650208.asp.

3. Thomas Jefferson, *The Works of Thomas Jefferson*, Federal Edition (New York and London: G. P. Putnam's Sons, 1904–1905), vol. 5, http://oll.libertyfund.org/titles/802. Jefferson wrote this in 1787 in a letter to James Madison.

4. For more information about civilization's energy transitions, see Richard W. Unger, ed., "Energy Transitions in History: Global Cases of Continuity and Change," *RCC Perspectives*, 2 (2013), http://www.environmentandsociety.org/perspectives/2013/2/energy-transitions-history-global-cases-continuity-and-change.

5. Adlai Stevenson II was America's ambassador to the United Nations from 1961 to 1965. The complete passage from this address to the UN is: "We travel together, passengers on a little spaceship, dependent on its vulnerable reserves of air and soil; all committed, for our safety, to its security and peace; preserved from annihilation only by the care, the work and the love we give our fragile craft. We cannot maintain it half fortunate, half miserable, half confident, half despairing, half slave – to the ancient enemies of man – half free in the liberation of resources undreamed of until this day. No craft, no crew can travel safely with such vast contradictions. On their resolution depends the survival of us all." The speech was his most famous and his last. He died of a heart attack five days later on July 14, 1965, http://www.adlaitoday.org/articles/connect2_geneva_07-09-65.pdf.

6. "Earth Day: The History of the Movement," Earth Day Network, http://www.earthday.org/earth-day-history-movement.

7. Ibid.

8. Al Reinert, "The Blue Marble Shot: Our First Complete Photograph of Earth," *The Atlantic*, April 12, 2011, http://www.theatlantic.com/technology/archive/2011/04/the-blue-marble-shot-our-first-complete-photograph-of-earth/237167. Previous photographs of the Earth from space showed only partial views, often stitched together by NASA.

9. Researchers at the Virginia Institute of Marine Science have counted more than 400 dead zones in coastal waters worldwide, affecting 95,000 square miles. The largest is in the United States at the mouth of the Mississippi River. Professor Bob Diaz and Swedish researcher Rutger Rosenberg found that dead zones – where too little oxygen is present for most marine life – increased a third between 1995 and 2007, http://www.vims.edu/research/topics/dead_zones.

10. "Our Living Oceans," World Bank, last modified April 12, 2012, http://web.world.worldbank.org/WBSITE/EXTERNAL/TOPICS/.

11. Bruce Pengra, *One Planet, How Many People? A Review of Earth's Carrying Capacity* (UNEP Global Environmental Alert Service [GEAS], June 2012), https://na.unep.net/geas/archive/pdfs/geas_Jun_12_carrying_capacity.pdf.

12. The Intergovernmental Panel on Climate Change, an international panel that periodically reviews emerging climate science, established in 1988 by the United Nations. More than 2,000 scientists from 154 nations participate.

13. *Powering Forward: Presidential and Executive Agency Actions to Drive Clean Energy in America* (Fort Collins: Colorado State University, Center for the New Energy Economy, January 2014), http://cnee.colostate.edu/graphics/uploads/CNEE-Powering-Forward-Full-Report.pdf.

14. "Top 10 States with Most Property Damage from Severe Weather," Insurance Institute for Business and Home Safety, August 8, 2014, https://www.disastersafety.org/blog/top-10-states-property-damage-severe-weather/.

15. Peter Mayer and Sonya Wytinck, *Colorado Drought and Water Supply Update 2007* (Denver: Colorado Water Conservation Board, December 1, 2007), http://cwcbweblink.state.co.us/WebLink/ElectronicFile.aspx?docid=140143&searchid=2757c42a-04b6-40fd-aea2-1cc10917b121&dbid=0.

16. Jon Gertner, "The Future Is Drying Up," *New York Times*, October 21, 2007, http://www.nytimes.com/2007/10/21/magazine/21water-t.html?pagewanted=all&_r=0.

17. Walter E. Hecox, PhD, Bryan Hurlbutt, and Caitlin O'Brady, *The 2006 Colorado College State of the Rockies Report Card* (Colorado Springs: Colorado College, 2006), https://www.coloradocollege.edu/dotAsset/a68bd37f-4ca0-472a-bb73-69ab7e4941ae.pdf.

18. *The Colorado Promise* (Denver, CO: Bill Ritter for Governor, 2006), https://coyotegulch.files.wordpress.com/2009/03/ritter_policy_book.pdf.

19. Renewable Energy Requirement, C.R.S. Amendment 37 (2004), http://www.leg.state.co.us/2003a/initrefr.nsf/dac421ef79ad243487256def0067c1de/060d847c-87be114987256f38004a69c5/$FILE/Amendment%2037%20-%20Renewable%20Energy.pdf.

20. Traditional gas and oil deposits were found in pools of oil that were relatively easy to extract. As those deposits ran low, oil and gas companies began exploring unconventional deposits locked in shale and coal formations. The dominant form of natural gas production now is in these formations, using the hydraulic fracturing process to free the gas.

21. The greater threat to the industry is carbon pricing and the possibility that production will be limited to reduce greenhouse gas emissions.

22. Anu K. Mittal, *Unconventional Oil and Gas Production: Opportunities and Challenges of Oil Shale Development* (Washington, DC: US Government Accountability Office, 2012), http://www.gao.gov/products/GAO-12-740T.

23. Julia Haggerty, *Fossil Fuel Extraction and Western Economies: Executive Summary* (Bozeman, MT: Headwaters Economics, April 2011), http://headwaterseconomics.org/wphw/wp-content/uploads/Fossilfuel_West_ExSummary.pdf.

24. *Climate Change 2007: Synthesis Report* (Geneva, Switzerland: International Panel on Climate Change, 2007), https://www.ipcc.ch/publications_and_data/ar4/syr/en/spms1.html.

25. *Colorado: An Energy and Economic Analysis* (Institute for Energy Research, September 10, 2013), http://instituteforenergyresearch.org/analysis/colorado-an-energy-and-economic-analysis.

26. See John Morrison, "Business and Society: Defining the 'Social License,'" *Guardian*, September 29, 2014, http://www.theguardian.com/sustainable-business/2014/sep/29/social-licence-operate-shell-bp-business-leaders. Morrison, the executive director of the Institute for Human Rights and Business, points out that to maintain its social license, an industry must be transparent, accountable, clear about its benefits, and diligent against negative impacts. "Consent is also an essential component," he says. "It is a mistake for any company to proceed on any activity without securing adequate social permission... Social license can never be self-awarded. It requires that an activity enjoys sufficient trust and legitimacy, and has the consent of those affected. Business cannot determine how much prevention or mitigation it should engage in to meet environmental or social risks – stakeholders and rights-holders have to be involved for thresholds of due diligence to be legitimate (sometimes even if these are clearly determined in law)."

27. By comparison, a new coal plant in Pueblo, Colorado, resulted in a rate increase of approximately 35% for utility customers.

28. Colorado's original RPS in the 2004 ballot initiative included a 4% "carve out," or specific mandate, for solar energy – 2% from utility-scale systems and 2% from small-scale distributed systems. In subsequent legislation, we changed this to 3% of the total RPS requirement and opened it up to other distributed resources.

29. Testimony of Leland B. Deck before the Public Utilities Commission of Colorado on behalf of Western Resource Advocates, Docket No. 10M-245E, September 17, 2010, file:///Users/billbecker/Downloads/WRA%20answer%20testimony%20-%20Deck%209-17-10.pdf.

30. The Colorado Act limits the net impact on customers' annual electric bills to 2% and prohibits utility companies from compounding the rate increase annually.

31. Heeter et al., *A Survey of State-Level Cost and Benefits Estimates of Renewable Portfolio Standards* (Golden, CO: National Renewable Energy Laboratory, and Berkeley, CA: Lawrence Berkeley National Laboratory, May 2014), http://www.nrel.gov/docs/fy14osti/61042.pdf.

32. In other words, 1% above the rates electric customers would have been charged without the RPS during the 2010 to 2012 period.

33. We found that existing econometric models were not capable of quantifying counterfactual external cost savings. For example, they could not determine how much more Colorado residents would have paid in health care and other external costs if the state had *not* passed its clean energy laws.

34. *Colorado Climate Action Plan: A Strategy to Address Global Warming* (Denver: Colorado State Energy Office, November 2007), http://www.tribesandclimatechange.org/docs/tribes_57.pdf.

35. Brandon Gee, "Ritter Praises South Routt," *Steamboat Pilot*, May 2008, http://www.mckinstry.com/news/view/id/29.

36. "The Nine Planetary Boundaries," Stockholm Resilience Centre, last modified January 22, 2015, http://www.stockholmresilience.org/21/research/research-programmes/planetary-boundaries/planetary-boundaries/about-the-research/the-nine-planetary-boundaries.html.

37. I discuss the moral dimensions of energy policy in Chapter 17.

38. The number of jobs and ventures fluctuated over the years due in part to uncertainty about the federal Production Tax Credit for wind power development.

39. *Energy – Colorado Industry Cluster Profile* (Denver, CO: Metro Denver Economic Development Corporation, January 2014), http://www.metrodenver.org/media/230125/energy_2014_co_012915.pdf.

40. Daniel Cusick. "Solar Power Sees Unprecedented Boom in U.S.," *Scientific American*, March 10, 2015, http://www.scientificamerican.com/article/solar-power-sees-unprecedented-boom-in-u-s.

41. "National Solar Jobs Census 2014," The Solar Foundation, http://www.thesolarfoundation.org/solar-jobs-census/national.

42. "U.S. Solar Market Insight: Residential Solar Grows by 76% over Q1 2014, Forecast for 2015 Remains Strong," Solar Energy Industries Association, June 9, 2015, http://www.seia.org/research-resources/us-solar-market-insight.

43. "Short-Term Energy Outlook: Renewables and Carbon Dioxide Emissions," US Energy Information Administration, July 2015, http://www.eia.gov/forecasts/steo/report/renew_co2.cfm.

44. Jordan Schneider and Rob Sargent, *Lighting the Way: The Top Ten States That Helped Drive America's Solar Energy Boom in 2013* (Environment America, August 2014), http://environmentamericacenter.org/sites/environment/files/reports/EA_Lightingtheway_scrn.pdf.

45. Nicole D'Alessandro, "Top 10 States Leading the U.S. in Energy Growth," *EcoWatch*, August 5, 2014, http://ecowatch.com/2014/08/05/top-10-states-leading-solar-energy-growth.

46. Stephanie Paige Ogburn, "Colorado First State to Limit Methane Pollution from Oil and Gas Wells," *Climate Wire*, February 25, 2014, http://www.scientificamerican.com/article/colorado-first-state-to-limit-methane-pollution-from-oil-and-gas-wells.

47. The biosphere consists of the land, oceans, atmosphere, and all the life they support on the planet.

48. David Orr, "Systems Thinking and the Future of Cities," Post Carbon Institute, May 30, 2014, http://www.postcarbon.org/systems-thinking-and-the-future-of-cities/.

49. "The Nine Planetary Boundaries," Stockholm Resilience Centre, last modified January 22, 2015, http://www.stockholmresilience.org/21/research/research-programmes/planetary-boundaries/planetary-boundaries/about-the-research/the-nine-planetary-boundaries.html. International scientists have identified nine "planetary boundaries" we cannot cross without major damage to nature and to ourselves.

50. "Anthropocene," *Wikipedia*, last modified June 24, 2015, http://en.wikipedia.org/wiki/Anthropocene. Anthropocene is the combination of the Greek roots for "human" and "new." At this writing, the scientific community has not yet accepted it as the official title of an epoch. Opinions vary greatly about when it began, ranging from 1610 to 1945 and 1964.

51. For a good overview: Gayarthri Vaidyanathan, "When Did Man Dominate Changes on Earth? A Rock-Hard Question for Scientists," *E&E News*, March 12, 2015, http://www.eenews.net/climatewire/stories/1060014908. Simon Lewis and Mark Maslin, "Defining the Anthropocene," *Nature* 519 (March 12, 2015): 171–180, http://www.nature.com/nature/journal/v519/n7542/full/nature14258.html.

52. "The best-known exercise to assign a monetary value to ecological systems was done by a team of researchers in 1997. They concluded that the global value was $46 trillion annually. An updated study published in 2014 estimated the

value at between $125 trillion and $145 trillion annually. The study also estimated that the loss of ecosystem services from land use changes alone was as much as $20 trillion annually from 1997 to 2011 (in 2007 dollars)." Robert Costanza et al., "Changes in the Global Value of Ecosystem Services," *Global Environmental Change* 26 (May 2014): 152–158, http://www.sciencedirect.com/science/article/pii/S0959378014000685.

53. Intergovernmental Panel on Climate Change, *Climate Change 2013: The Physical Science Basis, Summary for Policymakers*, p. 5, Intergovernmental Panel on Climate Change, https://www.ipcc.ch/pdf/assessment-report/ar5/wg1/WG1AR5_SummaryVolume_FINAL.pdf. The IPCC says this is the globally averaged combined land and ocean surface temperature as calculated by a linear trend. The Goddard Institute for Space Studies has calculated a similar number: 0.8°C, http://climate.nasa.gov/climate_resources/28.

54. Some of these geoengineering approaches qualify as problem switching rather than problem solving. I describe the difference in Chapter 8.

55. Susan Solomon et al., "Irreversible Climate Change Due to Carbon Dioxide Emissions," *Proceedings of the National Academy of Sciences in the USA* 106, no. 6 (January 2009): 1704–1709, http://www.noaanews.noaa.gov/stories2009/20090126_climate.html.

56. "Climate Change Statements from World Religions," Forum on Religion and Ecology at Yale, http://fore.yale.edu/climate-change/statements-from-world-religions/. An encyclical – officially a letter from a pope to the church's bishops – is considered the most authoritative expression of Catholic doctrine. While Francis is the most visible religious leader to take a stand on climate action, action is advocated by a wide variety of religious leaders of different faiths.

57. For example, Pope Francis has said, "I would like to ask all those who have positions of responsibility in economic, political and social life, and all men and women of goodwill: let us be 'protectors' of creation, protectors of God's plan inscribed in nature, protectors of one another and of the environment." Pope Francis, "Homily of Pope Francis" (Homily, Saint Peter's Square, March 19, 2013). And, "A way has to be found to enable everyone to benefit from the fruits of the earth, and not simply to close the gap between the affluent and those who must be satisfied with the crumbs falling from the table, but above all to satisfy the demands of justice, fairness and respect for every human being." Pope Francis, "Address of His Holiness Pope Francis to Participants in the 38th Conference of the Food and Agricultural Organization of the United Nations" (Address, Clementine Hall, June 20, 2013).

58. President Obama offered this assessment after climate change was included in the national security strategy the White House released in February 2015. A White House spokesman explained that "there are many more people on an annual basis who have to confront the direct impact on their lives of climate change or on the spread of a disease than on terrorism," Clare Foran, "White House: Climate Change Threatens More Americans Than Terrorism," *National Journal*, February 10, 2015, http://www.nationaljournal.com/energy/white-house-climate-change-threatens-more-americans-than-terrorism-20150210. As explained by the World Watch Institute: "As early as 1988, scientists cautioned that human tinkering with the Earth's climate amounted to 'an unintended, uncontrolled globally pervasive experiment whose ultimate consequences could be second only to a global nuclear war'... A growing number of international leaders now warn that climate change is, in the words of U.K. Chief Scientific Advisor

David King, 'the most severe problem that we are facing today – more serious even than the threat of terrorism'... A recent report by the International Climate Change Taskforce, co-chaired by Republican U.S. Senator Olympia Snowe, concludes that climate change is the 'single most important long term issue that the planet faces,'" Janet Sawin, *Global Security Brief #3: Climate Change Poses Greater Security Threat Than Terrorism* (World Watch Institute, 2013), http://www.worldwatch.org/node/77.

59. Carl Sagan and Ann Druyan, *The Demon-Haunted World: Science as a Candle in the Dark* (New York: Ballantine Books, 1997), http://www.goodreads.com/book/show/17349.The_Demon_Haunted_World. In another example, 200 evangelical scientists wrote to Congress to urge action against climate change. "As evangelical scientists and academics, we understand climate change is real and action is urgently needed... We as a society risk being counted among 'those who destroy the earth' (Revelation 11:18)." Tom Ackerman et al. to Speaker Boehner, Senate Majority Leader Reid, and members of the United States Congress, July 10, 2013 (EE News, July 7, 2015), http://www.eenews.net/assets/2013/07/15/document_cw_02.pdf.

60. Donella Meadows, "Down to Earth Speech," Vimeo Video, 32:32, Donella Meadows' "Down to Earth" speech delivered in 1993 at a sustainable conference in Costa Rica, posted by Donella Meadows Institute, 2013, https://vimeo.com/30752926.

61. Catherine L. Langford, "George Bush's Struggle with the 'Vision Thing,'" in *The Rhetorical Presidency of George H. W. Bush*, ed. Martin. J. Medhurst (College Station: Texas A&M University Press, 2006), pp. 19–36.

62. While the reference to America as a "shining city on a hill" is often attributed to President Reagan, it is believed to have originated in Jesus's Sermon on the Mount (Matthew 5:14) where he says, "You are the light of the world. A city that is set on a hill cannot be hidden." Other American politicians have also used the metaphor.

63. The Pearl Street Station was also the nation's first cogeneration plant, providing not only electricity but also steam heat to nearby buildings.

64. Matt Novak, "Where the Future Came From: A Trip Through the 1893 Chicago World's Fair," *Paleofuture*, July 12, 2013, http://paleofuture.gizmodo.com/where-the-future-came-from-a-trip-through-the-1893-chi-743942247. The fair was known officially as the World Columbian Exposition.

65. As reported by Erik Larson in his book *The Devil in the White City: Murder, Magic, and Madness at the Fair That Changed America* (New York: Crown Publishing, 2003).

66. Carl Kitchens and Price Fishback, "Flip the Switch: The Spatial Impact of the Rural Electrification Administration 1935–1940," The National Bureau of Economic Research (2013), http://www.nber.org/papers/w19743.

67. *2013 Report Card for America's Infrastructure* (Reston, VA: American Society of Civil Engineers, 2013), http://www.infrastructurereportcard.org/a/#p/energy/conditions-and-capacity.

68. George Constable and Bob Somerville, *The Greatest Engineering Achievements of the 20th Century* (Arlington, VA: National Academy of Sciences, 2015), http://www.greatachievements.org/.

69. Meagan Clark, "Aging US Power Grid Blacks Out More Than Any Other Developed Nation," *International Business Times*, July 17, 2014,

http://www.ibtimes.com/aging-us-power-grid-blacks-out-more-any-other-developed-nation-1631086.

70. Executive Office of the President, *Economic Benefits of Increasing Electric Grid Resilience to Weather Outages*, August 2013, http://energy.gov/downloads/economic-benefits-increasing-electric-grid-resilience-weather-outages.

71. As I will describe later, we also have had power interruptions in the United States caused by shortages of water for cooling generating plants.

72. Executive Office of the President, *Economic Benefits of Increasing Electric Grid Resilience to Weather Outages*, August 2013, http://energy.gov/downloads/economic-benefits-increasing-electric-grid-resilience-weather-outages. For example, an ice storm blacked out power to a half million Michigan residents in December 2013; 650,000 customers lost power in the northeastern United States because of a nor'easter in February 2013; high winds and flood waters during Hurricane Sandy blacked out power for an estimated 8 million customers in eastern states; thunderstorms and hurricane-force winds interrupted power for nearly 4 million people in the Midwest, East, and South in June 2013. Similar mass power outages occurred due to a snowstorm along the East Coast in October 2011; Hurricane Irene in August 2011; high winds in Chicago that July; a cluster of tornadoes that knocked out more than 300 transmission towers in Alabama that April; and cold weather that forced outages at two coal power plants that February in Texas.

73. "Frequently Asked Questions: How Much Electricity Is Lost in Transmission and Distribution in the United States?" Energy Information Administration, last modified May 7, 2014, http://www.eia.gov/tools/faqs/faq.cfm?id=105&t=3.

74, *Transmission & Distribution Infrastructure: A Harris Williams & Co. White Paper* (Richmond, VA: Harris Williams & CO., Summer 2010), http://www.harriswilliams.com/sites/default/files/industry_reports/final%20TD.pdf.

75. This estimate assumes that the boom in oil and gas production could continue, an issue I will address later.

76. "Futurama 1939," YouTube Video, 3:15, posted by KC Area Development Council, April 13, 2010, https://www.youtube.com/watch?v=-JFgpxYaeJQ.

77. "Futurama (New York World's Fair)," *Wikipedia*, last modified May 27, 2015, https://en.wikipedia.org/wiki/Futurama_(New_York_World's_Fair). This description of Futurama was drawn from *Wikipedia's* feature on the 1939 New York World's Fair.

78. "The History of American Technology: The Automobile Industry, Since 1960," Bryant University, last modified Fall 1998, http://web.bryant.edu/~ehu/h364/materials/cars/cars%20_90.htm.

79. *2013 Report Card for America's Infrastructure, 2013* (Reston, VA: American Society of Civil Engineers), http://www.infrastructurereportcard.org/a/#p/roads/overview.

80. *National Conference of State Legislatures (NCSL), Transport Report*, March 2014, http://www.ncsl.org/documents/transportation/trn-march2014.pdf. The US Department of Transportation reports that per capita vehicle miles declined in 2013 for the ninth straight year. The State Smart Transportation Initiative posted an analysis by Chris McCahill: "Unlike other past dips in driving, this recent downward shift has had no clear, lasting connection to economic trends or gas prices. Evidence suggests that the decline is likely due to changing demo-

graphics, saturated highways, and a rising preference for compact, mixed-use neighborhoods, which reduce the need for driving. Some key factors that pushed VMT upward for decades – including a growing workforce and rising automobile ownership – have also slowed considerably." Chris McCahill, "Per Capita VMT Drops for Ninth Straight Year; DOTs Taking Notice," State Smart Transportation Initiative, February 24, 2014, http://www.ssti.us/2014/02/vmt-drops-ninth-year-dots-taking-notice/.

81. Movement to city centers is being led by millennials, but baby boomers also are part of the trend. Between 2000 and 2010, more than a million baby boomers moved out of areas 40 to 80 miles from city centers and about the same number moved to within 5 miles of city centers, according to an analysis by the real estate brokerage Redfin, http://www.washingtonpost.com/local/2013/08/05/1a21c1b2-fba7-11e2-a369-d1954abcb7e3_story.html. Other research indicates that smart growth neighborhoods, both urban and suburban, are the locations of choice across age groups. In its 2011 Community Preference Survey, the National Association of Realtors found that 56% of Americans would like to live in walkable communities where shops, restaurants, and local business are within an easy walk from their homes, http://www.realtor.org/reports/2011-community-preference-survey.

82. Shared energy extends to solar electric systems today, including community solar systems that generate power for multiple buildings.

83. "Moving Ahead for Progress in the 21st Century Act (MAP-21)," US Department of Transportation, last modified April 3, 2015, http://www.transportation.gov/map21. While there is debate about whether it qualifies as a true national policy, a de facto policy is codified periodically by Congress in its multiyear reauthorization of funding for highways and transit systems. The most recent is the Moving Ahead for Progress in the 21st Century Act (MAP-21). "Grow America," US Department of Transportation, last modified April 7, 2015, http://www.transportation.gov/grow-america. The president's 2016 transportation budget represents the administration's current transportation vision.

84. Rebecca Riffkin, "Climate Change Not a Top Worry in U.S.," Gallup, March 12, 2014, http://www.gallup.com/poll/167843/climate-change-not-top-worry.aspx.

85. Neil King Jr. and Patrick O'Connor, "New WSJ/NBC Poll: 'Addressing Climate Change' Is the Dead-last, Lowest Priority Issue for Americans," The Hockey Schtick (blog), The Wall Street Journal, January 28, 2014, http://hockeyschtick.blogspot.com/2014/01/new-wsjnbc-poll-addressing-climate.html.

86. Colleen McCain Nelson, "Obama Climate-Change Push Faces a Lukewarm Public: Polls Show Climate Change Ranks Low When Voters Are Asked to Assess Priorities," The Wall Street Journal, May 7, 2014, http://www.wsj.com/news/articles/SB10001424052702303701304579548270013580820.

87. Daniel J. Weiss and Jackie Weidman, "Disastrous Spending: Federal Disaster-Relief Expenditures Rise amid More Extreme Weather" (Washington, DC: Center for American Progress, April 29, 2013), https://www.americanprogress.org/issues/green/report/2013/04/29/61633/disastrous-spending-federal-disaster-relief-expenditures-rise-amid-more-extreme-weather/. Analysis by the Center for American Progress found that federal spending on disaster relief and recovery totaled $136.5 billion from 2011 to 2013, the equivalent of nearly $400 for every American household. Daniel Lashof and Andy Stevenson, Who Pays for Climate Change? U.S. Taxpayers Outspend Private Insurers Three-to-One to Cover Climate Disruption Costs (New York: National Resources Defense Council,

May 2013), http://www.nrdc.org/globalwarming/files/taxpayer-climate-costs-IP.
pdf. While outlays by property and casualty insurers also have been increasing, a study issued by the Natural Resources Defense Council (NRDC) in 2013
concluded that outlays by taxpayers were three times higher than outlays by
private insurers. "Despite the lengthy debate on the federal budget in Congress,
climate change rarely gets mentioned as a deficit driver," the NRDC reported.
Yet paying for climate disruption was one of the largest nondefense discretionary budget items in 2012. Indeed, when all federal spending on last year's
droughts, storms, floods, and forest fires are added up, the US Climate Disruption
Budget was nearly $100 billion. The federal government spent more taxpayer
money on the consequences of 2012 extreme weather than on education or
transportation. Climate doesn't show up as a line item in the budget, but what
the NRDC calls the Climate Disruption Budget for 2012 is equal to one out of
every six dollars spent on nondefense discretionary programs, making it the
number-one item in that part of the federal budget.

88. *Quadrennial Defense Review* (Washington, DC: Department of Defense, March
2014): 8, http://www.defense.gov/pubs/2014_Quadrennial_Defense_Review.
pdf. In its most recent *QDR*, issued in 2014, the Defense Department concludes
"pressures caused by climate change will influence resource competition while
placing additional burdens on economies, societies, and governance institutions around the world. These effects are threat multipliers that will aggravate
stressors abroad such as poverty, environmental degradation, political instability, and social tensions – conditions that can enable terrorist activity and other
forms of violence."

89. "Americans Support Limits on CO2," Yale Project on Climate Change Communication: Bridging Science and Society, last modified April 2014, http://environ-
ment.yale.edu/climate-communication/article/americans-support-limits-on-co2.

90. "Global Warming National Poll" (Stanford University/Resources for the Future
National Global Warming Survey, June 2014), p. 3, http://www.rff.org/Documents/
Stanford-RFF-Global-Warming-Poll-June-2014-TOPLINE.pdf.

91. Andrew Dugan, "Americans Most Likely to Say Global Warming Is Exaggerated,"
Gallup, March 17, 2014, http://www.gallup.com/poll/167960/americans-like-
ly-say-global-warming-exaggerated.aspx.

92. Lydia Saad, "One in Four in U.S. Are Solidly Skeptical of Global Warming," Gallup, April 22, 2014, http://www.gallup.com/poll/168620/one-four-solidly-skepti-
cal-global-warming.aspx.

93. "Conspiracy Theory Poll Results," Public Policy Polling, April 2, 2013, http://www.
publicpolicypolling.com/main/2013/04/conspiracy-theory-poll-results-.html.

94. "Poll: 3 in 8 Americans Believe Global Warming Is a Hoax," Weather Channel,
April 4, 2013, http://beforeitsnews.com/environment/2013/04/poll-3-in-8-amer-
icans-believe-global-warming-is-a-hoax-2465858.html. Oddly, the poll tucked
its question about global warming among questions about whether people
believed in aliens and UFOs, that the moon landing was faked, that the government allowed 9-11 to happen, that President Obama is the anti-Christ, and that
"shape-shifting reptilian people control our world by taking on human form and
gaining political power to manipulate our societies."

95. Anthony Leiserowitz et al., *Public Support for Climate and Energy Policies in
November 2013* (Yale Project on Climate Change Communication and George
Mason University Center for Climate Change Communication, November 2013),

http://environment.yale.edu/climate-communication/files/Climate-Policy-Report-November-2013.pdf.

96. Darren Goode, "Polls Show Energy Doesn't Spark Americans' Interest," *Politico*, October 28, 2013, http://www.politico.com/story/2013/10/polls-show-energy-doesnt-spark-americans-interest-98904.html.

97. Gayathri Vaidyanathan, "Big Gap between What Scientists Say and Americans Think about Climate Change," *Scientific American*, January 30, 2015, http://www.scientificamerican.com/article/big-gap-between-what-scientists-say-and-americans-think-about-climate-change.

98. Ibid. See source for a more detailed explanation.

99. Sheldon R. Gawiser and G. Evans Witt, "20 Questions a Journalist Should Ask About Poll Results," 3rd ed. National Council on Public Polls, http://www.ncpp.org/?q=node/4. The American Association for Public Opinion Research also has published standards for research professionals: *The Code of Professional Ethics and Practices*, revised 2015 (American Association for Public Opinion Research, May 11, 2015), https://www.aapor.org/AAPORKentico/Standards-Ethics/AAPOR-Code-of-Ethics.aspx.

100. "History of Climate Science," *Skeptical Science* (blog), last modified April 7, 2013, http://www.skepticalscience.com/history-climate-science.html. See link for a more complete history.

101. Colin M. MacLeod et al., *Restoring the Quality of Our Environment: Report of the Environmental Pollution Panel*, President's Science Advisory Committee (Washington, DC: White House: President's Science Advisory Committee, 1965), pp. 126–127, http://dge.stanford.edu/labs/caldeiralab/Caldeira%20downloads/PSAC,%201965,%20Restoring%20the%20Quality%20of%20Our%20Environment.pdf.

102. "Legislation on Conservation and the Environment 1965–1968," LBJ for Kids!, last modified 2001, http://www.lbjlib.utexas.edu/johnson/lbjforkids/enviro_timeline.shtm. Link includes the Clean Air Act, Wilderness Act, and several others.

103. In his famous "moral equivalent of war" speech on April 18, 1977, President Jimmy Carter announced goals for the nation to significantly increase energy conservation and to use solar energy in more than 2.5 million homes. But he also called on utilities to use more coal and for coal production to increase by two-thirds. Carter did not mention climate change; the theme of his speech was that the United States was increasingly vulnerable to energy shortages because the world was running out of oil and natural gas, http://www.presidency.ucsb.edu/ws/index.php?pid=7369#axzz1R3qJn3vT.

104. R. E. Dunlap and A. M. McCright, *The Oxford Handbook on Climate Change and Society* (Oxford, UK: Oxford University Press, 2011), pp. 144–160, http://www.scottvalentine.net/yahoo_site_admin/assets/docs/dunlap_cc_denial.302183828.pdf. Sharon Begley, "The Truth about Denial," *Newsweek*, August 13, 2007, p. 20, http://academic.evergreen.edu/curricular/energy/0708/articles/TruthDenialNewsweek07Aug.pdf. *Dealing in Doubt: The Climate Denial Industry and Climate Science, A Brief History of Attacks on Climate Science, Climate Scientists and the IPCC* (Netherlands: Greenpeace International, 2010), http://www.greenpeace.org/international/Global/international/planet-2/report/2010/3/dealing-in-doubt.pdf. See above sources for a detailed analysis of the roots of global warming denial.

105. *The Environment: A Cleaner, Safer, Healthier America* (Luntz Research Companies, 2002), https://www2.bc.edu/~plater/Newpublicsite06/suppmats/02.6.pdf.

106. John Cook et al., "Quantifying the Consensus on Anthropogenic Global Warming in the Scientific Literature," *IOP Science* 8, no. 2 (2013), http://iopscience.iop.
org/1748-9326/8/2/024024/article. Their study was published in the journal *Environmental Research Letters*. It is the source of the frequently cited conclusion
that 97% of the world's climate scientists agree. A similar review of more than
900 peer-reviewed papers in 2004 found that none rejected the conclusion that
climate change was human caused.

107. Robert J. Bruelle, PhD, "New Study Exposes Flood of Dark Money Feeding
Climate Change Denial," *EcoWatch*, December 23, 2013, http://ecowatch.
com/2013/12/23/dark-money-feeding-climate-change-denial. According to
researchers at Drexel University, wealthy organizations and individuals, often
with vested interests in fossil fuels, have spent an average of $1 billion each
year to build a climate change countermovement, funding conservative trade
associations, think tanks, and advocacy groups. The funding has been characterized as "dark money" because it is channeled to the "denial industry" in
untraceable ways.

108. Mark Sanford, "A Conservative Conservationist?" *Washington Post*, February
23, 2007, http://www.washingtonpost.com/wp-dyn/content/article/2007/02/22/
AR2007022201455.html.

109. The Republican Platform: We Believe in America (Republican National Committee, 2012), https://gop.com/platform. Climate change all but disappeared
in the GOP's 2012 platform. It mentioned "climate change" only once in the
context of criticizing the Obama administration's National Security Strategy for
classifying climate change as a severe threat. At the same time, prominent
Republicans who previously acknowledged global warming, including several
of the presidential candidates, backed off or reversed their positions.

110. Climate scientists note that global warming could be beneficial to some parts of
the world, for example, by lengthening growing seasons for crops. However, the
net impacts would be profoundly negative.

111. "Who We Are," RepublicEN, last modified 2014, http://republicen.org/who-we-
are/.

112. William D. Ruckelshaus et al., "A Republican Case for Climate Action," *New York
Times*, August 1, 2013, http://www.nytimes.com/2013/08/02/opinion/a-republi-
can-case-for-climate-action.html?r=0.

113. Henry M. Paulson Jr., "The Coming Climate Crash: Lessons for Climate Change
in the 2008 Recession," *New York Times*, June 21, 2014, http://www.nytimes.
com/2014/06/22/opinion/sunday/lessons-for-climate-change-in-the-2008-reces-
sion.html.

114. "About the Project," Risky Business, http://riskybusiness.org/about.

115. Teresa A. Myers, "Simple Messages Help Set the Record Straight about Scientific Agreement on Human-Caused Climate Change: The Results of Two
Experiments," *PLOS One* (March 26, 2015), http://journals.plos.org/plosone/arti-
cle?id=10.1371/journal.pone.0120985.

116. A caution here: Not all extreme weather has been linked to global warming.
Scientists have low confidence, for example, in any link with tornadoes. They
also have concluded that climate change is not likely to increase the frequency

of hurricanes, but it does have an influence on their severity. It is important for climate action advocates to sustain their credibility with accuracy.

117. "About the Project," Risky Business, http://riskybusiness.org/about.

118. Mario Molina et al., *What We Know: The Reality, Risks, and Response to Climate Change* (Washington, DC: American Association for the Advancement of Science, July 2014), http://whatweknow.aaas.org/wp-content/uploads/2014/07/whatweknow_website.pdf.

119. For example, senior retired military officers convened by the Center for Naval Analysis concluded that climate change and our dependence on fossil fuels are "threat multipliers" that will create political instability, social tensions, conflict, and terrorist activity around the world. "The potential security ramifications of global climate change should be serving as catalysts for cooperation and change," the officers concluded. "Instead, climate change impacts are already accelerating instability in vulnerable areas of the world and are serving as catalysts for conflict." In its latest *Quadrennial Defense Review*, the Department of Defense warns, "The pressures caused by climate change will influence resource competition while placing additional burdens on economies, societies, and governance institutions around the world. These effects are threat multipliers that will aggravate stressors abroad such as poverty, environmental degradation, political instability, and social tensions – conditions that can enable terrorist activity and other forms of violence." The Government Accountability Office calls climate adaptation "a risk-management strategy to help protect vulnerable sectors and communities that might be affected by changes in the climate." The global reinsurance company Swiss Re concludes, "Climate adaptation is an urgent priority for national and city authorities… It is cheaper to start adapting now than to bear the costs of future disasters tomorrow." The fifth and most recent IPCC report, issued in the spring of 2014, updates the findings of climate scientists as usual, but it also describes climate change repeatedly as a risk management issue. As one IPCC expert, Stanford professor Christopher Field, notes, "The essence of dealing with climate change is not so much about identifying specific impacts at a specific time in the future; it's about managing risk."

120. *National Security Strategy* (Washington, DC: The White House, February 2015), p. 2, https://www.whitehouse.gov/sites/default/files/docs/2015_national_security_strategy.pdf.

121. *Quadrennial Defense Review 2014* (Washington, DC: Department of Defense, 2014), VI, http://www.defense.gov/pubs/2014_Quadrennial_Defense_Review.pdf.

122. L. Feldman et al., "Media 'Echo Chambers' and Climate Change," *Journal of Communication* (2014), http://environment.yale.edu/climate-communication/article/media-echo-chambers-and-climate-change.

123. Andrew Beaujon, "Survey: NPR's Listeners Best-Informed, Fox Viewers Worst-Informed," *Poynter*, May 23, 2012, http://www.poynter.org/latest-news/mediawire/174826/survey-nprs-listeners-best-informed-fox-news-viewers-worst-informed.

124. Dan Bernhardt, Stefan Krassa, and Mattias Polborn. "Political Polarization and the Electoral Effects of Media Bias," *Journal of Public Economics*, 92 (2007): 1092–1104, http://www.econ.uiuc.edu/~skrasa/media_bias_december_2007.pdf.

125. Ibid.

126. Ibid.

127. "SPJ Code of Ethics," Society of Professional Journalists, last modified September 6, 2014, http://www.spj.org/ethicscode.asp.

128. Cameron Davis, "The Media's Climate Change Misinformation Campaign," *The Triple Helix Online* (blog), September 20, 2014, http://triplehelixblog. com/2014/09/the-medias-climate-change-misinformation-campaign. These are among several criticisms of media coverage on climate and energy issues and how it contributes to public misinformation or misinterpretation of climate science.

129. Paul Thornton, "On Letters from Climate-Change Deniers," *LA Times*, October 8, 2013, http://www.latimes.com/opinion/opinion-la/la-ol-climate-change-letters-20131008-story.html#axzz30rnARope.

130. In a 6–3 decision in 2012, the US Supreme Court struck down a federal law called the Stolen Valor Act, under which a California man had been convicted of falsely claiming he had be awarded the Medal of Honor. The court found that while the lie was "pathetic," it was protected speech.

131. Christophe McGlade and Paul Ekins, "The Geographical Distribution of Fossil Fuels Unused When Limiting Global Warming to 2°C," *Nature* 517 (January 8, 2015): 187–190, http://www.nature.com/nature/journal/v517/n7533/full/nature14016.html. This paper, published in the journal *Nature* in January 2015, concludes that a third of global oil reserves, half of gas reserves, and 80% of coal reserves "should remain unused from 2010 to 2050" to keep global warming to no more than 2°C above preindustrial levels, the target agreed on by the international community to give the world an even chance of avoiding the worst consequences of warming.

132. Henry M. Paulson Jr., "The Coming Climate Crash: Lessons for Climate Change in the 2008 Recession," *New York Times*, June 21, 2014, http://www.nytimes. com/2014/06/22/opinion/sunday/lessons-for-climate-change-in-the-2008-recession.html?_r=0. Former treasury secretary Henry Paulson warned of this in June 2014, writing, "We're staring down a climate bubble that poses enormous risks to both our environment and economy. The warning signs are clear and growing more urgent as the risks go unchecked."

133. *Energy and Carbon – Managing the Risks* (ExxonMobil, 2014), http://cdn. exxonmobil.com/~/media/Files/Other/2014/Report%20-%20Energy%20and%20 Carbon%20-%20Managing%20the%20Risks.pdf.

134. "Energy Facts Every American Needs to Know," Plant Fossils of West Virginia, last modified February 20, 2010, http://www.geocraft.com/WVFossils/WhatNew.html.

135. Daily Comp. Pres. Docs., 2012 DCPD No. 000048, http://www.gpo.gov/fdsys/pkg/ DCPD-201200048/pdf/DCPD-201200048.pdf. See link for the complete 2012 State of the Union Address.

136. Daily Comp. Pres. Docs., 2014 DCPD No. 000050, http://www.gpo.gov/fdsys/pkg/ DCPD-201400050/pdf/DCPD-201400050.pdf. See link for the complete 2014 State of the Union Address.

137. One assumption among fossil energy advocates is that new technology – for example, carbon capture and sequestration (CCS) – will minimize or eliminate greenhouse gas emissions from carbon fuels. CCS is one of the technical fixes I describe later in this chapter, a solution whose viability remains to be seen.

138. Christopher Helman, "Itemizing the Oil Bust: 75,000 Layoffs and Count-ing," *Forbes*, March 18, 2015, http://www.forbes.com/sites/christopherhel-man/2015/03/16/oil-layoffs-itemized-75000-and-counting/.

139. "The Origins of the Financial Crisis: Crash Course," *The Economist*, September 7, 2013, http://www.economist.com/news/schoolsbrief/21584534-effects-financial-crisis-are-still-being-felt-five-years-article.

140. "Over the last five years, wind and solar PV have become increasingly cost-competitive with conventional generation technologies, on an unsubsi-dized basis, in light of material declines in the pricing of system components (e.g., panels, inverters, racking, turbines, etc.), and dramatic improvements in efficiency, among other factors," Lazard reports. *Lazard's Levelized Cost of Energy Analysis – Version 8.0* (Lazard, September 2014), http://www.lazard.com/PDF/Levelized%20Cost%20of%20Energy%20-%20Version%208.0.pdf.

141. LCOE is used by the utility industry and energy analysts to compare the costs of different options for producing electricity. It considers all of an energy system's anticipated lifetime costs including construction, financing, fuel, maintenance, taxes, insurance, and incentives. The costs are then divided by the system's lifetime expected power output (kWh). Among other things, this method allows fairer comparisons between renewable energy resources that have no fuel costs and fossil resources that do by including the fact that renewable energy systems require energy for manufacture, transport, installation, and so on.

142. Peter Sopher, "5 Reasons the Future of Clean Energy Investing Looks Stronger Than Ever," *Forbes*, January 28, 2015, http://www.forbes.com/sites/edfenergyex-change/2015/01/28/5-reasons-the-future-of-clean-energy-investing-looks-stron-ger-than-ever.

143. Benjamin Hulac, "Oil and Gas CEOs Call for Carbon Price as Exxon, Chevron Outline Climate Strategy," *E&E News*, June 2, 2015, http://www.eenews.net/cli-matewire/stories/1060019472. In June 2015, the CEOs of six of the world's largest energy companies called for national and regional carbon pricing. "For us to do more (to meet the world's energy demand), we need governments across the world to provide us with clear, stable, long-term ambitious policy frame-works," the CEOs wrote in a letter to Christiana Figueres, executive secretary of the UN Framework Convention on Climate Change. *Energy and Carbon – Managing the Risks* (ExxonMobil, 2014), p. 18, http://cdn.exxonmobil.com/~/media/Files/Other/2014/Report%20-%20Energy%20and%20Carbon%20-%20Managing%20the%20Risks.pdf. In an assessment of its climate risks, ExxonMobil says it "advocates an approach that ensures a uniform and predictable cost of carbon; allows market prices to drive solutions; maximizes transparency to stake-holders; reduces administrative complexity; promotes global participation; and is easily adjusted to future developments in climate science and policy impacts. We continue to believe a revenue-neutral carbon tax is better able to accom-modate these key criteria than alternatives such as cap-and-trade."

144. Michael Taylor, *Renewable Power Generation Costs in 2014* (IRENA, January 2015), http://www.irena.org/menu/index.aspx?mnu=Subcat&PriMenuID=36&-CatID=141&SubcatID=494.

145. *Renewable Portfolio Standard Policies* (Raleigh, NC: DSIRE, June 2015), http://ncsolarcen-prod.s3.amazonaws.com/wp-content/uploads/2014/11/Renew-able-Portfolio-Standards.pdf.

146. Peter Sopher, "5 Reasons the Future of Clean Energy Investing Looks Stronger Than Ever," *Forbes*, January 28, 2015, http://www.forbes.com/sites/edfenergyexchange/2015/01/28/5-reasons-the-future-of-clean-energy-investing-looks-stronger-than-ever.

147. Mark Fulton and Reid Capalino, *Investing in the Clean Trillion: Closing the Clean Energy Investment Gap* (CERES, January 2014), http://www.ceres.org/resources/reports/investing-in-the-clean-trillion-closing-the-clean-energy-investment-gap-executive-summary.

148. "Green Climate Fund" (home page), last modified 2015, http://news.gcfund.org.

149. *A World Awash in Money: Capital Trends through 2020* (Bain & Company, 2012), http://www.bain.com/images/bain_report_a_world_awash_in_money.pdf.

=. Alex Morales, "Fossil Fuels with $550 Billion Subsidies Hurt Renewables," *Bloomberg Business*, November 11, 2014, http://www.bloomberg.com/news/2014-11-12/fossil-fuels-with-550-billion-in-subsidy-hurt-renewables.html. The subsidies are perverse incentives that encourage carbon emissions. They also are ineffective. The IEA reports that 43% of the money goes to the richest 20% of households. A number of experts have concluded that direct cash payments to low-income consumers would be better.

151. Benedict Clements et al., "Energy Subsidy Reform: Lessons and Implications" (press release, IMF, January 2013), https://www.imf.org/external/np/sec/pr/2013/pr1393.htm.

152. See David Orr's advocacy of systems thinking in Chapter 9.

153. Joel Kirkland, "At Cushing Oil Hub, Emergency Drill Foretells Hard Reality in Tornado Alley," *E&E News*, May 28, 2013, http://www.eenews.net/energywire/stories/1059981838.

154. *Department of Energy Loan Guarantees: $8 Billion Allocated for Fossil Fuel Projects* (Washington, DC: Taxpayers for Common Sense, August 2013), http://www.taxpayer.net/library/article/department-of-energy-loan-guarantees-8-billion-allocated-for-fossil-fuel-pr.

155. Chris Berdik, "From the Labs: Six Geoengineering Ideas," the *Boston Globe*, October 20, 2013, http://www.bostonglobe.com/magazine/2013/10/19/geoengineering-schemes-from-cloud-brightening-space-mirrors/Dw9xmqdbtdV8cGv4K-93cJN/story.html.

156. Brian Angliss, "Three New Studies Illustrate Significant Risks and Complications with Geoengineering Climate," *Skeptical Science*, August 5, 2010, http://www.skepticalscience.com/Three-studies-illustrate-significant-risks-complications-geo-engineering-climate.html.

157. *2013 Report Card for America's Infrastructure* (Reston, VA: American Society of Civil Engineers, 2013), http://www.infrastructurereportcard.org/a/#p/energy/conditions-and-capacity. The stranded assets issue also exists at the global level. The International Institute for Applied Systems Analysis in Australia figures that nearly 40% of the world's investments in coal power plants over the next 40 years would become stranded if nations do not soon agree on a plan to limit carbon emissions. "Delaying cclimate action) encourages utilities to build more coal-fired power plants in the near term," the institute says. "Then, when policies are finally introduced, we have to phase out coal even more quickly and more investments go to waste."

158. *Quadrennial Energy Review* (Washington, DC: Department of Energy, April 2015), http://energy.gov/epsa/quadrennial-energy-review-qer.

159. *Clean Power Plan Proposal* (Washington, DC: Environmental Protection Agency, 2014), http://111d.naseo.org/Data/Sites/5/media/clean-power-plan-overview. pdf. EPA points out that the benefits of the power plant rule will far outweigh its costs. Public health and climate benefits will range from $55 billion to $93 billion in 2030, EPA estimates, while the cost of complying with the new standards will be $7.3 billion to $8.8 billion in 2030.

160. Steven Groves, "The 'Kyoto II' Climate Change Treaty: Implications for American Sovereignty," Heritage Foundation, November 17, 2009, http://www.heritage. org/research/reports/2009/11/the-kyoto-ii-climate-change-treaty-implica-tions-for-american-sovereignty.

161. *The Climate Has Changed* (We Mean Business, 2014), http://www.wemeanbusi-nesscoalition.org/sites/default/files/The%20Climate%20Has%20Changed_1.pdf.

162. I will use "full-cost accounting" and "life-cycle costing" more or less inter-changeably here. More precisely, life-cycle costing refers to the costs and ben-efits of a product or resource from cradle to grave, while full-cost accounting refers to quantifying all of the costs, internal and external, direct and indirect.

163. "About Eco Machines," John Todd Ecological Design, last modified 2012, http://www.toddecological.com/eco-machines/.

164. "FSA Pollinator Information," Farm Service Agency, last modified August 23, 2013, http://www.apfo.usda.gov/FSA/webapp?area=home&subject=ecpa&topic=n-ra-pl.

165. The urban heat-island effect refers to the fact that urban areas are usually sever-al degrees warmer than surrounding countryside because of asphalt and other dark-colored surfaces along with fewer trees. Those few degrees of temperature difference exacerbate heat waves, which now cause more deaths in the United States than any other weather event.

166. Robert Costanza et al., "The Value of the World's Ecosystem Services and Natural Capital," *Nature* 387 (May 1997): 253–260, http://www.esd.ornl.gov/benefits_conference/nature_paper.pdf.

167. Robert Costanza et al., *Valuing Ecosystem Services: Toward Better Environmen-tal Decision-Making* (Washington, DC: National Academies Press, 2004), p. 181, http://esanalysis.colmex.mx/Sorted%20Papers/2010/2010%20USA%20-3F%20 Econ%203.pdf.

168. The Costanza team put the total value at between $16 trillion and $54 trillion, and used the mean value of $33 trillion in the report. They evaluated seventeen ecosystem services from wetlands, forests, grasslands, estuaries, and other ma-rine and terrestrial systems.

169. Robert Costanza et al., "Changes in the Global Value of Ecosystem Service," *Global Environmental Change* 26 (May 2014): 152–158, http://www.sciencedi-rect.com/science/article/pii/S0959378014000685.

170. The National Academy of Sciences is a nongovernment not-for-profit research organization established by Congress to advise the federal government.

171. *Hidden Costs of Energy: Unpriced Consequences of Energy Production and Use* (Washington, DC: The National Academies Press, 2010), http://www8.nation-alacademies.org/onpinews/newsitem.aspx?RecordID=12794.

172. "Social Cost of Carbon," US Environmental Protection Agency, last modified No-vember 26, 2013, http://www.epa.gov/climatechange/EPAactivities/economics/scc.html.

173. Ibid.

174. Ibid.

175. The National Environmental Policy Act of 1970 requires federal agencies to evaluate the environmental impacts of their actions. At this writing in early 2015, CEQ still had not finalized the guidance.

176. Paul R. Epstein et al., "Full Cost Accounting for the Life Cycle of Coal," *Annals of the New York Academy of Sciences* (February 2011): 73–98, http://onlinelibrary. wiley.com/doi/10.1111/j.1749-6632.2010.05890.x/full. The late Dr. Paul Epstein of the Harvard Medical School, chief author of the report, said his estimate still did not represent the full societal and environmental burden of coal. "In quantifying the damages," he wrote, "we have omitted the impacts of toxic chemicals and heavy metals on ecological systems and diverse plants and animals; some ill-health endpoints (morbidity) aside from mortality related to air pollutants released through coal combustion that are still not captured; the direct risks and hazards posed by coal sludge, coal slurry, and coal waste impoundments; the full contributions of nitrogen deposition to eutrophication of fresh and coastal sea water; the prolonged impacts of acid rain and acid mine drainage; many of the long-term impacts on the physical and mental health of those living in coal-field regions and nearby MTR sites; some of the health impacts and climate forcing due to increased tropospheric ozone formation; and the full assessment of impacts due to an increasingly unstable climate." For more information on any of these additional pollutants created by the combustion of coal please visit SourceWatch, The Center for Media and Democracy, last modified June 12, 2015, http://www.sourcewatch.org/index.php/SourceWatch.

177. "Current Issues and Trends," US Energy Information Administration, last modified June 25, 2015, http://www.eia.gov/electricity/?t=epmt_5_3.

178. Paul R. Epstein et al., "Full Cost Accounting for the Life Cycle of Coal," *Annals of the New York Academy of Sciences* (February 2011): 73–98, http://onlinelibrary. wiley.com/doi/10.1111/j.1749-6632.2010.05890.x/full.

179. "Making Nature's Values Visible," The Economics of Ecosystems and Biodiversity, http://www.teebweb.org/about/.

180. "TEEB Mainstreaming the Economics of Nature," Ecosystem Marketplace, last modified 2014, http://www.ecosystemmarketplace.com/pages/dynamic/resources.library.page.php?page_id=7784&section=biodiversity_market&eod=1.

181. For example, someone who does not own a car and only rides a bike can suffer from air pollution from vehicles, while those who buy and burn gasoline may not. If the principle of "polluter pays" were applied, the indirect costs of gasoline would be reflected in its price.

182. Costs that are not reflected in the price of fuel and are passed on to other parts of society are called "indirect" or "external" costs. For example, air pollution and associated health problems are well-known consequences of coal-fired power plants, but the price we pay for electricity from those plants doesn't include costs like these.

183. Andrew Blackman, "Can Money Buy You Happiness?" *Wall Street Journal*, November 10, 2014, http://www.wsj.com/articles/can-money-buy-happiness-heres-what-science-has-to-say-1415569538. There has been interesting recent research on the age-old question of whether money can buy happiness. The answer appears to be both yes and no, depending on how money is spent. The

ability to purchase material goods, for example, leads to "hedonic adaptation," a fancy way of saying that people get bored with it. Susan Adams, "Money Does Buy Happiness, Says New Study," *Forbes*, May 10, 2013, http://www.forbes.com/sites/susanadams/2013/05/10/money-does-buy-happiness-says-new-study. Other studies have shown that people in the United States appear to be no happier than people in less-developed nations. The point here is that happiness is derived from many sources beyond money and cannot be fully measured by national GDP.

184. Robert Costanza et al., "A Short History of GDP: Moving Towards Better Measurements of Human Well-Being," *Solutions for a Sustainable and Desirable Future* 5, 1 (June 2014): 91–97, http://www.thesolutionsjournal.org/node/237164?page=1 6%2C0%2C0%2C0%2C0%2C0. Review this source for a detailed explanation of the history and purpose of the GDP and a summary of alternative indicators of genuine progress.

185. Robert F. Kennedy, "Robert F. Kennedy Challenges Gross Domestic Product," YouTube video, posted by ipyramid, 2:11, September 11, 2008, https://www.youtube.com/watch?v=77IdKFqXbUY.

186. Costanza et al. "Development: Time to Leave GDP Behind," *Nature* 505 (January 15, 2014): 283–285, http://www.nature.com/news/development-time-to-leave-gdp-behind-1.14499#/supplementary-information. See the article and its supplemental information for a more complete listing of international national indicators of well-being.

187. Sara Gates, "World Happiness Report 2013 Ranks Happiest Countries around Globe," *Huffington Post*, September 9, 2013, http://www.huffingtonpost.com/2013/09/09/world-happiness-report-happiest-countries_n_3894041.html.

188. According to their website, "The Happy Planet Index (HPI) is the Leading Global Measure of Sustainable Well-Being," Happy Planet Index, last modified 2015, http://www.happyplanetindex.org/about/.

189. Michel E. Porter, *Social Progress Index 2013* (Washington DC: Social Progress Imperative, 2013), http://www.socialprogressimperative.org/system/resources/W1si-ZiIsIjiwMTMvMDQvMTAvMTgvMTUvNDQvNzk4L3NvY2lhbF9wcm9ncmVzc19pbm-RleF8yMDEzLnBkZiJdXQ/social_progress_index_2013.pdf.

190. "MDG Progress Index," Center for Global Development, last modified 2011, http://www.cgdev.org/page/mdg-progress-index-gauging-country-level-achievements.

191. "OECD Better Life Index," Organization for Economic Development and Cooperation, last modified 2015, http://www.oecdbetterlifeindex.org/.

192. "Gross National Happiness Homepage," Center for Bhutan Studies, last modified 2015, http://www.grossnationalhappiness.com/.

193. Mijin Cha, *What's Missing from GDP?* (New York: Demos Explainer, January 2013).

194. Lew Daly and Sean McElwee, "Forget the GDP. Some States Have Found a Better Way to Measure Our Progress," February 3, 2014, http://www.newrepublic.com/article/116461/gpi-better-gdp-measuring-united-states-progress. Provides a February 2014 report on use of GPI. Maryland began using a Genuine Progress Indicator in 2010, becoming the first state to do so. From 2011 to 2012, the state's GPI increased 4.5%.

195. Marta Ceroni, "Beyond GDP: US States Have Adopted Genuine Progress Indicators," *Guardian*, September 23, 2014, http://www.theguardian.com/sustainable-business/2014/sep/23/genuine-progress-indicator-gdp-gpi-vermont-maryland.

196. Ibid.

197. "Social Progress Index 2015," Social Progress Imperative, last modified 2015, http://www.socialprogressimperative.org/.

198. Anthony B. Atkinson, Thomas Piketty, and Emmanuel Saez, "Top Incomes in the Long Run of History," *Journal of Economic Literature* 49, 1 (2011): 3–71, http://eml.berkeley.edu/~saez/atkinson-piketty-saezJEL10.pdf.

199. Robert Costanza et al., "A Short History of GDP: Moving Towards Better Measurements of Human Well-Being," *Solutions for a Sustainable and Desirable Future* 5, 1 (June 2014): 91–97, http://www.thesolutionsjournal.org/node/237164?page=16%2C0%2C0%2C0%2C0%2C0.

200. *Stern Review Report on the Economics of Climate Change* (UK National Archives, 2005), http://webarchive.nationalarchives.Governoruk/20100407172811/, http://www.hm-treasury.Governoruk/stern_review_report.htm.

201. *National Energy Policy Inventory of Major Federal Energy Programs and Status of Policy Recommendations* (Washington, DC: US Government Accountability Office, June 2005), http://www.gao.gov/new.items/d05379.pdf.

202. Gregory McNamee, "Mark Twain on the Weather," *Encyclopedia Britannica Blog*, April 21, 2010, http://blogs.britannica.com/2010/04/mark-twain-on-the-weather/. This quote often is attributed to Mark Twain, but others attribute it to a friend of his, Charles Dudley Warner.

203. "2030 Framework for Climate and Energy Policies," European Commission, last modified July 15, 2015, http://ec.europa.eu/clima/policies/2030/index_en.htm. Several other nations and regions have energy technology and/or carbon reduction roadmaps. Members of the European Union have developed a plan to reduce greenhouse gas emission by at least 40% by 2030 compared to 1990. "Technology Roadmaps," International Energy Agency, last modified 2015, https://www.iea.org/roadmaps. In response to interest from several nations, the International Energy Agency has developed a collection of technology roadmaps designed to achieve a 50% reduction in energy-related CO_2 emissions by 2050.

204. "Energy and Environment," the CATO Institute, http://www.cato.org/research/energy-environment.

205. We Believe in America: 2012 Republican Platform (The Republican Party, 2012), p. 16, https://cdn.gop.com/docs/2012GOPPlatform.pdf.

206. The Institute for the Analysis of Global Security writes, "Oil and terrorism are entangled. If not for the West's oil money, most Gulf states would not have had the wealth that allowed them to invest so much in arms procurement and sponsor terrorist organizations." "Fueling Terror," Institute for Analysis of Global Security, last modified 2004, http://www.iags.org/fuelingterror.html. Other analysts have come to the same conclusion.

207. "California Electricity Crisis," *Wikipedia*, last modified June 8, 2015, https://en.wikipedia.org/wiki/California_electricity_crisis. As described on *Wikipedia*, "The California electricity crisis, also known as the Western US Energy Crisis of 2000 and 2001, was a situation in which the state of California had a shortage

of electricity supply caused by market manipulations, illegal shutdowns of pipelines by the Texas energy consortium Enron, and capped retail electricity prices. The state suffered from multiple large-scale blackouts, one of the state's largest energy companies collapsed, and the economic fall-out greatly harmed Governor Gray Davis's standing."

208. Doug Koplow, *Subsidies in the US Energy Sector: Magnitude, Causes, and Options for Reform* (Cambridge, MA: Earth Track, Inc., November 2006), http://www.earthtrack.net/files/legacy_library/SubsidyReformOptions.pdf. For an exploration of the political forces behind energy subsidies.

209. There are many other ways, both direct and indirect, that the federal government favors fossil energy production. In addition, some of the tax code's major incentives for private investment in energy resources, among them Master Limited Partnerships, apply to fossil energy but not to renewable energy. While many oil and gas subsidies do not require periodic reauthorization by Congress, renewable energy subsidies typically do. As a result, federal support for solar and wind energy has been on-again, off-again, with Congress allowing the subsidies to expire before reauthorizing them again. The starts and stops have produced spasmodic progress for renewable energy resources, especially the wind industry. A precise number for energy subsidies is difficult to identify for several reasons.

210. Jeff Donn, "Aging Nukes: A Four-Part Investigative Series," Associated Press, 2011, http://www.ap.org/company/awards/aging-nukes.

211. For a detailed description of government subsidies for nuclear power, see Doug Koplow, *Nuclear Power: Still Not Viable without Subsidies* (Cambridge, MA: Union of Concerned Scientists, February 2011), http://www.ucsusa.org/sites/default/files/legacy/assets/documents/nuclear_power/nuclear_subsidies_report.pdf.

212. Ibid. The federal government's (taxpayer) liability is established in the Price-Anderson Act of 1957, which applies to nonmilitary nuclear facilities built in the United States prior to 2026. In effect, the nuclear power industry is responsible for damage claims from a nuclear accident, up to about $13 billion. Claims above that amount would be the responsibility of taxpayers. For other examples of public subsidies for the industry, see this source.

213. James Bovard, *Archer Daniels Midland: A Case Study In Corporate Welfare* (CATO Policy Analysis no. 241, September 26, 1995), http://www.cato.org/pubs/pas/pa-241.html.

214. Alternatives include natural gas and electricity, depending on how they are produced. Cellulosic ethanol, also called second-generation ethanol, is a variety made from wood, grasses, and inedible crop wastes rather than food crops. As a result, it requires less energy and water and produces fewer emissions from farm equipment. It has not yet been widely commercialized, although large corporations such as DuPont as well as the Department of Energy are involved in research and development.

215. National Energy Policy Plan, 42 U.S.C. §7321 (2015), http://uscode.house.gov/view.xhtml?req=(title:42%20section:7321%20edition:prelim).

216. Ibid.

217. Alaine Ginocchio, Esq., *The Boundaries of Executive Authority: An Evaluation of Priority Proposals from the Presidential Climate Action Plan* (Center for Environment and Energy Security, July 2008), p. 8, http://www.climateactionproject.com/docs/Executive_CEES_PCAP_II_Report_Jul_17.pdf.

218. Jeffrey Logan and Ted L. James, *A Comparative Review of a Dozen National Energy Plans: Focus on Renewable and Efficient Energy* (Golden, CO: National Renewable Energy Laboratory, March 2009), http://www.nrel.gov/docs/fy09osti/45046.pdf. The Department of Energy's National Renewable Energy Laboratory reported in March 2009, only three months after President Obama took office, that the new administration already had received energy, environmental, and economic recovery plans from dozens of organizations.

219. Kenneth R. Harney, "A Cut-Off of the Mortgage Interest Deduction for Big Houses?" *Realty Times*, August 26, 2007, http://realtytimes.com/consumeradvice/homeownersadvice1/item/6577-20070827_interestdeduct.

220. GE Grid Resiliency Survey (Atlanta, GA: General Electric, August 14, 2014), http://www.gedigitalenergy.com/press/gepress/grid-resiliency-survey.htm. In August 2014, respondents told General Electric they were willing to pay $10 more each month on their electric bills in exchange for a reliable grid. Lisa Lerer, "Poll: Americans Would Pay More for Energy to Curb Climate Change" (Bloomberg), *Houston Chronicle*, June 11, 2014, http://fuelfix.com/blog/2014/06/11/poll-americans-would-pay-more-for-energy-to-curb-climate-change. Sixty-two percent of Americans are willing to pay the costs of combatting climate change, according to a poll in June 2014. Amy Westervelt, "Study Finds Americans Willing to Pay More for Water," *Forbes*, November 29, 2012, http://www.forbes.com/sites/amywestervelt/2012/11/29/study-finds-americans-willing-to-pay-more-for-water. In 2012, a poll sponsored by the water technology firm Xylem found that 75% of Americans were willing to pay more for energy-conserving water systems, and 70% were willing to payer higher prices for water if it meant that all Americans had access to clean water.

221. Jeff Goodell, BrainyQuote.com, Xplore Inc., 2015, http://www.brainyquote.com/quotes/authors/j/jeff_goodell.html.

222. Matthew Yglesias, "Earl Blumenauer's Carbon Audit," *ThinkProgress*, December 11, 2009, http://thinkprogress.org/yglesias/2009/12/11/195414/earl-blumenauers-carbon-audit/.

223. Nordhaus et al., *Effects of U.S. Tax Policy on Greenhouse Gas Emissions*, (Washington, DC: National Academies Press, 2013), pp. 1–182, http://www.nap.edu/openbook.php?record_id=18299.

224. It is important to note that reducing the growth of emissions and reducing emissions are different things. The Obama administration's goal is an 80% reduction from 2005 emissions by mid-century.

225. *Oil and Gas Resources: Actions Needed for Interior to Better Ensure a Fair Return* (Washington, DC: US Government Accountability Office, December 2013), http://www.gao.gov/assets/660/659515.pdf. In 2012, oil and gas companies reportedly received more than $66 billion from the sale of fuels produced on public lands, while the Department of Interior collected about $9.7 billion in royalties and other payments.

226. Ibid.

227. "Interior Department Seeks Public Dialogue on Reform of Federal Onshore Oil and Gas Regulations" (press release, Department of the Interior, April 17, 2015), http://www.blm.gov/wo/st/en/info/newsroom/2015/april/interior_department.html. In April 2015, the Department of Interior finally issued a notice that it would begin work on rules that would allow it to increase royalty fees. The department said it currently lacks the flexibility to adjust the fees.

228. *Federal Oil and Gas Leases: Opportunities Exist to Capture Vented and Flared Natural Gas, Which Would Increase Royalty Payments and Reduce Greenhouse Gases* (Washington, DC: US Government Accountability Office, November 29, 2010), http://www.gao.gov/products/GAO-11-34. GAO's estimate did not include venting and flaring at offshore production sites. Its estimate was based on data from the EPA and technology vendors that about 40% of the flared and vented gas could be captured cost effectively with currently available technologies.

229. Nordhaus et al., *Effects of U.S. Tax Policy on Greenhouse Gas Emissions*, (Washington, DC: National Academies Press, 2013), pp. 1–182, http://www.nap.edu/openbook.php?record_id=18299.

230. *Federal Financial Support for the Development and Production of Fuels and Energy Technologies* (Washington, DC: Congressional Budget Office, March 2012), p. 9, http://www.cbo.gov/sites/default/files/03-06-FuelsandEnergy_Brief.pdf.

231. Ibid.

232. Koplow is the founder of Earth Track, a Massachusetts-based organization that "works to make government subsidies that harm the environment easier to see, value and eliminate," http://www.earthtrack.net.

233. Doug Koplow, *Subsidies in the US Energy Sector: Magnitude, Causes, and Options for Reform* (Cambridge, MA: Earth Track, Inc., November 2006), http://www.earthtrack.net/files/legacy_library/SubsidyReformOptions.pdf.

234. Maura Allaire and Stephen P. A. Brown, *U.S. Energy Subsidies: Effects on Energy Markets and Carbon Dioxide Emissions* (Philadelphia: The Pew Charitable Trusts, August 2012), http://www.pewtrusts.org/~/media/legacy/uploadedfiles/wwwpewtrustsorg/reports/fiscal_and_budget_policy/EnergySubsidiesFINALpdf.pdf.

235. By Pew's reckoning, there was a shift in subsidies during the study period. In 2005, federal subsidies that increased carbon emissions totaled $9.12 billion compared to $3.4 billion to reduce carbon emissions.

236. Doug Koplow, *Subsidies in the US Energy Sector: Magnitude, Causes, and Options for Reform* (Cambridge, MA: Earth Track, Inc., November 2006), http://www.earthtrack.net/files/legacy_library/SubsidyReformOptions.pdf. Koplow estimated in 2006 that energy subsidies totaled $74 billion each year in the United States, with 49% going to oil, gas, and coal, while the remainder was split between nuclear power, ethanol, conservation, and other renewable resources.

237. William S. Becker, "The Ideal Climate Deal," *Huffington Post*, April 15, 2015, http://www.huffingtonpost.com/william-s-becker/todd-sterns-mission-impos_b_6670212.html.

238. Laura Merrill et al., *Fossil-Fuel Subsidies and Climate Change Options for Policy-makers within Their Intended Nationally Determined Contributions* (Copenhagen, Denmark: Nordic Council of Ministers and the International Institute for Sustainable Development, 2015), http://www.iisd.org/gsi/sites/default/files/FFS_Climate.pdf.

239. David Coady et al., *How Large Are Global Energy Subsidies?* (International Monetary Fund, May 2015), http://www.imf.org/external/pubs/ft/survey/so/2015/new070215a.htm.

240. Damian Carrington, "G20 Countries Pay over $1,000 per Citizen in Fossil Fuel Subsidies, Says IMF," *Guardian*, August 4, 2015, http://www.theguardian.com/environment/2015/aug/04/g20-countries-pay-over-1000-per-citizen-in-fossil-fuel-subsidies-say-imf.

241. "World Energy Outlook," International Energy Agency, January 17, 2012, http://www.worldenergyoutlook.org/pressmedia/quotes/37/.

242. For a more detailed explanation of the challenges involved in tracking international energy subsidies, along with recommendations for improvement, see Doug Koplow, "Subsidies to Energy: A Review of Current Estimates and Estimation Challenges" (presentation, International Workshop on Fossil Energy Subsidy Reform, Beijing, China, September 4, 2014), http://earthtrack.net/files/uploaded_files/Sep14%20Beijing%20meeting_Koplow%20slides%20final.pdf.

243. "World Needs $48 Trillion in Investment to Meet Its Energy Needs to 2035" (press release, International Energy Agency, June 3, 2014), https://www.iea.org/newsroomandevents/pressreleases/2014/june/world-needs-48-trillion-in-investment-to-meet-its-energy-needs-to-2035.html.

244. David Coady et al., IMF Working Paper: How Large Are Global Energy Subsidies? (International Monetary Fund, May 2015), https://www.imf.org/external/pubs/ft/wp/2015/wp15105.pdf.

245. "Energy Subsidies," International Energy Agency, last modified 2015, http://www.worldenergyoutlook.org/resources/energysubsidies.

246. "Fossil Fuel Subsidies," Global Subsidies Initiative, last modified 2015, https://www.iisd.org/gsi/fossil-fuel-subsidies.

247. Benedict Clements and Vitor Gaspar, "Act Local, Solve Global: The $5.3 Trillion Energy Subsidy Problem," IMF Direct (blog), May 18, 2015, http://blog-imfdirect.imf.org/2015/05/18/act-local-solve-global-the-5-3-trillion-energy-subsidy-problem. The IMF says the $5.3 trillion is the difference between what consumers pay for energy and its true costs to society and the environment, including global warming, air pollution, traffic congestion and accidents, road damage, and other expenses typically born by local populations. David Coady et al., IMF Working Paper: How Large Are Global Energy Subsidies? (International Monetary Fund, May 2015), https://www.imf.org/external/pubs/ft/wp/2015/wp15105.pdf. Coal is the biggest beneficiary of these indirect subsidies because of its high environmental damage and because "no country imposes meaningful excises on its consumption."

248. David Coady et al., IMF Working Paper: How Large Are Global Energy Subsidies? (International Monetary Fund, May 2015), 7, http://www.imf.org/external/pubs/ft/wp/2015/wp15105.pdf.

249. This is a net calculation that accounts for higher energy costs for consumers. It amounts to 2.2% of global GDP.

250. "World Energy Investment Outlook 2014 Factsheet Overview," International Energy Agency, https://www.iea.org/media/140603_WEOinvestment_Factsheets.pdf.

251. "Climate, Environment, and the IMF: Fact Sheet," The International Monetary Fund, last modified April 9, 2015, http://www.imf.org/external/np/exr/facts/enviro.htm.

252. The EIA reported in 2014 that nations were investing more than $1 trillion annually to extract, transport, and refine fossil fuels and to build fossil fuel power plants, https://www.iea.org/media/140603_WEOinvestment_Factsheets.pdf.

253. "The Nine Planetary Boundaries," Stockholm Resilience Centre, last modified January 22, 2015, http://wwwstockholmresilience.org/21/research/research-programmes/planetary-boundaries/planetary-boundaries/about-the-research/the-nine-planetary-boundaries.html. As I mentioned in Chapter 4, international scientists have identified nine planetary boundaries we cannot cross without major damage to nature and to ourselves.

254. Ronald Regan, "President Regan's Remarks Following the Loss of the Space Shuttle *Challenger* and Her Crew," NASA archive, broadcast, 5 p.m. EST, January 28, 1986, http://www.nasa.gov/audience/fo, rmedia/speeches/reagan_challenger.html. This quote from aviator and poet John Gillespie Magee Jr. is best known today because President Ronald Reagan used it in 1986 in his emotional eulogy for the crew killed in the space shuttle *Challenger* disaster. The actual passages from Magee's sonnet "High Flight" were, "Oh! I have slipped the surly bonds of earth… Put out my hand and touched the face of God." Magee, who served in the Royal Canadian Air Force, died in a mid-air collision at the age of nineteen. "John Gillespie Magee, Jr.," *Wikipedia*, last modified August 11, 2015, https://en.wikipedia.org/wiki/John_Gillespie_Magee,_Jr.

255. "Understanding Global Warming Potentials," US Environmental Protection Agency, last modified July 21, 2015, http://www.epa.gov/climatechange/ghgemissions/gwps.html. EPA expresses the impact of each greenhouse gas as Global Warming Potential (GWP), the amount of energy one ton of a gas will absorb over time, compared to CO_2. The higher the GWP, the more a gas warms the Earth. In its role as a baseline, CO_2 has a GWP of 1. Methane's GWP is 28–36 over 100 years; nitrous oxide remains in the atmosphere for more than a century on average, and has a GWP of 265–298. Fluorocarbons have GWPs in the thousands and tens of thousands, trapping substantially more heat than CO_2 for a given amount of mass.

256. For a more detailed explanation of thermal inertia, see Alan Marshall, "Climate Change: The 40 Year Delay Between Cause and Effect," *Skeptical Science*, September 22, 2010, http://www.skepticalscience.com/Climate-Change-The-40-Year-Delay-Between-Cause-and-Effect.html. This range was estimated by James Hansen, formerly the chief climate scientist at NASA.

257. David Wogan, "U.S. Energy Transitions in One Graph," *Plugged In* (blog), *Scientific American*, July 8, 2013, http://blogs.scientificamerican.com/plugged-in/u-s-energy-transitions-in-one-graph.

258. Ibid.

259. Eric Holthaus, "The Point of No Return: Climate Change Nightmares Are Already Here," *Rolling Stone*, August 5, 2015, http://www.rollingstone.com/politics/news/the-point-of-no-return-climate-change-nightmares-are-already-here-20150805. This article reports on several other serious impacts under way, including damages to oceans.

260. "Dr. Silvia Earle: One Big Ocean," Climate One, last modified 2015, http://climateone.org/events/dr-sylvia-earle-one-big-ocean.

261. Phyllis Cuttino, *Power Shifts: Emerging Clean Energy Markets* (Philadelphia: The PEW Charitable Trusts, May 2015), http://www.pewtrusts.org/~/media/Assets/2015/05/Emerging-Markets-Report_WEB.pdf.

262. "Issues and Policies: Photovoltaic (Solar Electric)," Solar Energy Industries Association, http://www.seia.org/policy/solar-technology/photovoltaic-solar-electric. Three researchers at Bell Laboratories are credited with making the world's first photovoltaic cell in 1954.

263. Ucilia Wang, "Guess Who Are the Top 10 Solar Panel Makers in the World?" *Forbes*, December 3, 2014, http://www.forbes.com/sites/uciliawang/2014/12/03/guess-who-are-the-top-10-solar-panel-makers-in-the-world.

264. "Top 10 Wind Turbine Suppliers," Energy Digital, April 10, 2015, http://www.energydigital.com/top10/3705/Top-10-Wind-Turbine-Suppliers. The first power-

producing wind turbine was invented in 1888 in Cleveland, Ohio, by Charles F. Brush. Jake Richardson, "America's First Wind Turbine Generated Electricity In 1888," CleanTechnica, June 22, 2014, http://cleantechnica.com/2014/06/22/americas-first-wind-turbine-generated-electricity-1888.

265. Tim Fernholz, "More People around the World Have Cell Phones Than Ever Had Land-lines," Quartz, February 25, 2014, http://qz.com/179897/more-people-around-the-world-have-cell-phones-than-ever-had-land-lines. For example, the digital news service Quartz reports that fewer than 2 people in 100 have fixed telephone lines on the continent of Africa, while nearly 64 per 100 people have cell subscriptions.

266. "At Home," *The War*, directed and produced by Ken Burns and Lynn Novick (Washington, DC: Public Broadcasting Service, 2007), http://www.pbs.org/thewar/. Data drawn from the "At Home" episode in the PBS series *The War*.

267. Adam Browning, "When There Is a Huge Solar Energy Spill, It's Called 'A Nice Day.'" Vote Solar, April 12, 2012, http://votesolar.org/2012/04/12/when-there-is-a-huge-solar-energy-spill-its-called-a-nice-day/. Quote attributed to Colin Murchie from Solar City.

268. Harvey J. Kaye, *The Fight for the Four Freedoms: What Made FDR and the Greatest Generation Truly Great* (New York: Simon & Schuster, 2014).

269. Richard Howitt et al., *Preliminary Analysis: 2015 Drought Economic Impact Study* (California Department of Food and Agriculture, May 31, 2015), https://watershed.ucdavis.edu/files/biblio/2015Drought_PrelimAnalysis.pdf.

270. Tom Knudson, "California Is Drilling for Water That Fell to Earth 20,000 Years Ago," *Mother Jones*, March 13, 2015, http://www.motherjones.com/environment/2015/03/california-pumping-water-fell-earth-20000-years-ago.

271. Casey Chan, "A Texas Town Is Drinking Recycled Pee Water Because of a Drought," Gizmodo, August 6, 2011, http://gizmodo.com/5828295/a-texas-town-is-drinking-recycled-pee-water-because-of-a-drought. At its peak in 2011, the Texas drought put more than 97% of the state in water crisis. Combined with drought-connected wildfires, Texas suffered billions of dollars in damages. The drought appeared to have been broken in the spring of 2015 by weather on the other extreme – deluges of rain that caused billions of dollars in flood damage and killed more than twenty people. While the storms were attributed to El Niño, both of the weather disasters were consistent with the observations of climate scientists that global warming is turning natural weather patterns into extreme events.

272. Patrick M. Sheridan, "Water Becoming More Valuable Than Gold," CNN Money, April 24, 2014, http://money.cnn.com/2014/04/24/news/water-gold-price. The value of water is the subject of what has been called the "paradox of value." Gold and diamonds, among other things, have had higher value than water in the marketplace. Yet gold and diamonds are not essential to human survival. Water is. It appears that markets may now be resolving the paradox. Over the last decade, the S&P Global Water Index has outperformed gold and energy indices, as well as the stock market.

273. Claudia Copeland, *Energy-Water Nexus: The Water Sector's Energy Use* (Washington, DC: Congressional Research Service, January 3, 2014), 3, https://www.fas.org/sgp/crs/misc/R43200.pdf.

274. Ibid, p. 5.

275. "The Water Cycle – USGS Water Science School," US Geological Survey, last modified March 18, 2014, http://water.usgs.gov/edu/watercycle.html.

276. "Water Cooperation," United Nations Educational, Scientific, and Cultural Organization, last modified 2013, http://www.unwater.org/water-cooperation-2013/water-cooperation/facts-and-figures/en/.

277. *Environmental Outlook to 2030, Organization of Economic Cooperation and Development* (Paris: OECD, 2012), http://www.oecd.org/env/indicators-modelling-outlooks/40200582.pdf. The World Economic Forum ranked water availability worldwide as the third most serious global risk in 2014. In 2012, the 16 intelligence agencies in the US government predicted that within a decade, "many countries important to the United States will experience water problems that will increase the risk of instability and state failure, exacerbate regional tensions, and distract them from working with the United States on important policy objectives." Controlling access to water already is a military tactic in Africa. In Somalia, where a civil war has been under way for several years, the Islamist terrorist organization al-Shabaab is using "water terrorism," shutting off water supplies in cities under government control. ISIS also uses water as a weapon in the Middle East. "Isis and the Water Crisis in the Middle East," *Polemics*, December 10, 2014, http://dapolemics.com/2014/12/10/isis-and-the-water-crisis-in-the-middle-east.

278. *2013 Report Card for America's Infrastructure: Drinking Water: Conditions and Capacity* (Reston, VA: American Society of Civil Engineers, 2013), http://www.infrastructurereportcard.org/a/#p/drinking-water/conditions-and-capacity. These numbers vary from source to source. The Congressional Research Service reported in 2014 that there are about 200,000 drinking water treatment systems in the United States, including 52,000 community water systems. Claudia Copeland, *Energy-Water Nexus: The Water Sector's Energy Use* (Washington, DC: Congressional Research Service, January 3, 2014), https://www.fas.org/sgp/crs/misc/R43200.pdf.

279. "Percent Area in U.S. Drought Monitor Categories," United States Drought Monitor, last modified June 20, 2015, http://droughtmonitor.unl.edu/MapsAndData/DataTables.aspx.

280. Mike Bostock and Kevin Quealy, "Mapping the Spread of Drought Across the U.S.," *New York Times*, April 9, 2015, http://www.nytimes.com/interactive/2014/upshot/mapping-the-spread-of-drought-across-the-us.html.

281. "Tri-State Water Wars (AL, GA, FL)," Southern Environmental Law Center, last modified June 16, 2015, http://www.southernenvironment.org/cases/tri_state_water_wars_al_ga_fl.

282. Anne-Marie Fennel, *Freshwater Supply Concerns Continue, and Uncertainties Complicate Planning* (Washington, DC: Government Accountability Office, May 2014), http://www.gao.gov/assets/670/663344.pdf.

283. "Climate Change, Water, and Risk: Current Water Demands Are Not Sustainable," National Resources Defense Council, last modified July 16, 2010, http://www.nrdc.org/globalwarming/watersustainability/index.asp.

284. *Water on Tap: What You Need to Know* (Washington, DC: US Environmental Protection Agency, December 2009), http://www.epa.gov/ogwdw/wot/pdfs/book_waterontap_full.pdf. Anaya Groner, "The Politics of Drinking Water," *The Atlantic*, December 30, 2014, http://www.theatlantic.com/technology/archive/2014/12/the-politics-of-drinking-water/384081.

285. "Water Sense," US Environmental Protection Agency, last modified June 25, 2015, http://www.epa.gov/WaterSense/pubs/fixleak.html.

286. Abrahm Lustgarten, "How the West Overcounts Its Water Supplies," *New York Times*, July 16, 2015, http://www.nytimes.com/2015/07/19/opinion/sunday/how-the-west-overcounts-its-water-supplies.html?_r=0.

287. Olivia Wolfertz, "Water Main Breaks, Power Outage and a Thinning Hourglass for Federal Highway Funds," American Society of Civil Engineers, April 10, 2015, http://www.infrastructurereportcard.org/asce-news-tag/water-infrastructure.

288. *2013 Report Card for America's Infrastructure: Drinking Water: Conditions and Capacity* (Reston, VA: American Society of Civil Engineers, 2013), http://www. infrastructurereportcard.org/drinking-water.

289. "Water Efficiency Strategies," US Environmental Protection Agency, last modified September 14, 2012, http://water.epa.gov/infrastructure/sustain/wec_wp.cfm. Urban areas set acceptable range between 10 and 15%. In addition, household leaks can waste more than 1 trillion gallons annually nationwide, an amount equal to water use of 11 million homes.

290. *Buried No Longer: Confronting America's Water Infrastructure Challenge* (Denver, CO: American Water Works Association, 2011), http://www.awwa.org/ Portals/0/files/legreg/documents/BuriedNoLonger.pdf.

291. Darryl Fears, "Study Says U.S. Can't Keep Up with Loss of Wetlands," *Washington Post*, December 8, 2013, http://www.washingtonpost.com/national/health-science/study-says-us-cant-keep-up-with-loss-of-wetlands/2013/12/08/ c4801be8-5d2e-11e3-95c2-13623eb2b0e1_story.html. The Environmental Protection Agency, the US Fish and Wildlife Service, and the National Oceanic and Atmospheric Administration issued the study in 2013. Others report we have lost between 54 and 87% of all wetlands, with the majority (64–71%) of all wetlands lost occurring since 1900. Nick C. Davidson, "How Much Wetland Has the World Lost? Long-Term and Recent Trends in Global Wetland Area," *Marine and Freshwater Research* 65, 10 (September 2014): 934–941, http://dx.doi. org/10.1071/MF14173.

292. Burnell C. Fischer et al., *The 2007 Bloomington Street Tree Report: An Analysis of Demographics and Ecosystem Services* (Bloomington: Indiana University, 2007), https://bloomington.in.gov/documents/viewDocument.php?document_id=7063. For a good description of urban storm water issues and management, see the paper produced by the city of Bloomington, Indiana.

293. Larry West, "Tap Water in 42 States Contaminated by Chemicals: EWG Tap Water Probe Reveals 141 Unregulated Chemicals Flowing into U.S. Homes," About News, http://environment.about.com/od/waterpollution/a/tap_water_probe.htm. Researchers from the US Geological Survey (USGS) and the US Environmental Protection Agency (EPA) found that an astounding one-third of US water systems contain traces of at least 18 unregulated and potentially hazardous contaminants, many of which are linked to causing endocrine disruption and cancer. They included 11 perfluorinated compounds, an herbicide, 2 solvents, caffeine, an antibacterial compound, a metal, and an antidepressant. Overall, 134 chemicals, bacteria, viruses, and microbes were detected in drinking water. *Abstract Book: Society of Environmental Toxicology and Chemistry North America 34th Annual Meeting* (Annual Meeting, Nashville, TN, November 17–21, 2013), http://www.environmentalhealthnews.org/ehs/news/2013/pdf-links/SETAC-Nashville-abstract-book-1.pdf.

294. "Total Water Use in the United States, 2005," US Geological Survey, last modified March 17, 2014, http://water.usgs.gov/edu/wateruse-total.html. Overall, power plants draw more freshwater from rivers, lakes, and other surface sources than any other activity in the economy, 41% compared to 31% by the next highest use, crop irrigation.

295. "Thermoelectric Power Water Use," US Geological Survey, accessed July 16, 2015, last modified March 17, 2015, http://water.usgs.gov/edu/wupt.html.

296. Edward J. Markey, *Energy and Water: Connection and Conflict* (Washington, DC: House Natural Resources Committee, August 2012), http://democrats. naturalresources.house.gov/sites/democrats.naturalresources.house.gov/files/ documents/FactSheet_081612_final.pdf. It is important to make a distinction between water withdrawal and water consumption. There are several ways that power plants can use water for cooling. They can recirculate water in a closed-loop system, use "once-through" cooling in which water is returned to the source from which it was withdrawn, or employ dry cooling technologies. Each involves trade-offs. Dry cooling costs more. Once-through cooling withdraws as much as 100 times more water per unit of electric generation than recirculating cooling methods, while recirculating methods consume at least twice as much water as once-through cooling, according to DOE's National Renewable Energy Laboratory. Jordan Macknick et al., *A Review of Operational Water Consumption and Withdrawal Factors for Electricity Generating Technologies* (National Renewable Energy Laboratory, March 2011), http://www.nrel.gov/docs/fy11osti/50900.pdf. The US Geological Survey says that 99% of the water withdrawn by thermoelectric power plants is returned to the sources from which it was taken. The remaining 1% is consumed – that is, lost through evaporation during the cooling process. Improvements in power plant efficiency and the use of recycled or gray water are other ways that utilities can reduce their freshwater demands.

297. Ibid.

298. According to the World Nuclear Association, "Hardly any U.S. generating capacity uses dry cooling." It is less efficient than cooling with water and costs three to four times more than a recirculating wet cooling system, according to a 2009 study by the DOE. "Cooling Power Plants," World Nuclear Plants, last modified April 30, 2015, http://www.world-nuclear.org/info/Current-and-Future-Generation/Cooling-Power-Plants.

299. Tom Plant, "The Energy Collective, Water, the West, and the Clean Power Plan," The Energy Collective, May 29, 2015, http://www.theenergycollective.com/ coley-girouard/2233376/water-west-and-clean-power-plan.

300. Michael E. Webber, "Will Drought Cause the Next Blackout?" *New York Times*, July 23, 2012, http://www.nytimes.com/2012/07/24/opinion/will-drought-cause-the-next-blackout.html?ref=opinion&_r=0, and Jonathan Marshall, "Climate Change Comes to the Power Industry," PG&E Currents, August 7, 2012, http:// www.pgecurrents.com/2012/08/07/climate-change-comes-to-the-power-industry/.

301. *Inventory of U.S. Greenhouse Gas Emissions and Sinks: 1990–2010* (US Environmental Protection Agency, 2012), http://www.epa.gov/climatechange/ ghgemissions/sources/electricity.html. As I note elsewhere, an estimated 679 widespread power outages occurred due to severe weather between 2003 and 2012, costing the US economy $18 billion to $33 billion each year, http://energy. gov/sites/prod/files/2015/05/f22/QER%20Full%20Report_0.pdf.

302. US EPA, *Assessment of the Potential Impacts of Hydraulic Fracturing for Oil and Gas on Drinking Water Resources* (External Review Draft) (Washington, DC: US Environmental Protection Agency, 2015), http://cfpub.epa.gov/ncea/hfstudy/recordisplay.cfm?deid=244651. EPA emphasized that this study was a draft for review purposes only and did not reflect the agency's policies or final findings.

303. Ibid.

304. In March 2015, the Interior Department issued a rule that established requirements for hydraulic fracturing in gas production on public lands. It included a number of "best practice" requirements for managing wastewater and preventing groundwater contamination. "Interior Department Releases Final Rule to Support Safe, Responsible Hydraulic Fracturing Activities on Public and Tribal Land," US Bureau of Land Management, March 20, 2015, http://www.blm.gov/wo/st/en/info/newsroom/2015/march/nr_03_20_2015.html.

305. US EPA. *Assessment of the Potential Impacts of Hydraulic Fracturing for Oil and Gas on Drinking Water Resources* (External Review Draft) (Washington, DC: US Environmental Protection Agency, 2015), http://cfpub.epa.gov/ncea/hfstudy/recordisplay.cfm?deid=244651.

306. "What Is Coal Slurry?" Sludge Safety Project of Ohio Valley Environmental Coalition, http://www.sludgesafety.org/what-coal-slurry.

307. Coal slurry and ash spills in the United States have occurred in West Virginia in 1972, where 125 people were killed; in Martin County, Kentucky, in 2000, where 306 million gallons were released into two creeks; in 2008, when a retention pond collapsed at a Tennessee Valley Authority plant in Tennessee; and in 2009 at a TVA plant in Alabama.

308. David Biello, "How Dangerous Is the Coal-Washing Chemical Spilled in West Virginia?" *Scientific American*, January 10, 2014, http://www.scientificamerican.com/article/how-dangerous-is-the-chemical-spilled-in-west-virginia/.

309. Claudia Copeland, *Mountaintop Mining, Background on Current Controversies* (Washington, DC: Congressional Research Service, April 20, 2015), https://www.fas.org/sgp/crs/misc/RS21421.pdf.

310. Ibid. Also, US EPA, *The Effects of Mountaintop Mines and Valley Fills on Aquatic Ecosystems of the Central Appalachian Coalfields* (External Review Draft) (Washington, DC: US Environmental Protection Agency, 2010), http://cfpub.epa.gov/ncea/cfm/recordisplay.cfm?deid=215267#Download.

311. "How Does Carbon Capture Affect Water Consumption?" Global CCS Institute, January 2, 2015, https://www.globalccsinstitute.com/insights/authors/guidomagneschi/2015/01/02/how-does-carbon-capture-affect-water-consumption. The water demands of different CCS technologies are expected to vary. Some studies indicate water consumption will double; others estimate it will increase 30%. I will discuss other issues raised by CCS in Chapter 15.

312. Over its life cycle, nuclear power does produce carbon emissions from uranium mining and, like all other energy systems, the manufacture and construction of equipment.

313. M. Hightower and S. A. Pierce, "The Energy Challenge," *Nature* 452, 7185 (March 20, 2008): 285–286.

314. "Decommissioning Projects – USA," World Information Service on Energy, last modified May 2, 2015, http://www.wise-uranium.org/udusa.html.

315. "What Is U.S. Electricity Generation by Energy Source?" Energy Information Administration, last modified March 31, 2015, http://www.eia.gov/tools/faqs/faq.cfm?id=427&t=3.

316. *Effects of Climate Change on Federal Hydropower: Report to Congress* (Washington, DC: US Environmental Protection Agency, August 2013), http://www1.eere.energy.gov/water/pdfs/hydro_climate_change_report.pdf. For more detailed information on the regional water impacts of climate change, see EPA's analysis: "Water Resources," US Environmental Protection Agency, last modified March 25, 2015, http://www.epa.gov/climatechange/impacts-adaptation/water.html#Impacts.

317. "Short-Term Energy Outlook: Renewables and CO2 Emission," US Energy Information Administration, last modified July 2015, http://www.eia.gov/forecasts/steo/report/renew_co2.cfm.

318. "Total Energy," US Energy Information Administration, last modified June 25, 2015, http://www.eia.gov/totalenergy/, and "What Is U.S. Electricity Generation by Energy Source?" Energy Information Administration, last modified March 31, 2015, http://www.eia.gov/tools/faqs/faq.cfm?id=427&t=3.

319. Ibid. PV and wind turbines convert sunlight and wind directly into electricity, while thermoelectric power plants use water to create steam that both drives turbines and cools equipment. However, PV power plants use some water to wash panels and to suppress dust that can collect on PV panels and reduce their efficiency.

320. Michael Goggin, "Wind Energy Saves 2.5 Billion Gallons of Water Annually in Drought-Parched California," *Into the Wind* (blog), American Wind Energy Association, April 2, 2015, http://www.aweablog.org/wind-energy-saves-2-5-billion-gallons-of-water-annually-in-drought-parched-california.

321. Dry cooling technologies are an alternative for thermoelectric power equipment including CSP plants, but cost more than wet cooling.

322. Second-generation ethanol made from nonfood crops (called cellulosic ethanol) will require less water, but these fuels are not yet commercially available.

323. "How Geothermal Really Works," Union of Concerned Scientists, December 22, 2014, http://www.ucsusa.org/clean_energy/our-energy-choices/renewable-energy/how-geothermal-energy-works.html#.VY2OFxNVhBc.

324. Ibid.

325. N. Carter, *Energy's Water Demand: Trends, Vulnerabilities and Management* (Washington, DC: Congressional Research Service, CRS Publication No. R-41507, 2010).

326. Shuaizhang Fenga, Alan B. Kruegera, and Michael Oppenheimera, "Linkages among Climate Change, Crop Yields and Mexico–US Cross-Border Migration," *Proceedings of the National Academy of Sciences* 107, 32 (June 2010): 14257–14262, http://www.pnas.org/content/107/32/14257. As reported by David Biello, "Climate Change May Mean More Mexican Immigration," *Scientific American*, July 26, 2010, http://www.scientificamerican.com/article/climate-change-may-mean-more-mexican-immigration.

327. Daniel Potter, "Why Isn't Desalination the Answer to All California's Water Problems?" KQED Science, March 30, 2015, http://ww2.kqed.org/science/2015/03/30/why-isnt-desalination-the-answer-to-all-californias-water-problems.

328. Timothy Cama, *The Hill*, http://thehill.com/policy/energy-environment/243299-democrats-buck-obama-on-water-rule, and Michael Holtz, *The Christian Science Monitor*, http://www.csmonitor.com/Environment/2015/0831/Obama-s-Clean-Water-Act-rule-faces-deepening-opposition.

329. *2014 Strategic Directions: U.S. Water Industry* (Denver, CO: Black & Veatch, October 2014), http://www.circleofblue.org/waternews/wp-content/uploads/2014/10/BV_2014-sdr-water-industry-report.pdf.

330. Exec. Order No. 13693 (March 19, 2015), https://www.whitehouse.gov/the-press-office/2015/03/19/executive-order-planning-federal-sustainability-next-decade.

331. Tom Randall, "Fossil Fuels Just Lost the Race Against Renewables," Bloomberg Business, April 14, 2015, http://www.bloomberg.com/news/articles/2015-04-14/fossil-fuels-just-lost-the-race-against-renewables.

332. "Frequently Asked Questions: What Countries Are the Top Net Importers of Oil?" Energy Information Administration, last modified June 18, 2015, http://www.eia.gov/tools/faqs/faq.cfm?id=709&t=6. According to EIA, net oil imports by the United States were 7.39 million barrels per day in 2012, well ahead of second-place Japan's 4.66 million barrels.

333. "Renewables," International Energy Agency, last modified 2015, http://www.iea.org/topics/renewables/.

334. The liberated money would be more than enough for the world to transition to clean energy by mid-century.

335. J. Hansen et al., "Ice Melt, Sea Level Rise and Superstorms: Evidence from Paleoclimate Data, Climate Modeling, and Modern Observations that 2 °C Global Warming Is Highly Dangerous," *Atmospheric Chemistry and Physics* (July 23, 2015), http://www.atmos-chem-phys-discuss.net/15/20059/2015/acpd-15-20059-2015.html.

336. Kevin Anderson and Alice Bows, "Beyond 'Dangerous' Climate Change: Emission Scenarios for a New World," *Philosophical Transactions of the Royal Society* 369 (2011): 20–44, http://rsta.royalsocietypublishing.org/content/roypta/369/1934/20.full.pdf.

337. Michael E. Mann, "Earth Will Cross the Climate Danger Threshold by 2036," *Scientific American*, March 18, 2014, http://www.scientificamerican.com/article/earth-will-cross-the-climate-danger-threshold-by-2036/.

338. *Energy Technology Perspectives 2015: Mobilising Innovation to Accelerate Climate Action* (Paris: International Energy Agency, 2015), p. 3, http://www.iea.org/publications/freepublications/publication/EnergyTechnologyPerspectives2015ExecutiveSummaryEnglishversion.pdf.

339. "Frequently Asked Questions: How Much Carbon Dioxide Is Produced When Different Fuels Are Burned?" Energy Information Administration, last modified June 18, 2015, http://www.eia.gov/tools/faqs/faq.cfm?id=73&t=11. Among fossil fuels, the general ranking, from highest to lowest carbon emissions, is coal in its various forms, diesel fuel, and heating oil, gasoline, propane, and natural gas. The ranking is based on pounds of CO_2 emitted per million British thermal energy.

340. *Energy Technology Perspectives 2015: Mobilising Innovation to Accelerate Climate Action* (Paris: International Energy Agency, 2015), p. 3, http://www.iea.org/publications/freepublications/publication/EnergyTechnologyPerspectives2015ExecutiveSummaryEnglishversion.pdf.

341. Edward Wong, "In Step to Lower Carbon Emissions, China Will Place a Limit on Coal Use in 2020," *New York Times*, November 20, 2014, http://www.nytimes.com/2014/11/21/business/energy-environment/china-to-place-limit-on-coal-use-in-2020.html?_r=0.

342. Anna Yukhananov and Valerie Volcovici, "World Bank to Limit Financing of Coal-Fired Plants," Reuters, July 16, 2013, http://www.reuters.com/article/2013/07/16/us-worldbank-climate-coal-idUSBRE96F19U20130716.

343. John J. Conti et al., *Annual Energy Outlook 2015* (Washington, DC: Energy Information Administration, April 2015), http://www.eia.gov/forecasts/aeo/executive_summary.cfm.

344. Tim Mullaney, "The Biggest Energy Dog Bet of All, or Value Trap?" CNBC, January 12, 2015, http://www.cnbc.com/2015/01/12/has-war-on-coal-unearthed-the-ultimate-value-stocks.html.

345. Ibid.

346. Ibid.

347. Other ideas also are afoot for capturing greenhouse gases or removing them from the atmosphere. Under the general category of "geoengineering," they range from artificial trees to seeding oceans with iron to promote large algae blooms that would absorb carbon from the air and funnel it deep underwater to remain sequestered "for some time." These are controversial approaches, still conceptual with the likelihood of unintended consequences. CCS is much further along the R&D path.

348. Anthony Adragna, "McCarthy Defends Viability of Carbon Capture Technologies Before House Energy Panels," Bloomberg BNA, February 26, 2015, http://www.bna.com/mccarthy-defends-viability-n17179923414.

349. "Department of Energy Oversite: Status of Clean Coal Programs," YouTube video, posted by Subcommittee on Oversite and Investigations, 1:58, February 11, 2014, https://www.youtube.com/watch?v=DNtjOpj3Kys&feature=youtube. In testimony before Congress, DOE's deputy decretary for clean coal predicted that first-generation CCS would double the wholesale cost of coal-fired electricity; as the technology evolves, it would increase the wholesale price by 25%.

350. One prominent environmental issue is mountaintop removal coal mining in Appalachia. It has destroyed large expanses of forest and 2,000 freshwater streams that have been buried in mining spoils. Water supplies, communities, and families also have been affected by accidental releases of chemicals used to wash coal, failures of coal waste impoundments, and alleged drinking water contamination.

351. According to the EIA, "Short-Term Energy Outlook: Gasoline Consumption Is Forecast to Remain Relatively Flat in 2016 as a Long-Term Trend toward More Fuel-Efficient Vehicles Offsets the Effects of Continued Economic Growth," US Energy Information Administration, August 11, 2015, http://www.eia.gov/forecasts/steo/report/us_oil.cfm.

352. Emily Badger "The Many Reasons Millennials Are Shunning Cars," *Wonkblog*, *Washington Post*, October 14, 2014, http://www.washingtonpost.com/blogs/wonkblog/wp/2014/10/14/the-many-reasons-millennials-are-shunning-cars.

353. *FHWA Forecasts of Vehicle Miles Traveled (VMT)* (Washington, DC: Federal Highway Administration, May 2014), http://www.eenews.net/assets/2015/01/12/document_cw_01.pdf.

354. Robert Grattan, "U.S. Households to Spend $550 Less on Gasoline in 2015," *Fuel Fix* (blog), *Houston Chronicle*, December 16, 2014, http://fuelfix.com/blog/2014/12/16/u-s-households-to-spend-550-less-on-gasoline-in-2015-compared-to-2014-report-says/#29319101=0.

355. "Today in Energy: Fuel Economy Standards Drive Down Projected Gasoline Use; Diesel Use, Product Exports Rise," Energy Information Administration, June 26, 2014, http://www.eia.gov/todayinenergy/detail.cfm?id=16871.

356. Michael Levi, "Fracking and the Climate Debate," *Democracy: A Journal of Ideas* 37 (Summer 2015), http://www.democracyjournal.org/37/fracking-and-the-climate-debate.php.

357. Ibid.

358. Katie Gilbert, "Investors Confront the Risk of a Carbon Bubble," Institution Investor, July 1, 2013, http://www.institutionalinvestor.com/Article/3225130/Asset-Management-Green-Investing/Investors-Confront-the-Risk-of-a-Carbon-Bubble.html#.Vct_yJNVhBc.

359. Ibid.

360. Most conversations about a carbon tax propose that it be revenue neutral. One proposal is to use the revenues from a carbon tax to reduce the corporate income tax rate, presumably to blunt industry opposition.

361. *Options and Considerations for a Federal Carbon Tax* (Arlington, VA: Center for Climate and Energy Solutions, February 2013), http://www.c2es.org/publications/options-considerations-federal-carbon-tax.

362. Ibid.

363. Benjamin Hulac, "Oil and Gas CEOs Call for Carbon Price as Exxon, Chevron Outline Climate Strategy," *ClimateWire*, June 2, 2015, http://www.eenews.net/climatewire/stories/1060019472. The CEOs were from European oil and gas companies including GB Group PLC, BP PLC, Eni SpA, Royal Dutch Shell PLC, Statoil, and Total SA. Despite a number of shareholder resolutions encouraging them to address climate change, Chevron Corp. and ExxonMobil Corp. declined to sign the letter. An Exxon spokesman told the media, however, that the company wants a "uniform and stable price on carbon."

364. When Congress takes up the idea of taxing carbon – and sooner or later, it will – it should ask itself this question: Who should pay, the consumer of carbon fuels or the producers? There are several advantages to levying a surcharge on carbon at the point it enters the economy: the mine mouth, wellhead, refinery, pipeline, or port. A producer surcharge would involve several thousand payers rather than many millions. It would be more politically palatable to most voters to tax oil, coal, and gas companies instead of consumers. Most importantly, it would ensure that a carbon price applies not just to gasoline or coal-fired electricity or natural gas but also to whenever and however the fuel is used. The effects of the surcharge, including a correction in the price signals of fossil fuels, would be as ubiquitous as the fuels are themselves. It would apply even to fuels that are produced in the United States for export.

365. Christophe McGlade and Paul Elkins, "The Geographical Distribution of Fossil Fuels Unused When LImiting Global Warming to 2°C," *Nature* 517, 7533 (January 8, 2015): 187–190, http://www.nature.com/nature/journal/v517/n7533/full/nature14016.html. This paper, published in the journal *Nature* in January 2015, concludes that a third of global oil reserves, half of gas reserves, and 80% of coal reserves "should remain unused from 2010 to 2050" to keep global warming to no more than 2°C. Proved reserves, also known as proven reserves, are the fossil energy resources that can be extracted with a reasonable amount of certainty. They are determined by geologic and engineering studies. Improvements in extraction methods can increase proved reserves, as we

have seen happen to oil and gas in the United States with the use of hydraulic fracturing and horizontal drilling, the ability to reach out and harvest oil and gas in several directions from a single well.

366. Henry M. Paulson Jr., "The Coming Climate Crash, Lessons for Climate Change in the 2008 Recession," *New York Times*, June 21, 2014, http://www.nytimes.com/2014/06/22/opinion/sunday/lessons-for-climate-change-in-the-2008-recession.html.

367. "Global Forest Watch: United States of America," Global Forest Watch, last modified 2013, http://www.globalforestwatch.org/country/USA. Global Forest Watch is a partnership of more than 60 organizations that contribute data, technology, and expertise in an effort to monitor the status of forests worldwide. It operates a free interactive online forest monitoring and alert system at: http://www.globalforestwatch.org.

368. John DeCicco, "Rather Than Divest, Advocate for Carbon Balancing," The Energy Collective, May 22, 2015, http://www.theenergycollective.com/john-m-decicco/2231016/rather-divest-advocate-carbon-balancing.

369. "Sources of Greenhouse Gas Emissions," US Environmental Protection Agency, last modified May 7, 2015, http://www.epa.gov/climatechange/ghgemissions/sources/lulucf.html.

370. "About Us," Corporation for National and Community Service, last modified 2015, http://www.nationalservice.gov. AmeriCorps operates several subprograms that could engage young Americans in restoring ecosystem services, including the National Civilian Community Corps and FEMA Corps, in which men and women ages 18 to 24 help communities become more disaster resilient. Samantha Jo Warfield, "Public–Private Partnership Launches New AmeriCorps Program to Help Communities Build Resilience," Corporation for National and Community Service, July 9, 2015, http://www.nationalservice.gov/newsroom/press-releases/2015/public-%E2%80%93-private-partnership-launches-new-americorps-program-help. In a recent development, AmeriCorps, along with several federal agencies and the Rockefeller Foundation, announced the creation of Resilience AmeriCorps to help communities plan and implement projects that improve their resilience to climate impacts.

371. Robert Hudson Westover, "US Forest Service Reforestation Efforts a Win-Win for Healthy Forests" (*USDA blog*), US Department of Agriculture, April 27, 2011, http://blogs.usda.gov/2011/04/27/us-forest-service-reforestation-efforts-a-win-win-for-healthy-forests/.

372. "Reclaiming Abandoned Mine Lands," US Office of Surface Mining and Reclamation and Enforcement, last modified May 21, 2015, http://www.osmre.gov/programs/aml.shtm.

373. *Carbon Sequestration through Reforestation: A Local Solution with Global Implications* (US Environmental Protection Agency, March 2012), http://www.epa.gov/aml/revital/cseqfact.pdf. There are between 80,000 and 250,000 abandoned mine lands in the United States according to the US General Accounting Office. "Frequently Asked Questions," US Bureau of Land Management, last modified February 2, 2015, http://www.blm.gov/wo/st/en/prog/more/Abandoned_Mine_Lands/frequently_asked_questions.html. The Interior Department says that more than 40,000 of them are on lands managed by the federal government. Many are physical, health, and environmental hazards. Most have never been considered for reclamation and reuse.

374. Clifford Krauss, "Rockefeller Family Members Press for Change at Exxon," *New York Times*, May 26, 2008, http://www.nytimes.com/2008/05/26/business/worldbusiness/26iht-exxon.4.13223497.html?pagewanted=all&_r=0.

375. "Shareholder Resolutions," Ceres, last modified 2015, http://www.ceres.org/investor-network/resolutions.

376. Daniel Cusick, "CEOs Face Rising Shareholder Interest in Managing Corporate Climate Risks," *ClimateWire*, March 7, 2014, http://www.eenews.net/stories/1059995740.

377. *Energy and Carbon: Managing the Risks* (Irving, TX: ExxonMobil, 2014), http://cdn.exxonmobil.com/~/media/Files/Other/2014/Report%20-%20Energy%20and%20Carbon%20-%20Managing%20the%20Risks.pdf.

378. Ibid.

379. Nick Sundt, "Groundbreaking Analysis Reveals Route for Businesses to Uncover Billions in Hidden Profits from Climate Change Action," *World Wildlife Fund Climate Blog*, June 18, 2013, http://www.worldwildlife.org/blogs/wwf-climate-blog/posts/groundbreaking-analysis-reveals-route-for-businesses-to-uncover-billions-in-hidden-profits-from-climate-change-action.

380. "Western Landowners Alliance: Connecting for Solutions," Western Landowners Alliance, last modified February 20, 2015, www.westernlandownersalliance.org.

381. "Local Actions Against Fracking," Food & Water Watch, last modified 2015, http://www.foodandwaterwatch.org/water/fracking/anti-fracking-map/local-action-documents.

382. "About: Keep Tap Water Safe," Keep Tap Water Safe: Don't Frack the Delaware River Water Shed!, last modified 2012, http://keeptapwatersafe.org/about-us-2/.

383. Melissa Osgood, "Fracking Flowback Could Pollute Groundwater with Heavy Metals," Cornell University Media Relations, June 25, 2014, http://mediarelations.cornell.edu/2014/06/25/fracking-flowback-could-pollute-groundwater-with-heavy-metals/.

384. Shale Oil and Gas Production – Seismic Activity (Washington, DC: American Fuel and Petrochemical Manufacturers, 2012), https://www.afpm.org/uploadedFiles/Content/News/Shale%20Seismic%20Activity.pdf.

385. Marchese et al., "Methane Emissions from United States Natural Gas Gathering and Processing," Colorado State University, August 18, 2015, http://pubs.acs.org/doi/abs/10.1021/acs.est.5b02275. The study looked at the facilities located near gas wells to gather and process the fuel before it enters pipelines. Researchers concluded that leaks were roughly eight times higher than EPA estimates, constituted 30% of total net methane emissions from gas systems, and most were not being reported under EPA's greenhouse gas reporting rule.

386. A World Resources Institute study concluded that reducing leaks to less than 1% of total production is necessary to ensure that the climate impacts from natural gas are lower than those from coal or diesel fuel over any time horizon. Other researchers have concluded that the threshold is 3.2%.

387. Ramón A. Alvareza et al., "What Will It Take to Get Sustained Benefits from Natural Gas?" *Proceedings of the National Academy of Sciences* 109, 17 (December 21, 2011): 6435–6440, http://www.edf.org/energy/methaneleakage.

388. Jon Kamp, "Cheaper Heating Oil Fuels Billions in Savings in Northeast," *Wall Street Journal*, January 16, 2015, http://www.wsj.com/articles/cheaper-heating-oil-fuels-billions-in-savings-in-northeast-1421431800.

389. *Chapter 3: The Fuel Effect: What Is Being Burned Matters* (Concord, MA, and Washington, DC: M. J. Bradley and Associates LLC, and New York: Environmental Defense Fund, December 21, 2009), http://www.edf.org/sites/default/files/10071_EDF_BottomBarrel_Ch3.pdf.

390. Kit Kennedy, *The Role of Natural Gas Is America's Energy Mix* (Washington, DC: National Resource Defense Council, June 2012), http://www.nrdc.org/energy/files/energymixll.pdf.

391. Michael Levi, "Fracking and the Climate Debate," *Democracy: A Journal of Ideas* 37 (Summer 2015), http://www.democracyjournal.org/37/fracking-and-the-climate-debate.php.

392. Ernest J. Moniz et al., *The Future of Natural Gas: An interdisciplinary MIT Study* (Boston, MA: MIT Energy Initiative, 2011), p. 7, http://mitei.mit.edu/system/files/NaturalGas_ExecutiveSummary.pdf. The MIT Energy Initiative is a multidisciplinary team once led by Professor Ernest Moniz, who went on to become secretary of energy.

393. Ibid.

394. "Study Identifies Which Fossil Fuel Reserves Must Stay in the Ground to Avoid Dangerous Climate Change," University College London, January 7, 2015, http://www.bartlett.ucl.ac.uk/sustainable/sustainable-news/nature_fossil_fuels.

395. Christina Nunez, "Climate Mission Impossible: Scientists Say Fossil Fuels Must Go Untapped," *National Geographic*, January 7, 2015, http://news.nationalgeographic.com/news/energy/2015/01/150107-fossil-fuel-unburnable-2-degree-climate-target-study.

396. "Interior Department Releases Final Rule to Support Safe, Responsible Hydraulic Fracturing Activities on Public and Tribal Lands," US Department of the Interior, March 20, 2015, http://www.blm.gov/wo/st/en/info/newsroom/2015/march/nr_03_20_2015.html.

397. Benjamin Storrow, "Federal Judge Issues Stay on BLM Fracking Rule," *Casper Star Tribune*, June 23, 2015, http://trib.com/business/energy/federal-judge-issues-stay-on-blm-fracking-rule/article_7e14957f-11d9-5120-b1d9-e86bf382bb1c.html. Industry groups reportedly argued that BLM did not follow the law's rule-making requirements. Colorado, North Dakota, Utah, and Wyoming challenged BLM's authority to make the rule, arguing that the authority belongs to the Environmental Protection Agency.

398. The BLM rule is one of several actions the Obama administration has taken to address issues related to gas production. In January 2015 the president took executive action to reduce methane leaks in oil and gas operations, with the goal of reducing them 40–45% by 2015. EPA was to follow up with a rule that directly engages the industry in methane reduction.

399. Quoted in "Trends in Responsible Natural Gas Development," an unpublished report on natural gas symposia organized by the Colorado State University Energy Institute and the Center for the New Energy Economy.

400. "Colorado Water Watch," Center for Energy and Water Sustainability, last modified 2014, http://cewc.colostate.edu.

401. Kit Kennedy, *The Role of Natural Gas in America's Energy Mix* (Washington, DC: National Resources Defense Council, June 2012), http://www.nrdc.org/energy/files/energymixll.pdf.

402. Climatic temperatures affected by the sun produce winds. Winds produce ocean waves. Evaporation caused by the sun is an essential part of the water cycle that fills the rivers and streams used for hydropower.

403. Thermal mass is material that complies with the second law of thermodynamics: heat flows from hot to cold. Rocks, concrete, bricks, and several other materials absorb heat from the air when it is warmer than they are and put it back into the air when it is cooler. The practical effect in a passive solar home is to keep interior temperatures from overheating in the daytime and to help keep air warm during the night when the sun is down.

404. John J. Conti et al., *Annual Energy Outlook 2015* (Washington, DC: US Energy Information Administration, April 14, 2015), http://www.eia.gov/forecasts/aeo/executive_summary.cfm.

405. John Rodgers, "Annual Energy Outlook 2015: EIA Consistently Lowballs Renewables, Undercuts Climate Change Efforts," Union of Concerned Scientists, April 13, 2015, *The Equation* (blog), http://blog.ucsusa.org/eia-annual-energy-outlook-2015-renewable-energy-climate-change-704.

406. Thirty-one states have passed legislation that authorizes PACE financing, but only 12 states had active programs by the end of 2014, according to the National Conference of State Legislatures. In 2010, the Federal Housing Finance Authority (FHFA) put residential PACE financing in limbo, in part because of concerns that liens associated with standard mortgages would become secondary to liens under PACE financing. PACE loans for commercial properties were allowed to continue. The administration's latest announcement indicates that FHFA had developed criteria for residential PACE financing that satisfy its concerns.

407. See the American Council for an Energy Efficient Economy's explanation of on-bill financing at http://aceee.org/sector/state-policy/toolkit/on-bill-financing, and EPA's explanation of EEMs at https://www.energystar.gov/index.cfm?c=mortgages.energy_efficient_mortgages.

408. Rhone Resch, "New Report Shows Explosive Growth in Residential Solar Installations" (blog), Solar Energy Industries Association, June 9, 2015, http://www.seia.org/blog/new-report-shows-explosive-growth-residential-solar-installations.

409. Katie Fehrenbacher, "U.S. Solar Industry Shifting towards Consumers," *Fortune*, June 9, 2015, http://fortune.com/2015/06/09/solar-industry-shifting.

410. Rhone Resch, "New Report Shows Explosive Growth in Residential Solar Installations," (blog), Solar Energy Industries Association, June 9, 2015, http://www.seia.org/blog/new-report-shows-explosive-growth-residential-solar-installations.

411. Jose Zayas et al., *Enabling Wind Power Nationwide* (Washington, DC: US Department of Energy, May 2015), http://energy.gov/sites/prod/files/2015/05/f22/Enabling-Wind-Power-Nationwide_18MAY2015_FINAL.pdf.

412. Camilo Patrignani, "The Solar Industry Needs to Let Its Federal Tax Credit Die, Says This CEO," greentechmedia, January 13, 2015, http://www.greentechmedia.com/articles/read/the-solar-industry-needs-to-let-its-federal-tax-credit-die-says-this-ceo.

413. Ibid.

414. Diane Cardwell, "Solar and Wind Energy Start to Win on Price vs. Conventional Fuels," *New York Times*, November 23, 2014, http://www.nytimes.com/2014/11/24/business/energy-environment/solar-and-wind-energy-start-to-win-on-price-vs-conventional-fuels.html.

415. Susan Kraemer, "How Solar Energy Zones and Easy Permitting Helped Create 3-Cent Solar," Renewable Energy World, July 22, 2015, http://www.renewableenergyworld.com/articles/2015/07/how-solar-energy-zones-and-easy-permitting-helped-create-3-cent-solar.html.

416. Barbose and Darghouth et al., "Tracking the Sun VIII," Lawrence Berkeley National Laboratory and the US Department of Energy, August 2015, http://emp.lbl.gov/sites/all/files/lbnl-188238_1.pdf.

417. Ibid.

418. Vishal Shah, Deutsche Bank Markets Research: Industry Solar FITT for Investors (Deutsche Bank, February 27, 2015), https://www.db.com/cr/en/docs/solar_report_full_length.pdf.

419. "Fact Sheet: President Obama Announces New Actions to Bring Renewable Energy and Energy Efficiency to Households across the Country," The White House, August 24, 2015, https://www.whitehouse.gov/the-press-office/2015/08/24/fact-sheet-president-obama-announces-new-actions-bring-renewable-energy.

420. M. M. Hand et al., Renewable Electricity Futures Study (Golden, CO: National Renewable Energy Laboratory, 2012), http://www.nrel.gov/docs/fy13osti/52409-ES.pdf.

421. Nafeez Ahmed, "How Solar Power Could Slay the Fossil Fuel Empire by 2030," Motherboard, December 10, 2014, http://motherboard.vice.com/read/how-solar-power-could-slay-the-fossil-fuel-empire-by-2030.

422. Diane Cardwell, "Solar and Wind Energy Start to Win on Price vs. Conventional Fuels," New York Times, November 23, 2014, http://www.nytimes.com/2014/11/24/business/energy-environment/solar-and-wind-energy-start-to-win-on-price-vs-conventional-fuels.html.

423. Debbie Dooley, "A Tea Party Leader Explains Why She's Teaming Up with the Sierra Club to Push for Solar Power," Grist, August 12, 2013, http://grist.org/climate-energy/a-tea-party-leader-explains-why-shes-teaming-up-with-the-sierra-club-to-push-for-solar-power.

424. Debbie Dooley, "I Support Solar Energy Because of My Beliefs, Not Despite Them," Guardian, July 24, 2015, http://www.theguardian.com/commentisfree/2015/jul/24/-solar-energy-tea-party-beliefs-not-despite-them#comment-56320922.

425. Jeff St. John, "New York Plans $40M in Prizes for Storm-Resilient Microgrids," greentechmedia, January 9, 2014, http://www.greentechmedia.com/articles/read/new-york-plans-40m-in-prizes-for-storm-resilient-microgrids.

426. In 2008, the National Renewable Energy Laboratory estimated that fewer than one-third of the residential rooftops in the United States are suitable for on-site solar systems.

427. "Energy," Gallup, last modified 2015, http://www.gallup.com/poll/2167/energy.aspx. A Gallup poll in March 2015 found that 79% of Americans want more emphasis on solar energy, 70% want more attention to wind energy, and 55% want more emphasis on natural gas. Rebecca Riffkin, "U.S. Support for Nuclear Energy at 51%," Gallup, March 30, 2015, http://www.gallup.com/poll/182180/support-nuclear-energy.aspx?utm_source=POLITICS&utm_medium=topic&utm_campaign=tiles. Oil, nuclear power, and coal received favorable responses from 41%, 35%, and 28% respectively.

428. National Solar Jobs Census 2014 (The Solar Foundation, January 2015), http://www.thesolarfoundation.org/national-solar-jobs-census-2014/.

429. Joby Warrick, "Utilities Wage Campaign against Rooftop Solar," *Washington Post*, March 7, 2015, http://www.washingtonpost.com/national/health-science/utilities-sensing-threat-put-squeeze-on-booming-solar-roof-industry/2015/03/07/2d916f88-c1c9-11e4-ad5c-3b8ce89f1b89_story.html. The presentation was by David Owens of the Edison Electric Institute. David K. Owens, "Facing the Challenges of a Distribution System in Transition" (meeting, Edison Electric Board and Chief Executives Meeting, September 2012), https://www.documentcloud.org/documents/1374670-2012-eei-board-and-chief-executives-meeting.html#document/p48/a191712.

430. Herman K. Trabish, "ConEd Will Enter NY Rooftop Solar Market through Unregulated Subsidiary," Utility Dive, July 30, 2015, http://www.utilitydive.com/news/coned-will-enter-ny-rooftop-solar-market-through-unregulated-subsidiary/403145/.

431. Herman K. Trabish, "Has APS Invented a Rooftop Solar Business Model for Utilities?" Utility Dive, August 11, 2014, http://www.utilitydive.com/news/has-aps-invented-a-rooftop-solar-business-model-for-utilities/296019.

432. Lorraine Chow, "Elon Musk's Tesla Battery + SolarCity's Solar Systems = Clean Energy Future," *EcoWatch*, May 5, 2015, http://ecowatch.com/2015/05/05/elon-musk-tesla-battery-solarcity.

433. Lorraine Chow, "Google Invests $300 Million in SolarCity to Make Going Solar Easier," *EcoWatch*, February 26, 2015, http://ecowatch.com/2015/02/26/google-invests-300-million-solarcity.

434. "Alternative Fuels Data Center," US Department of Energy, last modified July 28, 2015, http://www.afdc.energy.gov. The data were for vehicles in 2011.

435. Brad Tuttle, "So About That Goal of 1 Million Electric Cars by 2015..." *Time*, January 22, 2015, http://time.com/money/3677021/obama-electric-cars-gas.

436. "History," Zentrum für Sonnenenergie- und Wasserstoff-Forschung Baden-Württemberg, last modified 2011, http://www.zsw-bw.de/en/the-zsw/history.html.

437. This estimate is difficult to confirm. The website Inside EVs reports that nearly 63,300 plug-in electric vehicles were sold in the United States between January and July 2015 and that more than 123,000 were sold in 2014, http://insideevs.com/may-2015-plug-electric-vehicle-sales-report-card. DOE reports that electric vehicle sales rose 128% in the United States from 2012 to 2014. HydbridCars.com reports that more than 330,000 all-electric and plug-in electric vehicles have been sold in the United States from 2011 to mid-2015, http://evobsession.com/us-electric-car-sales-other-info-in-charts-graphs.

438. See the Plugincars website at http://www.plugincars.com/cars.

439. "The Future of the Luxury Electric Vehicle Market," Frost & Sullivan, August 13, 2015, http://www.frost.com/sublib/display-report.do?id=MB40-01-00-00-00&bdata=bnVsbEB%2BQEJhY2tAfkAxNDQwNDQ0MzU4MDQz.

440. "Electric Storage and Plug-In Vehicles," Energy Storage Association, http://energystorage.org/energy-storage/technology-applications/electricity-storage-and-plug-vehicles.

441. David Pimentel and Anne Wilson, "World Population, Agriculture, and Malnutrition, "*World Watch Magazine* 17, 5 (September/October 2004): 22–25, http://www.worldwatch.org/node/554.

442. Paul Harris, "Population of World 'Could Grow to 15bn by 2100,'" *Guardian*, October 22, 2011, http://www.theguardian.com/world/2011/oct/22/population-world-15bn-2100.

443. Charlotte McDonald, "How Many Earths Do We Need?" BBC News, June 16, 2015, http://www.bbc.com/news/magazine-33133712.

444. Steffen et al., "Planetary Boundaries: Guiding Human Development on a Changing Planet," *Science* 347, 62232015 (2015), http://www. stockholmresilience.org/21/research/research-news/1-15-2015-planetary-boundaries-2.0---new-and-improved.html.

445. Robert Pollin et al., *Green Growth: A U.S. Program for Controlling Climate Change and Expanding Job Opportunities* (Washington, DC: Center for American Progress, and Amherst, MA: Political Economy Research Institute, September 2014), https://cdn.americanprogress.org/wp-content/uploads/2014/09/PERI.pdf.

446. *Global Risks 2015* (Geneva: World Economic Forum, January 15, 2015), http://reports.weforum.org/global-risks-2015.

447. *Our Common Future* (WCED, October 1987), http://www.un-documents.net/our-common-future.pdf.

448. *World Business Council for Sustainable Development Annual Review 2011/2012* (Geneva: WBCSD, 2011/2012), http://www.wbcsd.org/about.aspx.

449. "Principles," Natural Capitalism Solutions, last modified 2013, http://natcapsolutions.org/about/principles/#.VcOUrBNViko.

450. "About," Natural Capitalism Solutions, last modified 2013, http://natcapsolutions.org/about/#.VcOO7xNViko.

451. *Climate Action and Profitability: CDP S&P 500 Climate Change Report 2014* (CDP, 2014), https://www.cdp.net/CDPResults/CDP-SP500-leaders-report-2014.pdf.

452. Ibid.

453. John Fullerton, *Regenerative Capitalism: How Universal Principles and Patterns Will Shape Our New Economy* (Greenwich, CT: Capital Institute, April 2015), http://capitalinstitute.org/wp-content/uploads/2015/04/2015-Regenerative-Capitalism-4-20-15-final.pdf.

454. "Our Vision," The Natural Step, http://www.thenaturalstep.org/about-us.

455. "About," World Business Council for Sustainable Development, http://www.wbcsd.org/about.aspx.

456. "Overview," American Sustainable Business Council, last modified 2015, http://asbcouncil.org/about-us#.Vbupy5NVhBc.

457. David Mielach, "Small Business Owners See Value of Social Responsibility," *Business News Daily*, April 10, 2013, http://www.businessnewsdaily.com/4313-business-social-responsibility.html.

458. The list of companies included Alcoa, Apple, Bank of America, Berkshire Hathaway Energy, Cargill, Coca-Cola, General Motors, Goldman Sachs, Google, Microsoft, PepsiCo, UPS, and Walmart.

459. "Fact Sheet: White House Launches American Business Act on Climate Pledge," Washington, DC: Office of the Press Secretary, July 27, 2015, https://www.whitehouse.gov/the-press-office/2015/07/27/fact-sheet-white-house-launches-american-business-act-climate-pledge.

460. "Fact Sheet: Obama Administration Announces More Than $4 Billion in Private Sector Commitments and Executive Actions to Scale Up Investments in Clean Energy Innovation," Washington, DC: Office of the Press Secretary, June 16, 2015, https://www.whitehouse.gov/the-press-office/2015/06/16/fact-sheet-obama-administration-announces-more-4-billion-private-sector.

461. Larry Kramer and Carol Larson, "Foundations Must Move Fast to Fight Climate Change," *The Chronicle of Philanthropy* (April 20, 2015), https://philanthropy.com/article/Foundations-Must-Move-Fast-to/229509.

462. *Walmart 2015 Global Responsibility Report* (Bentonville, AK: Walmart, April 22, 2015), http://news.walmart.com/news-archive/2015/04/22/walmart-highlights-progress-in-2015-global-responsibility-report.

463. Mindy Lubber, "Why Businesses (Big and Small) Should Support Climate Action," *Inside Climate News*, May 22, 2009, http://insideclimatenews.org/news/20090522/why-businesses-big-and-small-should-support-climate-action.

464. Ibid.

465. John W. Schoen, "Where Big Oil Is Cutting Back," CNBC, April 9, 2015, http://www.cnbc.com/2015/04/09/where-big-oil-is-cutting-back.html. The industry reportedly is cutting back on oil exploration and production because low oil prices have made it unprofitable. CNBC reports that oil and gas companies worldwide are expected to cut spending on exploration and production by 17% in 2015.

466. Matthew Morton, "Is There Still a Role for Oil Companies in Renewables?" Greentechmedia, March 12, 2015, http://www.greentechmedia.com/articles/read/is-there-still-a-role-for-oil-companies-in-renewables. Morton is a consultant with Nextant's Energy and Chemicals Advisory Services Unit.

467. Ibid. The pressure is evident today, for example, in the divestment movement, in the Sierra Club's Beyond Coal campaign, and in shareholder pressures to acknowledge climate risks.

468. Pope Paul VI, "*Octogesima Adveniens*, Apostolic Letter of Pope Paul VI," Vatican website, May 14, 1971, 21, http://w2.vatican.va/content/paul-vi/en/apost_letters/documents/hf_p-vi_apl_19710514_octogesima-adveniens.html.

469. Christine Polzin, *Overconsumption? Our Use of the World's Natural Resources* (Sustainable Europe Research Institute [SERI], Austria and GLOBAL 2000 Friends of the Earth Austria, September 2009), http://www.academia.edu/223160/Overconsumption_Our_use_of_the_world_s_natural_resources.

470. Ibid.

471. Pope Francis, "Encyclical Letter of the Holy Father Francis, *Laudato Si'*, On Care for Our Common Home," 68, Vatican website, May 24, 2015, http://w2.vatican.va/content/francesco/en/encyclicals/documents/papa-francesco_20150524_enciclica-laudato-si.html.

472. Lee Peterson, "US Conservative Voices Grow Louder in Support of Renewable Energy" (blog), *Renewable Energy World*, October 7, 2013, http://blog.renewableenergyworld.com/ugc/blogs/2013/10/conservative-voices-grow-louder-in-support-of-renewable-energy.html.

473. Miles Unterreiner et al., Moving America Forward: State and Federal Leadership Is Producing Results in the Fight against Global Warming, *Environment America*, (Winter 2014): 8, http://www.eenews.net/assets/2014/03/13/document_pm_01.pdf. The study concluded that state and federal policies helped produce a 12% decline in US carbon emissions between 2007 and 2012. The recession also was a factor.

474. "About ICC" (International Code Council), last modified 2015, http://www.iccsafe.org/about-icc/overview/about-international-code-council/. Working with the building industry, the US Department of Energy and an organization called the International Code Council do create model building standards dealing with energy efficiency, but they are not mandatory.

475. "Summary Maps," DSIRE, last modified 2015, http://programs.dsireusa.org/system/program/maps. These are known as Renewable Energy Portfolio Standards (RPSs) or Renewable Energy Standards (RESs). For a current count of RPSs and RESs, see the DSIRE's "Renewables Portfolio Standards Summary Map" and "Database of State Incentives for Renewables and Efficiency."

476. Annie Gilleo and Maggie Molina, *State Energy Efficiency Resource Standards (EERS)* (Washington, DC: American Council for an Energy-Efficient Economy, April 7, 2015), http://aceee.org/sites/default/files/eers-04072015.pdf. Early in 2014, 26 states had EERS policies, but Indiana and Ohio rolled theirs back "due to political aversion to mandatory clean energy policies," according to ACEEE.

477. *State Energy Efficiency Resource Standards (EERS): February 2014 EERS Policy Approaches by State* (Washington, DC: American Council for an Energy-Efficient Economy, February 2014), http://aceee.org/files/pdf/policy-brief/eers-07-2014.pdf.

478. Seth Nowak et al., *Leaders of the Pack: ACEEE's Third National Review of Exemplary Energy Efficiency Programs* (Washington, DC: American Council for an Energy Efficient Economy, June 21, 2013), http://aceee.org/research-report/u132.

479. Ben Adler, "Why Michigan's Republican Governor Supports Clean Energy – or Does He?" *Grist*, January 3, 2014, http://grist.org/politics/why-michigans-republican-governor-supports-clean-energy-or-does-he.

480. Greg Bluestein and Kristi E. Swartz, "More Fights Ahead for Georgia Power After Loss on Solar," *Atlanta Journal Constitution*, July 11, 2013, http://www.ajc.com/news/news/state-regional-govt-politics/georgia-utility-regulators-back-unprecedented-sola/nYnBk/.

481. Todd Woody, "California Carbon Market to Generate Billions but Won't End Budget Woes," *Forbes*, May 17, 2012, http://www.forbes.com/sites/toddwoody/2012/05/17/california-carbon-market-to-generate-billions-but-wont-end-budget-woes/.

482. Duane Shimogawa, "Hawaii Legislation Sets 100 Percent Renewable Energy Goal for the State," *Pacific Business News*, May 5, 2015, http://www.bizjournals.com/pacific/news/2015/05/05/hawaii-legislation-sets-100-percent-renewable.html.

483. Davide Savenije and Claire Cameron, "Hawaii's Overhaul of the Utility Business Model: The Sun Is Setting on Traditional Cost-of-Service Regulation," Utility Dive, May 7, 2014, http://www.utilitydive.com/news/hawaiis-overhaul-of-the-utility-business-model/259923/.

484. Ibid.

485. Ibid.

486. *California Poised to Move Up in World Economy Rankings in 2013* (Palo Alto, CA: Center for Continuing Study of the California Economy, July 2013), http://www.ccsce.com/PDF/Numbers-July-2013-CA-Economy-Rankings-2012.pdf. In recent years, California has fluctuated between the eighth and ninth largest economy in the world.

487. "Assembly Bill 32 Overview," California Environmental Protection Agency Air Resources Board, last modified August 5, 2014, http://www.arb.ca.gov/cc/ab32/ab32.htm.

488. Ibid.

489. "The California Clean Energy Jobs Act (Proposition 39)," The California Energy Commission, last modified June 2015, http://www.energy.ca.gov/efficiency/proposition39.

490. Ibid.

491. "2015 U.S. Clean Tech Leadership Index," Clean Edge, June 2015, http://cleanedge.com/indexes/u.s.-clean-tech-leadership-index. Based on more than 70 technology, policy, and capital indicators, Clean Edge ranked California as the leading lean-tech state in 2015, the sixth year in a row. Next among the top five were Massachusetts, Oregon, Colorado, and New York.

492. Bethany K. Speer, "Connecticut's Solar Lease Program Demonstrates High Borrower Fidelity," NREL Renewable Energy Project Finance, October 22, 2012, https://financere.nrel.gov/finance/content/connecticut-s-solar-lease-program-demonstrates-high-borrower-fidelity.

493. Brad Copithorne, "The Spread of Green Banking Paves the Way for Clean Energy Investments" (blog), Environmental Defense Fund, May 13, 2014, http://www.edf.org/blog/2014/05/13/spread-green-banking-paves-way-clean-energy-investments.

494. "Nevada-SB 123-2013," Advanced Energy Legislative Tracker, Center for the New Energy Economy, last modified September 1, 2014, http://www.aeltracker.org/bill-details/737/nevada-2013-sb-123.

495. Powering Up Nevada: A Report on the Economic Benefits of Renewable Electricity Development (Washington, DC: A Renewable America, January 2015), http://arenewableamerica.org/wp-content/uploads/2014/11/Nevada-Economic-Development-Report.pdf.

496. Karlynn Cory, "Minnesota Values Solar Generation with New 'Value of Solar' Tariff," National Renewable Energy Laboratory, October 3, 2014, https://www.nrel.gov/tech_deployment/state_local_governments/blog/vos-series_minnesota.

497. For more detailed information about this complicated policy, see the series of articles on the Solar Industry website at Michael Puttre, "Guide Offers Regulators a Way to Put a Value on Distributed Solar," Solar Industry, October 10, 2013, http://www.solarindustrymag.com/e107_plugins/content/content.php?content.13325. Michael Puttre, "Minnesota PUC Approves Methodology for Measuring Solar Value," Solar Industry, March 24, 2014, http://www.solarindustrymag.com/e107_plugins/content/content.php?content.13943. Michael Puttre, "Minnesota PUC Passes on Value of Solar, But Likely Not for Long," Solar Industry, August 11, 2014, http://www.solarindustrymag.com/e107_plugins/content/content.php?content.14461.

498. "Non-hydro Renewables Now Routinely Surpass Hydropower Generation," US Energy Information Administration, last modified July 31, 2014, http://www.eia.gov/todayinenergy/detail.cfm?id=17351.

499. Michael Brower, "Despite Ohio Freeze, Renewable Energy Continues to Be Hot," CleanTechnica, July 10, 2014, http://cleantechnica.com/2014/07/10/despite-ohio-freeze-renewable-energy-continues-hot/.

500. Robert Bryce, The High Cost of Renewable-Electricity Mandates (New York: Manhattan Institute, February 2012), http://www.manhattan-institute.org/html/eper_10.htm.

501. Jenny Heeter et al., A Survey of State-Level Cost and Benefit Estimates of Renewable Portfolio Standards (Berkeley, CA: Electricity Markets and Policy Group, May 2014), http://emp.lbl.gov/publications/survey-state-level-cost-and-benefit-estimates-renewable-portfolio-standards.

502. Ibid. LBNL found that the benefits of avoided emissions ranged from $4–23/Mwh for renewable energy generation, $22–30/Mwh in economic development,

and $2–50/Mwh in wholesale electricity price suppression (the reduction in natural gas prices due to lower consumption as renewable energy replaces the uses of gas in generating plants). In sum, then, these indirect benefits ranged from $28–103/Mwh. The EIA reports that in 2012, the average household used about 900 kilowatt-hours of electricity each month, which equates to $25.2 to $92.7 per month. States interested in calculating the benefits and costs of RPSs will find guidance in Warren Leon, *Evaluating the Benefits and Costs of a Renewable Portfolio Standard* (Montpelier, VT: Clean Energy States Alliance, May 2012), http://www.cesa.org/assets/2012-Files/RPS/CESA-RPS-evaluation-report-final-5-22-12.pdf.

503. *Economic Impacts of Advanced Energy* (San Francisco, Washington, DC, and Boston: Advanced Energy Economy Institute, 2013), http://info.aee.net/economics-of-advanced-energy-download.

504. "Position Statements on Renewables and Climate Change," American Legislative Exchange Council, last modified 2015, http://www.alec.org/position-statement-renewables-climate-change/.

505. "Mission Statement," American Legislative Exchange Council, last modified 2015, http://www.alec.org/news/mission/.

506. Chris Martin, "U.S. States Turn against Renewable Energy as Gas Plunges," Bloomberg Business, April 23, 2013, http://www.bloomberg.com/news/articles/2013-04-23/u-s-states-turn-against-renewable-energy-as-gas-plunges.

507. *State Renewable Portfolio Standards Hold Steady or Expand in 2013* (Denver, CO: The Center for the New Energy Economy, 2013), http://www.aeltracker.org/graphics/uploads/2013-State-By-State-RPS-Analysis.pdf.

508. Chris Martin, "U.S. States Turn against Renewable Energy as Gas Plunges," Bloomberg Business, April 23, 2013, http://www.bloomberg.com/news/articles/2013-04-23/u-s-states-turn-against-renewable-energy-as-gas-plunges.

509. Ibid.

510. *State Renewable Portfolio Standards Hold Steady or Expand in 2013* (Denver, CO: The Center for the New Energy Economy, 2013), http://www.aeltracker.org/graphics/uploads/2013-State-By-State-RPS-Analysis.pdf.

511. Renewable Energy and Advanced Energy Requirement, Sub. S.B. 310, 130th General Assembly (May 2014). The Ohio legislation, SB 310, lowers renewable energy requirements each year starting in 2015. The requirement hits its maximum in 2026 at 12.5%. Under the original RPS, the 12.5% goal would have been required two years earlier.

512. The action by Governor Christie may backfire on the state as it now will have to submit a plan to achieve compliance with the EPA's Clean Power Plan without participation in RGGI. The regional effort is a default mechanism for states to comply with the new regulations.

513. "Multistate Climate Initiatives," Center for Climate and Energy Solutions, http://www.c2es.org/us-states-regions/regional-climate-initiatives.

514. Officially known as the Clean Power Plan.

515. Timothy Cama, "States to Sue Obama Administration over Climate Rules," *The Hill*, August 3, 2015, http://thehill.com/policy/energy-environment/250125-states-to-sue-obama-administration-over-climate-rules.

516. "Advanced Energy Legislation Tracker," The Center for the New Energy Economy, last modified July 2015, http://www.aeltracker.org/.

517. *Global Green Growth: Clean Energy Industrial Investments and Expanding Job Opportunities* (United Nations Industrial Development Organization and the Global Green Growth Institute, 2015), http://www.unido.org/fileadmin/user_media_upgrade/Resources/Policy_advice/GLOBAL_GREEN_GROWTH_REPORT_vol1_final.pdf.

518. Rush Limbaugh, "Everything I've Always Told You about Liberals Is Coming True," *The Rush Limbaugh Show*, http://www.rushlimbaugh.com/daily/2015/05/05/everything_i_ve_always_told_you_about_liberals_is_coming_true.

519. "Coal and Jobs in the United States," SourceWatch, last modified June 26, 2015, http://www.sourcewatch.org/index.php/Coal_and_jobs_in_the_United_States.

520. "Coal," US Environmental Protection Agency, last modified September 25, 2013, http://www.epa.gov/cleanenergy/energy-and-you/affect/coal.html. Both the federal government and many states regulate some pollutants created as coal is extracted, cleaned, and burned. Coal combustion produces carbon dioxide, sulfur dioxide, nitrogen oxides, and mercury compounds that create smog, acid rain, toxic air emissions, and global warming. Solid wastes include ash from coal combustion and sludge from coal cleaning. These wastes, along with chemicals used in cleaning, have been accidently released into soils and water in the past. In addition, strip mining causes significant damage to lands and in some cases to waterways.

521. John J. Conti et al., *Annual Energy Outlook 2015* (Washington, DC: US Energy Information Administration, April 14, 2015), http://www.eia.gov/forecasts/aeo/executive_summary.cfm.

522. Cathy Proctor, "State May Join Legal Battle to Halt Shutdown of Colowyo Coal Mine," *Denver Business Journal*, June 5, 2015, http://www.bizjournals.com/denver/blog/earth_to_power/2015/06/state-may-join-legal-battle-to-halt-shutdown-of.html.

523. "Northwest Colorado Cultural Heritage Homepage," Northwest Colorado Cultural Heritage, http://nwcoloradoheritagetravel.org/new-castle-colorado/home.

524. "New Castle Homepage," Town of New Castle, http://www.newcastlecolorado.org/.

525. Heidi Rice, "New Castle Scraps Solar Park Site Due to Protests," *Post Independent/Citizen Telegram*, July 25, 2014, http://www.postindependent.com/news/12347067-113/solar-castle-location-energy. Protests also have slowed wind power development off the coast of Cape Cod and a few other areas on the East Coast where property owners felt turbines would ruin their views of the ocean and harm tourism.

526. Sandra Fish, "Fighting to Save Colorado Mining Town," Aljazeera America, November 3, 2013, http://america.aljazeera.com/articles/2013/11/3/fighting-to-saveacoloradominingtown.html.

527. Ibid.

528. "History of Rifle," Rifle Area Chamber of Commerce, http://riflechamber.com/relocate-do-business/history-of-rifle/.

529. Carrie Click, "Black Sunday – Rifle Rebounds and How," *Post Independent*, June 15, 2008, http://www.postindependent.com/article/20070426/NEWS/664343124.

530. Judee Burr et al., *Shining Cities: Harnessing the Benefits of Solar Energy in America* (America Research and Policy Center, March 26, 2015), http://www.environmentamerica.org/sites/environment/files/reports/EA_ShiningCities2015_scrn.pdf.

531. "Garfield Clean Energy Homepage," Garfield Clean Energy, http://www.garfieldcleanenergy.org.

532. Randy Essex, "In Solar Energy, Rifle Shines Most Brightly," *Post Independent/ Citizen Telegram*, April 22, 2015, http://www.postindependent.com/ news/16013885-113/in-solar-energy-rifle-shines-most-brightly.

533. Major shale gas plays include Barnette Shale in Texas; Haynesville Shale in Texas and Louisiana; Marcellus Shale in New York, Pennsylvania, Ohio, Maryland and West Virginia; and Utica Shale in the Marcellus states plus Virginia and Tennessee. Joseph Reed, "The Top U.S. Shale Gas Plays," OilPro, http://oilpro. com/post/646/the-major-shale-gas-plays-in-the-us.

534. "Put Just Transition at the Heart of a European Position on Climate in Durban and a Roadmap on Sustainability at Rio+20," European Trade Union Confederation, last modified October 10, 2010, https://www.etuc.org/put-just-transition-heart-european-position-climate-durban-and-roadmap-sustainability-rio20.

535. *Global Green Growth: Clean Energy Industrial Investments and Expanding Job Opportunities* (United Nations Industrial Development Organization and the Global Green Growth Institute, 2015), http://www.unido.org/fileadmin/user_media_upgrade/Resources/Policy_advice/GLOBAL_GREEN_GROWTH_REPORT_vol1_final.pdf.

536. Ibid.

537. "Fact Sheet: President Obama's Promise Zones Initiative," Washington, DC: Office of the Press Secretary, January 8, 2014, https://www.whitehouse.gov/the-press-office/2014/01/08/fact-sheet-president-obama-s-promise-zones-initiative.

538. *President's 2016 Budget Fact Sheet: Investing in Coal Communities, Workers, and Technology: The POWER+ Plan* (Washington, DC: White House, 2015), https://www.whitehouse.gov/sites/default/files/omb/budget/fy2016/assets/fact_sheets/investing-in-coal-communities-workers-and-technology-the-power-plan.pdf. He also proposed up to $2 billion in tax credits for technology to reduce carbon emissions from coal-fired power plants and $1 billion to reclaim abandoned coal mines in ways that promote sustainable development.

539. Data on Americans in poverty is drawn from *Income and Poverty in the United States: 2013* (Washington, DC: US Census Bureau, September 2014), https://www.census.gov/content/dam/Census/library/publications/2014/demo/p60-249.pdf. Data on children in poverty come from "Basic Facts and Low-Income Children," Columbia University Mailman School of Public Health, January 2015, http://www.nccp.org/publications/pub_1100.html. Researchers defined children as those under age 18. The study was based on 2013 data. Low income was defined as at or above 200% of the federal poverty threshold; poor was defined as below 100% of the threshold.

540. "Department of Energy Weatherization Assistance Program Fact Sheet," http://www1.eere.energy.gov/wip/pdfs/wap_factsheet.pdf.

541. See David R. Baker, "Low Income Homeowners Get Free Solar Panels Thanks to Cap and Trade," San Francisco Gate, http://www.sfgate.com/business/article/Low-income-homeowners-get-free-solar-panels-6281762.php#photo-8030588. The Clean Power Plan – EPA's regulation of carbon emissions from power plants – is expected to result in more states collaborating in regional cap-andtrade programs, generating revenues that could be used to help low-income households cope with carbon pricing.

542. See Timothy Gardner, "U.S. Government Outlines Solar Power Boost for the Poor," Reuters, http://www.reuters.com/article/2015/07/07/us-usa-solar-poor-idUSKCN0PH0WM20150707.

543. The CRA, enacted by Congress in 1977, grades local lending institutions on how well they meet the credit needs of the communities in which they operate, https://www.ffiec.gov/cra. The grading is important because it influences whether local banks can receive federal approval for mergers and acquisitions. The Office of the Comptroller of the Currency, which administers the CRA, has issued guidance that financing for green buildings, wind farms, solar panels, and other renewable energy systems can qualify for credit if community development is the primary purpose of the financing. Kathleen Rogers, "Community Reinvestment Act Can Boost Energy-Efficiency, Funding for Low-Income Schools, *The Hill* (blog), http://thehill.com/blogs/congress-blog/education/233494-community-reinvestment-act-can-boost-energy-efficiency-funding.

544. See a National Governors Association fact sheet on public benefit funds at http://www.nga.org/files/live/sites/NGA/files/pdf/1008CLEANENERGYEFFICIENCYFUNDS.pdf.

545. *Improving the Fuel Efficiency of American Trucks – Bolstering Energy Security, Cutting Carbon Pollution, Saving Money and Supporting Manufacturing Innovation* (Washington, DC: The White House, February 2014), https://www.whitehouse.gov/sites/default/files/docs/finaltrucksreport.pdf.

546. "Appliance and Equipment Standards Program," US Office of Energy Efficiency and Renewable Energy, http://energy.gov/eere/buildings/appliance-and-equipment-standards-program.

547. DOE reports that 42 states and US territories, plus the District of Columbia, have adopted energy codes for commercial buildings; 40 have adopted energy codes for residences. As of August 2015, however, only two have adopted the most current model code, https://www.energycodes.gov/status-state-energy-code-adoption.

548. David Frankel and Humayun Tai, "Giving U.S. Energy Efficiency a Jolt," McKinsey & Company, December 2013, http://www.mckinsey.com/insights/energy_resources_materials/giving_us_energy_efficiency_a_jolt.

549. I described some of these financing options in Chapter 16. They include on-bill financing by utilities, residential and commercial PACE financing by municipalities, energy efficiency mortgages from private lenders and the federal government, and third-party financing that allows homeowners and businesses to install solar energy equipment with no up-front costs.

550. "State & Trends Report Charts Global Growth of Carbon Pricing," The World Bank, May 2014, http://www.worldbank.org/en/news/feature/2014/05/28/state-trends-report-tracks-global-growth-carbon-pricing.

551. Paul J. Hibbard et al., *The Economic Impacts of the Regional Greenhouse Gas Initiative on Nine Northeast and Mid-Atlantic States: Review of RGGI's Second Three-Year Compliance Period (2012– 2014)* (Denver, CO: Analysis Group, July 14, 2015), http://www.analysisgroup.com/uploadedfiles/content/insights/publishing/analysis_group_rggi_report_july_2015.pdf. A "job year" is one job for one year. It is a metric that combines all jobs, whether full or part time, into the equivalent of full-time jobs.

552. California's Global Warming Solutions Act of 2006 (AB32).

553. See Evan Lehmann, "Support for Carbon Tax Reaches Almost 70%," *ClimateWire*, http://www.eenews.net/stories/1060016859.

554. Kevin Kennedy et al., *Putting a Price on Carbon: A Handbook for U.S. Policymakers* (Washington, DC: World Resources Institute, April 2015), p. 24, http://www.wri.org/publication/putting-price-carbon.

555. *Global Green Growth: Clean Energy Industrial Investments and Expanding Job Opportunities*, p. 18 (United Nations Industrial Development Organization and the

Global Green Growth Institute, 2015), http://www.unido.org/fileadmin/user_media_
upgrade/Resources/Policy_advice/GLOBAL_GREEN_GROWTH_REPORT_vol1_final.pdf.

556. "Energy Efficiency and Economic Opportunity Fact Sheet," American Council for
an Energy Efficient Economy, http://aceee.org/files/pdf/fact-sheet/ee-economic-
opportunity.pdf.

557. Travis Hoium, "How Renewable Energy Jobs Are Changing America," The Motley
Fool, December 6, 2014, http://www.fool.com/investing/general/2014/12/06/how-
renewable-energy-jobs-are-changing-america.aspx.

558. Ibid.

559. Todd K. BenDor et al., Exploring and Understanding the Restoration Economy,
Final Report to the Walton Family Fund, January 2014, https://curs.unc.edu/
files/2014/01/RestorationEconomy.pdf.

560. Robert Pollin et al., A U.S. Program for Controlling Climate Change and
Expanding Job Opportunities (Washington, DC: Center for American Progress,
September 18, 2014), https://www.americanprogress.org/issues/green/
report/2014/09/18/96404/green-growth/.

561. A report by the Center for Climate and Energy Solutions estimates that a $16 per
ton tax on CO_2 would raise more than $1.1 trillion in the first 10 years and more
than $2.7 trillion over 20 years. Broadening the tax to include other greenhouse
gases would produce even higher revenues. Adele Morris and Aparna Mathur,
"A Carbon Tax in Broader U.S. Fiscal Reform: Design and Distributional Issues,"
(Arlington, VA: Center for Climate and Energy Solutions), http://www.c2es.org/
publications/carbon-tax-broader-us-fiscal-reform-design-distributional-issues.

562. CAP says that to reach this goal, the United States would have to cut its oil
consumption 40% and its gas consumption 30% while reducing energy
consumption a third and achieving a fourfold increase in the use of low-carbon
renewable energy. No additional nuclear power plants would be required.

563. "Protecting Your Businesses," Federal Emergency Management Agency, last
modified June 15, 2015, https://www.fema.gov/protecting-your-businesses.

564. John Arensmeyer, "Extreme Weather Puts Economic Chill on Small Businesses,"
Huffington Post Blog, May 7, 2014, http://www.huffingtonpost.com/john-
arensmeyer/extreme-weather-puts-econ_b_4914752.html.

565. Todd K. BenDor et al., Exploring and Understanding the Restoration Economy,
Final Report to the Walton Family Fund, January 2014, https://curs.unc.edu/
files/2014/01/RestorationEconomy.pdf.

566. Ibid.

567. Ibid.

568. Steve Berry, "Why Preserving History Matters," Huffington Post Blog, April 23,
2012, http://www.huffingtonpost.com/steve-berry/why-preserving-history-
matters_b_1446631.html.

569. Appalachia: Turning Assets into Opportunities (Ashville, NC: Appalachian
Regional Commission, October 2004), http://www.climateactionproject.com/
appalachia/docs/ARC_Asset_based_Development.pdf.

570. Pope Francis, "Encyclical Letter of the Holy Father Francis, Laudato Si', On Care
for Our Common Home," 68, Vatican website, May 24, 2015, http://w2.vatican.
va/content/francesco/en/encyclicals/documents/papa-francesco_20150524_
enciclica-laudato-si.html.

571. Matthew DiLallo, "What Is the Richest Country in the World? (Hint: It's Not
America)," The Motley Fool, June 24, 2015, http://www.fool.com/investing/
general/2015/06/24/what-is-the-richest-country-in-the-world-hint-it-2.aspx.

572. Tierney Smith, "5 Countries Leading the Way Toward 100% Renewable Energy," *EcoWatch*, January 9, 2015, http://ecowatch.com/2015/01/09/countries-leading-way-renewable-energy.

573. "World's Top 500 Universities," Academic Ranking of World Universities, last modified 2015, http://www.shanghairanking.com/.

574. "Honors and Awards: DOE Nobel Laureates," US Department of Energy, Office of Science, last modified May 20, 2014, http://science.energy.gov/about/honors-and-awards/doe-nobel-laureates/.

575. Catherine Clifford, "The Top 10 Most Innovative Countries in the World," *Entrepreneur*, July 18, 2014, http://www.entrepreneur.com/article/235756. Peter Coy, et al. *The Bloomberg Innovation Index* (Bloomberg, 2015), http://www.bloomberg.com/graphics/2015-innovative-countries/.

576. Peter Coy, et al. *The Bloomberg Innovation Index* (Bloomberg, 2015), http://www.bloomberg.com/graphics/2015-innovative-countries/.

577. Pat Adams, "20 Amazing Things the National Labs Have Done," US Department of Energy, July 27, 2015, http://energy.gov/articles/20-amazing-things-national-labs-have-done.

578. Amy Levin, "Topline Results on International Climate Change Action," Benenson Strategy Group, March 25, 2015, http://big.assets.huffingtonpost.com/BSGSCpoll.pdf.

579. Ibid, pp. 41 and 45.

580. Anthony Leiserowitz et al., *Climate Change in the American Mind* (New Haven, CT: Yale Project on Climate Change Communication and George Mason University Center for Climate Change Communication, March 2015), p. 25, http://environment.yale.edu/climate-communication/files/Global-Warming-CCAM-March-2015.pdf.

581. Phyllis Cuttino, *Power Shifts: Emerging Clean Energy Markets* (Philadelphia: The Pew Charitable Trusts, May 2015), http://www.pewtrusts.org/en/research-and-analysis/reports/2015/05/power-shifts.

582. Richard Wike, Bruce Stokes, and Jacob Poushter, "Global Publics Back U.S. on Fighting ISIS, but Are Critical of Post-9/11 Torture," Pew Research Center, June 23, 2015, http://www.pewglobal.org/2015/06/23/global-publics-back-u-s-on-fighting-isis-but-are-critical-of-post-911-torture/.

583. Eric Zuesse, "United States Is Now the Most Unequal of All Advanced Economies," *Huffington Post Politics* (blog), December 8, 2013, http://www.huffingtonpost.com/eric-zuesse/us-is-now-the-most-unequa_b_4408647.html.

584. The rulings were in Citizens United v. Federal Election Commission (2010) and McCutcheon v. FEC (2014). As a result of these and earlier rulings, wealthy corporations and individuals can spend unlimited amounts of money in support of a political candidate, and can do so anonymously, so long as the expenditures are not direct donations to the candidate or his or her campaign organization.

585. Opinion of the Court McConnell v. Federal Election Commission, 540 U.S. §323(a) (2003), https://supreme.justia.com/cases/federal/us/540/93/opinion.html. Justice Breyer quoted former Republican senator Alan Simpson and former Oklahoma Democratic senator David Boren in his opinion.

586. "Interview with Senator Bernie Sanders," RealClearPolitics, May 16, 2012, http://www.realclearpolitics.com/articles/2012/05/16/interview_with_senator_bernie_sanders_114188.html.

587. Joseph E. Stiglitz, "Of the 1 percent, by the 1 percent, for the 1 percent," *Vanity Fair*, May 2011, http://www.vanityfair.com/news/2011/05/top-one-percent-201105.

588. Martin Gilens and Benjamin I. Page, "Testing Theories of American Politics: Elites, Interest Groups, and Average Citizens," *Perspectives on Politics* 12, 3 (September 2014): 564–581, http://journals.cambridge.org/action/displayAbstract?fromPage=online&aid=9354310.

589. "The Money Behind the Elections," Open Secrets.org: Center for Responsive Politics, https://www.opensecrets.org/bigpicture/.

590. Lawrence Mishel, Elise Gould, and Josh Bivens, "Wage Stagnation in Nine Charts," Economic Policy Institute, January 6, 2015, http://www.epi.org/publication/charting-wage-stagnation/.

591. Ibid.

592. "Congressional Performance: Is Congress for Sale?" Rasmussen Reports, July 9, 2015, http://www.rasmussenreports.com/public_content/politics/mood_of_america/congressional_performance.

593. "Retirements Drain Congress of Leaders amid Frustration over Gridlock, Dysfunction," *Fox News Politics Blog*, April 6, 2014, http://www.foxnews.com/politics/2014/04/06/retirements-drain-congress-leaders-hint-at-frustration-over-gridlock.

594. Jennifer Steinhauer, "Weighing the Effect of an Exit of Centrists," *New York Times*, October 8, 2012, http://www.nytimes.com/2012/10/09/us/politics/pool-of-moderates-in-congress-is-shrinking.html?_r=0.

595. Russ Choma, "One Member of Congress = 18 American Households: Lawmakers' Personal Finances Far From Average," OpenSecrets.org: Center for Responsive Politics, January 12, 2015, http://www.opensecrets.org/news/2015/01/one-member-of-congress-18-american-households-lawmakers-personal-finances-far-from-average/.

596. Stephanie Condon, "Why Is Congress a Millionaires Club?" CBS News, March 27, 2012, http://www.cbsnews.com/news/why-is-congress-a-millionaires-club.

597. Ibid.

598. Republicans controlled both the Senate and the House, giving them the majority of members on key congressional committees. The blog *Climate Progress* did the math and reported that in the 114th Congress, 62% of the GOP's members on the House Science Committee denied climate change along with 91% of the Republican members of the Senate Energy and Public Works Committee.

599. "Are Voters Warming Up to Congress?" Rasmussen Reports, February 20, 2015, http://www.rasmussenreports.com/public_content/archive/mood_of_america_archive/congressional_performance/are_voters_warming_up_to_congress.

600. Sheldon Richman, "How the Rich Rule," *The American Conservative*, December 5, 2012, http://www.theamericanconservative.com/articles/how-the-rich-rule.

601. Ariel Edwards-Levy, "America's Tax System Is Widely Seen as Favoring the Rich, Poll Shows," *Huffington Post*, January 28, 2015, http://www.huffingtonpost.com/2015/01/28/tax-system-poll_n_6566388.html.

602. Bruce Drake, "Americans See Growing Gap between Rich and Poor," Pew Research Center, December 5, 2013, http://www.pewresearch.org/fact-tank/2013/12/05/americans-see-growing-gap-between-rich-and-poor/.

603. "Robert F. Kennedy," Speech in the United States Senate, May 9, 1966, https://en.wikiquote.org/wiki/Robert_F._Kennedy.

References

Adams, Pat. "20 Amazing Things the National Labs Have Done." Energy.gov, July 27, 2January 6, 2015.015. http://energy.gov/articles/20-amazing-things-national-labs-have-done.

American Council for an Energy Efficient Economy. *Energy Efficiency and Economic Opportunity Fact Sheet.* Washington, DC: ACEEE. http://aceee.org/files/pdf/factsheet/ee-economic-opportunity.pdf.

Appalachian Regional Commission. *Appalachia: Turning Assets into Opportunities,* Ashville, NC: Appalachian Regional Commission, October 2004. http://www.climateactionproject.com/appalachia/docs/ARC_Asset_based_Development.pdf.

Arensmeyer, John. "Extreme Weather Puts Economic Chill on Small Businesses." *Huffington Post Blog*, May 7, 2014. http://www.huffingtonpost.com/john-arensmeyer/extreme-weather-puts-econ_b_4914752.html.

Baker, David R. "Low-Income Homeowners Get Free Solar Panels Thanks to Cap and Trade," *San Francisco Chronicle*, May 22, 2015. http://www.sfgate.com/business/article/Low-income-homeowners-get-free-solar-panels-6281762.php#photo-8030588.

BenDor, Todd K. et al. *Exploring and Understanding the Restoration Economy.* Final Report to the Walton Family Fund, January 2014. https://curs.unc.edu/files/2014/01/RestorationEconomy.pdf.

Berry, Steve. "Why Preserving History Matters." *Huffington Post Blog*, April 23, 2012. http://www.huffingtonpost.com/steve-berry/why-preserving-history-matters_b_1446631.html.

Black & Veatch. *2014 Strategic Directions: U.S. Water Industry.* Denver, CO: Black & Veatch, October 2014. http://www.circleofblue.org/waternews/wp-content/uploads/2014/10/BV_2014-sdr-water-industry-report.pdf.

Burr, Judee, Lindsey Hallock, and Rob Sargent. *Shining Cities: Harnessing the Benefits of Solar Energy in America.* Boston, MA: America Research and Policy Center, March 26, 2015. http://www.environmentamerica.org/sites/environment/files/reports/EA_ShiningCities2015_scrn.pdf.

Cama, Timothy. "Obama's Clean Water Act Rule Faces Deepening Opposition." *The Christian Science Monitor*, August 31, 2015. http://www.csmonitor.com/Environment/2015/0831/Obama-s-Clean-Water-Act-rule-faces-deepening-opposition.

Choma, Russ. "One Member of Congress = 18 American Households: Lawmakers' Personal Finances Far from Average." OpenSecrets.org: Center for Responsive Politics. http://www.opensecrets.org/news/2015/01/one-member-of-congress-18-american-households-lawmakers-personal-finances-far-from-average/.

Click, Carrie. "Black Sunday – Rifle Rebounds and How." *Post Independent*, June 15, 2008. http://www.postindependent.com/article/20070426/NEWS/664343124.

Clifford, Catherine. "The Top 10 Most Innovative Countries in the World." *Entrepreneur Magazine*, July 18, 2014. http://www.entrepreneur.com/article/235756.

Condon, Stephanie. "Why Is Congress a Millionaires Club?" CBS News. http://www.cbsnews.com/news/why-is-congress-a-millionaires-club.

Coy, Peter et al. *The Bloomberg Innovation Index*, Bloomberg, 2015. http://www.bloomberg.com/graphics/2015-innovative-countries.

Cuttino, Phyllis. *Power Shifts: Emerging Clean Energy Markets*. Philadelphia: The Pew Charitable Trusts, May 2015. http://www.pewtrusts.org/en/research-and-analysis/reports/2015/05/power-shifts.

DeNavas-Walt, Carmen, and Bernadette D. Proctor. *Income and Poverty in the United States: 2013*. Washington, DC: US Census Bureau, September 2014. https://www.census.gov/content/dam/Census/library/publications/2014/demo/p60-249.pdf.

DiLallo, Matthew. "What Is the Richest Country in the World? (Hint: It's Not America)." *The Motley Fool*, June 24, 2015. http://www.fool.com/investing/general/2015/06/24/what-is-the-richest-country-in-the-world-hint-it-2.aspx.

Drake, Bruce. "Americans See Growing Gap between Rich and Poor." Pew Research Center, December 5, 2013. http://www.pewresearch.org/fact-tank/2013/12/05/americans-see-growing-gap-between-rich-and-poor/.

Edwards-Levy, Ariel. "America's Tax System Is Widely Seen as Favoring the Rich, Polls Show." *Huffington Post Politics* (blog). http://www.huffingtonpost.com/2015/01/28/tax-system-poll_n_6566388.html.

Essex, Randy. "In Solar Energy, Rifle Shines Most Brightly." *Post Independent/Citizen Telegram*, April 22, 2015. http://www.postindependent.com/news/16013885-113/in-solar-energy-rifle-shines-most-brightly.

European Trade Union Confederation. "Put Just Transition at the Heart of a European Position on Climate in Durban and a Roadmap on Sustainability at Rio+20." ETUC, last modified October 10, 2010. https://www.etuc.org/put-just-transition-heart-european-position-climate-durban-and-roadmap-sustainability-rio20.

Exec. Order No. 13693. *Planning for Federal Sustainability in the Next Decade*. Washington, DC: White House, March 19, 2015. https://www.whitehouse.gov/the-press-office/2015/03/19/executive-order-planning-federal-sustainability-next-decade.

Federal Emergency Management Agency. "Protecting Your Businesses," last modified June 15, 2015. https://www.fema.gov/protecting-your-businesses.

Federal Financial Institutions Examination Council. Community Reinvestment Act. Washington, DC: FFIEC. https://www.ffiec.gov/cra.

Fish, Sandra. "Fighting to Save Colorado Mining Town." Aljazeera America, November 3, 2013. http://america.aljazeera.com/articles/2013/11/3/fighting-to-saveacoloradominingtown.html.

FoxNews.com. "Retirements Drain Congress of Leaders amid Frustration over Gridlock, Dysfunction," *Fox News Politics Blog*, April 6, 2014. http://www.foxnews.com/politics/2014/04/06/retirements-drain-congress-leaders-hint-at-frustration-over-gridlock.

Frankel, David, and Humayun Tai. "Giving U.S. Energy Efficiency a Jolt." McKinsey & Company, December 2013. http://www.mckinsey.com/insights/energy_resources_materials/giving_us_energy_efficiency_a_jolt.

Gardner, Timothy. "U.S. Government Outlines Solar Power Boost for Poor." Reuters, July 7, 2015. http://www.reuters.com/article/2015/07/07/us-usa-solar-poor-idUSKCN-0PH0WM20150707.

"Garfield Clean Energy" (home page). Garfield Clean Energy. http://www.garfield-cleanenergy.org.

Gilens, Martin, and Benjamin I. Page. "Testing Theories of American Politics: Elites, Interest Groups, and Average Citizens." *Perspectives on Politics* 12, 3 (September 2014): 564–581. http://journals.cambridge.org/action/displayAbstract?fromPage=online&aid=9354310.

Hibbard, Paul J. et al. *The Economic Impacts of the Regional Greenhouse Gas Initiative on Nine Northeast and Mid-Atlantic States: Review of RGGI's Second Three-Year Compliance Period (2012–2014).* Analysis Group, July 14, 2015. http://www.analysisgroup.com/uploadedfiles/content/insights/publishing/analysis_group_rggi_report_july_2015.pdf.

"History of Rifle." Rifle Area Chamber of Commerce. http://riflechamber.com/relocate-do-business/history-of-rifle/.

Hoium, Travis. "How Renewable Energy Jobs Are Changing America." The Motley Fool, December 6, 2014. http://www.fool.com/investing/general/2014/12/06/how-renewable-energy-jobs-are-changing-america.aspx.

Holtz, Michael. "Democrats Buck Obama on Water Rule." *The Hill*, May 28, 2015. http://thehill.com/policy/energy-environment/243299-democrats-buck-obama-on-water-rule.

Jiang, Yang et al. *Basic Facts About Low-Income Children: Children under 19 Years, 2013.* New York: National Center for Children in Poverty, Columbia University Mailman School of Public Health, January 2015. http://www.nccp.org/publications/pub_1100.html.

Kennedy, Kevin et al. *Putting a Price on Carbon: A Handbook for U.S. Policymakers*, p. 24. World Resources Institute, April 2015. http://www.wri.org/publication/putting-price-carbon.

Kennedy, Robert F. Speech in the United States Senate, May 9, 1966. https://en.wikiquote.org/wiki/Robert_F._Kennedy.

Lehmann, Evan. "Public Opinion: Support for Carbon Tax Reaches Almost 70%." *ClimateWire*, April 16, 2015. http://www.eenews.net/stories/1060016859.

Leiserowitz, Anthony et al. *Climate Change in the American Mind*, p. 25. Yale Project on Climate Change Communication and George Washington University Center for Climate Change Communication, March 2015. http://environment.yale.edu/climate-communication/files/Global-Warming-CCAM-March-2015.pdf.

Levin, Amy. "Topline Results on International Climate Change Action." Benenson Strategy Group, March 25, 2015. http://big.assets.huffingtonpost.com/BSGSCpoll.pdf. Rush Limbaugh. "Everything I've Always Told You about Liberals Is Coming True." *The Rush Limbaugh Show*, May 5, 2015. http://www.rushlimbaugh.com/daily/2015/05/05/everything_i_ve_always_told_you_about_liberals_is_coming_true.

Mishel, Lawrence, Elise Gould, and Josh Bivens. "Wage Stagnation in Nine Charts." Economic Policy Institute, January 6, 2015. http://www.epi.org/publication/charting-wage-stagnation/.

Morris, Adele, and Aparna Mathur. *A Carbon Tax in Broader U.S. Fiscal Reform: Design and Distributional Issues.* Arlington, VA: Center for Climate and Energy Solutions. http://www.c2es.org/publications/carbon-tax-broader-us-fiscal-reform-design-distributional-issues.

National Governors Association. *Clean and Secure Actions Report: Energy Efficiency, Public Benefits Fund*, 2010. http://www.nga.org/files/live/sites/NGA/files/pdf/ 1008CLEANENERGYEFFICIENCYFUNDS.PDF.

"New Castle: Authentically Colorado" (home page). New Castle: Authentically Colorado. http://www.newcastlecolorado.org/.

"Northwest Colorado Cultural Heritage" (home page). Northwest Colorado Cultural Heritage. http://nwcoloradoheritagetravel.org/new-castle-colorado/home.

OpenSecrets.org. "The Money Behind the Elections." OpenSecrets.org: Center for Responsive Politics. https://www.opensecrets.org/bigpicture/.

Pollin, Robert et al. "A U.S. Program for Controlling Climate Change and Expanding Job Opportunities." Washington, DC: Center for American Progress, September 18, 2014. https://www.americanprogre"ss.org/issues/green/report/2014/09/18/96404/ green-growth/.

Pope Francis. "Encyclical Letter, *Laudato Si'*, of the Holy Father Francis On Care for Our Common Home." The Vatican website, May 24, 2015. http://w2.vatican.va/ content/francesco/en/encyclicals/documents/papa-francesco_20150524_enciclica-laudato-si.html

Proctor, Cathy. "State May Join Legal Battle to Halt Shutdown of Colowyo Coal Mine." *Denver Business Journal*, June 5, 2015. http://www.bizjournals.com/denver/blog/ earth_to_power/2015/06/state-may-join-legal-battle-to-halt-shutdown-of.html.

Rasmussen Reports. "Are Voters Warming Up to Congress?" Rasumussen Reports, February 20, 2015. http://www.rasmussenreports.com/public_content/archive/ mood_of_america_archive/congressional_performance/are_voters_warming_up_ to_congress.

———. "Congressional Performance: Is Congress for Sale?" Rasmussen Reports, July 9, 2015. http://www.rasmussenreports.com/public_content/politics/mood_of_america/congressional_performance.

Reed, Jeff. "The Top 5 U.S. Shale Gas Plays." Oilpro. http://oilpro.com/post/646/the-major-shale-gas-plays-in-the-us.

Rice, Heidi. "New Castle Scraps Solar Park Site due to Protests." *Post Independent/Citizen Telegram*, July 25, 2014. http://www.postindependent.com/news/12347067-113/solar-castle-location-energy.

Richman, Sheldon. "How the Rich Rule." *The American Conservative*, December 5, 2012. *http://www.theamericanconservative.com/articles/how-the-*rich-rule.

Rogers, Kathleen. Community Reinvestment Act Can Boost Energy-Efficiency, Funding for Low-Income Schools. *Congress Blog*, February 23, 2015. http:// thehill.com/blogs/congress-blog/education/233494-community-reinvestment-act-can-boost-energy-efficiency-funding.

Smith, Tierney. "5 Countries Leading the Way Toward 100% Renewable Energy." *EcoWatch*, January 9, 2015. http://ecowatch.com/2015/01/09/countries-leading-way-renewable-energy.

SourceWatch. "Coal and Jobs in the United States." Center for Media and Democracy/SourceWatch, last modified June 26, 2015. http://www.sourcewatch.org/index. php/Coal_and_jobs_in_the_United_States.

Steinhauer, Jennifer. "Weighing the Effect of an Exit of Centrists." *New York Times*, October 8, 2012. http://www.nytimes.com/2012/10/09/us/politics/pool-of-moderates-in-congress-is-shrinking.html?_r=0.

Stiglitz, Joseph. "Of the 1%, by the 1%, for the 1%," *Vanity Fair*, May 2011. http://www.vanityfair.com/news/2011/05/top-one-percent-201105.

United Nations Industrial Development and Global Green Growth Institute. *Global Green Growth: Clean Energy Industrial Investments and Expanding Job Opportunities*, 2015. http://www.unido.org/fileadmin/user_media_upgrade/Resources/Policy_advice/GLOBAL_GREEN_GROWTH_REPORT_vol1_final.pdf.

US Department of Energy. "Building Energy Codes Program." Energy Efficiency and Renewable Energy. https://www.energycodes.gov/status-state-energy-code-adoption.

———. *Department of Energy Weatherization Assistance Program Fact Sheet*. Washington, DC: Department of Energy, Weatherization and Intergovernmental Program, May 2009. http://www1.eere.energy.gov/wip/pdfs/wap_factsheet.pdf.

———. "Honors and Awards: DOE Nobel Laureates." DOE, Office of Science, last modified May 20, 2014. http://science.energy.gov/about/honors-and-awards/doe-nobel-laureates/.

US Energy Information Administration. *Annual Energy Outlook 2015*. Washington, DC: US Energy Information Administration, April 14, 2015. http://www.eia.gov/forecasts/aeo/executive_summary.cfm.

US Environmental Protection Agency. "Coal." EPA, last modified September 25, 2013. http://www.epa.gov/cleanenergy/energy-and-you/affect/coal.html.

US Office of Energy Efficiency and Renewable Energy. "Appliance and Equipment Standards Program." Energy.Gov. http://energy.gov/eere/buildings/appliance-and-equipment-standards-program.

White House. "Fact Sheet: President Obama's Promise Zones Initiative." White House, Office of the Press Secretary, January 8, 2014. https://www.whitehouse.gov/the-press-office/2014/01/08/fact-sheet-president-obama-s-promise-zones-initiative.

———. *Improving the Fuel Efficiency of American Trucks – Bolstering Energy Security, Cutting Carbon Pollution, Saving Money and Supporting Manufacturing Innovation*. Washington, DC: The White House, February 2014. https://www.whitehouse.gov/sites/default/files/docs/finaltrucksreport.pdf.

———. *President's 2016 Budget Fact Sheet: Investing in Coal Communities, Workers, and Technology: The POWER+ Plan*. Washington, DC: White House, 2015. https://www.whitehouse.gov/sites/default/files/omb/budget/fy2016/assets/fact_sheets/investing-in-coal-communities-workers-and-technology-the-power-plan.pdf.

Wike, Richard, Bruce Stokes, and Jacob Poushter. "Global Publics Back U.S. on Fighting ISIS, but Are Critical of Post-9/11 Torture." Pew Research Center, June 23, 2015. http://www.pewglobal.org/2015/06/23/global-publics-back-u-s-on-fighting-isis-but-are-critical-of-post-911-torture/.

The World Bank. "State and Trends Report Charts Global Growth of Carbon Pricing." The World Bank, May 2014. http://www.worldbank.org/en/news/feature/2014/05/28/state-trends-report-tracks-global-growth-carbon-pricing.

"World's Top 500 Universities." Academic Ranking of World Universities, last modified 2015. http://www.shanghairanking.com.

Zuesse, Eric. "United States Is Now the Most Unequal of All Advanced Economies," *Huffington Post Politics* (blog), December 8, 2013. http://www.huffingtonpost.com/eric-zuesse/us-is-now-the-most-unequa_b_4408647.html.

Index

solar photovoltaic cells (PV), 139

Solar PV installations, 171

South America, clear cutting of forests, 12

Spain, solar power, 35

Standard Oil, 157

Standard & Poor's, 149, 151

Stanford University, 61, 174, 214

Stern, Nicholas, 103, 118

Stevenson, Adlai, 11

Stevens, Wallace, 144

Steyer, Tom, 72

Stiglitz, Joseph, 229

Strategic Petroleum Reserve, 89

subsidies, 61, 81, 83–84, 93, 106, 108, 111–120, 210, 212, 216, 246n150, 251n208–209, 251n211–212

Sun Edison, 175

SunPower, 173

Sunrun, 180

T

Tennessee Valley Authority, 51

Tesla Motors, 182

Tesla, Nikola, 50

thermoelectric power plants, 135–136, 259n296, 261n319

Third Generation Environmentalism, 73

Thornton, Paul, 77

tidal power, 179

TIME magazine, Cuyahoga River fire, 11

Todd, John, 91

Trade Adjustment Assistance (TAA) program, 210

Tri-State Water Wars, 132, 257n281

Turner, Ted, 33, 161–162

U

Union of Concerned Scientists (UCS), 75, 154, 155

United Nations, 11, 88, 185

United Nations Framework Convention on Climate Change (UNFCCC), 67

United Nations Industrial Development Organization (UNIDO), 206, 210

University of California – Davis, 129

University of Colorado, 19

University of Illinois, 75–76

University of London's Institute for Sustainable Resources, 165

University of Massachusetts, 177, 184

University of Michigan Energy Institute, 156

US Chamber of Commerce, 67

US Department of Defense, 58, 73

US Department of Energy, 21, 210, 224

US electric transmission grid, 50

US Energy Information Administration (EIA), 38, 122, 139, 152, 154, 170, 199–200, 207, 254n252, 262n332, 263n351, 268n405, 275n502

US Fish and Wildlife Service, 161

US Forest Service, 157

US Geological Survey (USGS), 130, 135, 136, 158, 258n293, 259n294–296

US Government Accountability Office (GAO), 21, 103, 110, 114–115, 133, 137, 233n22

US Supreme Court, 110, 227–228

V

V-2 rockets, 11

Value of Solar Tariff (VOST), 199

Vatican, 223

vehicle mile traveled (VMT), 152

Vermejo Park Ranch, 161–162

Veterans Administration, 171

volatile organic compounds (VOCs), 39

W

Waldo Canyon fire, 17

Walmart, 189

Washington Post
millennials and automobile ownership, 151

Sanford article, 68–69

slowing down solar installations, 178

Wasserman, Dave, 229

wave power, 179

Weather Channel, 59

Weatherization Assistance Program (WAP), 212

Western Climate Initiative, 196

Western Landowners Alliance, 162

West Fork Fire, 17

Westinghouse, 50

wetlands, 34, 43, 92, 135, 141, 143, 156, 157, 158, 247n168

The White City, 49–50, 52

Willamette River, 90

wind energy, 5, 23, 28, 30, 31, 81–82, 140, 170, 175, 189, 206, 224, 251n209

"Wind Farms in Wheat Fields", 22–23, 65

wind turbines, 20–22, 26, 35–36, 125, 170, 175, 199, 223, 261n3199

Wirth, Timothy E., climate and energy challenges, 3–5

Wiser, Ryan H., 113

Wogan, David, 123, 255n257

World Bank, 13, 214

World Business Council for Sustainable Development (WBCSD), 184, 188, 271n448, 271n455

World Commission on Environment and Development, 184

World Economic Forum, 184, 257n277, 271n446

World Happiness Report, 98, 249n187

World Resources Institute (WRI), 215–216

World's Columbian Exposition, 49

World War I, 227

World War II, 15, 54, 84, 99, 106, 125–127, 227

Worldwatch Institute, 184

World Wildlife Fund, 159, 266n379

X

Xcel Energy, 25, 28–29, 31–32

Acknowledgments

I owe an infinite debt of gratitude to the following:

- To my entire staff at the Center for the New Energy Economy at Colorado State University, all of whom assisted in making this book a reality; specifically William S. (Bill) Becker, Jeff Lyng and Tom Plant for their help in editing and re-drafting so much of this book;

- To Jane Culkin, Katherine Heriot Hoffer, and Jeff Cook, for their careful and detailed research efforts;

- To a great group of Colorado State University Interns and Natural Capitalism Interns, Ayman Afifi, Annabelle Berklund, Divneet Dhillon, Matthew Flynn, Kirsten Frysinger, Josh Garcia, Wendy Keller, David Lagreca, Adam Mayer, Stephanie Mitts, Amy Russell, Mateo Schimpf, Leigha Silberman, and Chris Termyn for their many contributions to the research of this book;

- To Wendy Hartzell and Maury Golder-Dobbie of the Center for the New Energy Economy for their invaluable assistance with the administrative work and logistics necessary to publish this book;

- To my former staff in the Governor's office who helped conceive of and implement the Colorado Promise;

- To Tony Frank, President and Chancellor at Colorado State University, for helping me find a home at CSU following my time in public life;

- And finally, to my wife, Jeannie, and my children, August, Abraham, Sam, and Tally, for all of their love and support.

About the Author

Bill Ritter, Jr. is the founder and director of the Center for the New Energy Economy (CNEE) at Colorado State University, which launched on February 1, 2011.

The center works directly with governors, legislators, regulators, planners, policy makers, and other decision makers. It provides technical assistance to help officials create the policies and practices that will facilitate America's transition to a clean-energy economy.

Ritter was elected as Colorado's 41st governor in 2006, and built consensus to tackle some of the state's biggest challenges. During his four-year term, Ritter established Colorado as a national and international leader in clean energy by building a new energy economy. He signed 57 new energy bills into law, including a 30% Renewable Portfolio Standard and a Clean Air Clean Jobs Act that replaced nearly a gigawatt of coal-fired generation with natural gas. In total, the Colorado new energy economy created thousands of new jobs.

Ritter is a member of the board of the directors of the Energy Foundation and a senior fellow and member of the board of directors of the Advanced Energy Economy Institute. Ritter earned his bachelor's degree in political science from Colorado State University (1978) and his law degree from the University of Colorado (1981). With his wife, Jeannie, he operated a food distribution and nutrition center in Zambia. He then served as Denver's district attorney from 1993 to January 2005.

The Ritters have four children: August, Abe, Sam, and Tally.